Best Wishes

Jerome

Zimbabwe
WARM HEART UGLY FACE

Zimbabwe
WARM HEART UGLY FACE

Jerome Gardner

ZIMBABWE **WARM HEART** UGLY FACE

DEDICATION

Jason Andrew Gardner
12-09-1979 – 01-06-2008
Our Son *"Forever young"*

ZIMBABWE **WARM HEART** UGLY FACE

gardnerj@yoafrica.com

©World rights Jerome Gardner.

All rights reserved. With the exception of small extracts quoted for review purposes, no part of this publication may be reproduced, translated, adapted, stored in a retrieval system, or transmitted in any form or through any means including but limited to electronic, mechanical, photocopying, recording or otherwise without the written permission of the author.

First published in 2010

ISBN 978-0-620-46805-3

Book design by Sarel Greyling
Photographs by Jerome Gardner, Tori Hirst and Forma Photography, Somerset West
Edited by Rosemarie Harrison
Copy Edited by Mandy Freeman
Printed by Paarl Media, Paarl

Contents

ABBREVIATIONS AND LOCALISMS USED	8
ACKNOWLEDGEMENTS	9
INTRODUCTION	11
PROLOGUE	12
TIMELINE OF EVENTS	14
OUR FAMILY	19
BULAWAYO	23
THE GOOD TIMES [1997-2000]	29
THE BEGINNING OF THE END [2000-2005]	37
IT CAN'T GET ANY WORSE [2006]	55
IT CAN GET WORSE [2007]	73
HOPE AND SHATTERED DREAMS [2008]	109
TRAGEDY	133
STARTING FROM SCRATCH [2009…]	141
THE BULAWAYO GOLF CLUB – AND OTHER STORIES	169
EPILOGUE	190
APPENDIX	192

ABBREVIATIONS AND LOCALISMS USED

'A'-level – Post-matric "advanced" exam
BACOSSI – Basic Commodity Supply Side Intervention
Bakkie – small (often open-backed) truck
Bearer Cheques – form of promissory notes
Braai – barbecue
CBC – Christian Brothers College
CIO – Central Intelligence Organisation
COD – cash on delivery of the goods supplied
Down South – South Africa
FCA – Foreign Currency Account
FOLIWARS – Foreign Exchange Licenced Warehouses and Retail Shops
Lekker – nice, tasty
MDC – Movement for Democratic Change
Mopani – indigenous hardwood tree
NIPC – National Income and Pricing Commission
NOSTROS – A banking term to describe an account one bank holds with another bank in a foreign country, usually in the currency of that foreign country
Panga – knife with long blade, machete
PH – Professional hunter
Pungwe – all-night vigil with dancing and singing
R – (South African) Rand
Rondavel – circular, often thatched building
RTGS – Real Time Gross Settlement
SABC – South African Broadcasting Corporation
Sadza – mealie meal, cornmeal
SI – Statutory Instrument
SPCA – Society for the Prevention of Cruelty to Animals
Trek – long journey
US$ – United States dollar
Varsity – university
VAT – Value-added tax
ZANU-PF – Zimbabwe African National Union – Patriotic Front
ZAPU – Zimbabwe African People's Union
ZIMRA – Zimbabwe Revenue Authority
ZRP – Zimbabwe Republic Police
ZW$ – Zimbabwe dollar

Acknowledgements

I owe a huge amount of gratitude to so many people who made the writing of this book such a cathartic and satisfying task.

First and foremost, to my soulmate, best friend and wife, Jane. Her willingness to accompany me as I lived my dreams was, and still is, exceptional. To my children Jason, Candice, Jonathan, and my step children Bronwyn, Nicola, Brett and Tracy, for making my job as a father so fulfilling.

To the team of Giants I was privileged to lead – Elana, Fanuel, Larry, Richard and Randall – as well as the 1 500 Giants who are the organisation. Their support, through the darkest and most trying times, was what made the journey that more sustainable. The fact we survived as an organisation, to the extent we have, was for the most part their doing. The support from Head Office in Cape Town and in particular Pieter Erasmus, who, in my opinion, has the emotional intelligence of the Dalai Lama, combined with a razor-sharp mind, whose encouragement and support helped me through the toughest ten years of my business career.

To Rosemarie Harrison, to whom I was introduced through a mutual friend Maggie. Rosemarie's passion for literature and invaluable help in getting the layout and grammar into its present form, while preserving my original vision of what this book should be, made my task of putting the finishing touches so much easier.

To Jane, Tracy, Petra, Brett, Maggie and Colin, who read the manuscript in its rough form and whose comments and feedback helped shape its final form.

Finally I must thank my friends at Somerset West, Polokwane and Bulawayo Golf Clubs who gave me so much pleasure while enjoying the infuriating but great game week after week.

This book contains my own personal thoughts and experiences and does not necessarily reflect the opinions of any other person or organisation.

ZIMBABWE **WARM HEART** UGLY FACE

Introduction

The name of this book came to me one day as our management team and I were driving along a badly-potholed road in Bulawayo, Zimbabwe. We had just been visiting some of our shops. The state of the infrastructure, the polarised political atmosphere permeating every aspect of life in the country – all contrasted so dramatically with its beauty, and even during such dark days, its wonderfully warm and happy people. I commented to them,

"Zimbabwe is like a very loving, warm-hearted and patient woman but with an ugly face."

If you can see past her outer looks, you find something unique underneath.
 This book is not a political analysis of the Zimbabwean situation. There are those much better qualified and articulate than I to comment on that. This is simply a book on how my family and I experienced life in Zimbabwe, from arriving as new immigrants in 1997 to present-day 2009. How we handled situations, which very few are privileged to live through, and how with a dedicated team, we managed to keep a 196-store retail chain, employing over 1 500 people, afloat for ten years during arguably the worst hyper-inflation experienced by any country in the world.

Prologue

According to Wikipedia, the free encyclopaedia, "The name Zimbabwe derives from the Shona language words 'Dzimba dza mabwe' meaning 'great houses of stone.'" Its name is taken from the site of the Great Zimbabwe ruins, rambling structures of stone dating back hundreds of years and referred to as the "Capital of the great Empire of Zimbabwe".

In the 1880s the British arrived, organised by Cecil John Rhodes, naming the country Southern Rhodesia in 1898. Many wars, called Chimurengas, were fought between the local Ndebele people, Shona tribes and British Colonists.

In 1923 Southern Rhodesia became a self-governing British Colony.

Zimbabwe is a landlocked country. South Africa, its southern neighbour, lies across the great Limpopo River. Zambia stretches to the northwest across the mighty Zambezi, which in 1953 was dammed and created Lake Kariba, 240 kilometres long and 40 kilometres wide. Botswana forms the border in the southwest and Mozambique in the east.

In 1953, Britain consolidated Rhodesia and Nyasaland – now Malawi – into the Federation of Rhodesia and Nyasaland, a union the British dissolved in 1963. On 11th November 1965, the white-minority Rhodesian Government, led by Ian Smith, issued the unilateral declaration of independence from the United Kingdom. Smith declared Rhodesia a Republic in 1970.

A civil war broke out against the white-minority rule. Economic sanctions were imposed by the United Nations and the Smith Government was only recognised by South Africa, itself governed by an apartheid administration.

From 1965 to 1979, the guerrilla war against the Smith government intensified, with thousands killed on both sides. In 1979 Smith opened negotiations with the leaders of the Zimbabwe African National Union – ZANU – led by Robert Mugabe and the Zimbabwe African People's Union – ZAPU – lead by Joshua Nkomo.

This ultimately led to a meeting to determine a new constitution in 1979 and elections supervised by Lord Soames that same year. On 1st December 1979, delegations from all sides signed the Lancaster House Agreement, thus ending the civil war.

In 1980, Mugabe and his ZANU party won a landslide victory. This brought about an uprising in the Western-Matabeleland region of Zimbabwe with its predominantly Ndebele population. After Mugabe unleashed his Korean-trained soldiers from the 5th Brigade, the insurrection was quelled for a brief period, but in reality continued until 1985, and became known as the gukurahundi, a Shona word that means, "The early rain which washes away the chaff."

It has been estimated that close to 20 000 Ndebele were murdered. The conflict ended when in 1988 ZANU and ZAPU signed a unity accord and formed ZANU-PF.

In 1990 Mugabe once again won a landslide victory in the election.

From 1990 to 1996 civil unrest had been escalating for various reasons. The most important of these was the increased state control over the media, universities and the Trade Union movement.

In November 1997, Mugabe's government gave in to the protesting civil-war veterans and paid them gratuities that the state simply could not afford. As a direct result, on 14th November 1997, a day known as "Black Friday", the Zimbabwe dollar suddenly collapsed against all other currencies. Although the devaluation was substantial and continuous, it was only in 2002 that the so-called parallel market mushroomed as a result of the critical shortage of foreign currency.

This lack of hard currency was a direct consequence of the violent farm takeovers launched by Mugabe's government in 2000, which led to huge outflows of capital from the country and the total collapse of the agricultural sector. The transition from a net exporter of agricultural products in 1999 to a net importer by 2003, shows the sudden dramatic collapse of this sector.

Up until 2000, Zimbabwe was self-reliant in almost everything except petroleum products. Supermarket shelves were full of locally-produced goods, from cooking oil to jams, canned vegetables and fruit as well as all toiletries. Beef prices were the lowest in the region and the meat regarded as the best in the world, after Argentina's. Beef made up a sizable part of the country's total export earnings.

Life in Zimbabwe, up until the 2000 farm invasions, was truly enjoyable. Motor vehicles, which were locally assembled, were within the price range of the average working Zimbabwean. Mortgage loans were available; tobacco products were the cheapest in the region. There were no power cuts, and health and sanitation systems were some of the best in Southern Africa. Everyone drank water straight from the tap; garage attendants filled your tank, cleaned your windows and inflated your tyres.

And then everything began to change…

Timeline of events in this book

In order to really grasp the full impact of events on organisations and individuals in Zimbabwe, it is important to understand the sequence in which they occurred, from independence in 1980 to our arrival in 1997, up until the present time of writing in 2009.

1980	Independence – Mugabe elected Prime Minister. Zimbabwe dollar introduced: ZW$1 = US$1.47.
1987	Constitution changed to create presidential function. Prime Minister's position done away with – Mugabe elected president by parliament.
1990, 1996	Mugabe again elected President by popular vote for six-year term.
1997	February, we arrive in Bulawayo.
1997	14th November "Black Friday" ZW$ against US$ devalues from ZW$14: US$1 to ZW$26: US$1 as a direct result of gratuities paid to "War Veterans", which Government could not afford.
1999	September – Opposition MDC formed out of Trade Union Movement with Morgan Tsvangirai as its President.
2000	14th February – New Government-drafted constitution rejected in Referendum. Includes right of President Mugabe to stand for two more terms, immunity of prosecution for all Government ministers, and authorises government takeover of white-owned land. "Yes" votes 45%, "No" votes 54%. New constitution rejected by people of Zimbabwe.
2000	March – First farms invaded by so-called "War Veterans". Farmers killed and workers driven off white-owned land. Government endorses "Land Redistribution Programme."
2000	June Parliamentary elections. Opposition MDC captures 57 of 120 seats. Mugabe's ZANU-PF claims 62 with 1 Independent, despite localised violence and allegations of massive vote-rigging.
2001	28th January *Daily News* newspaper, critical of Government, destroyed in bomb blast, one day after Information Minister calls for it to be "silenced".
2002	Presidential Elections – Mugabe (ZANU-PF) wins 56%, Morgan Tsvangirai (MDC) wins 42%, with allegations of violence and vote-rigging.

TIMELINE

2002	November – Commonwealth suspends Zimbabwe from Council meetings for one year, after their observers declare Presidential election neither free nor fair.
2003	March – MDC leadership (Morgan Tsvangirai, Renson Gasela and Welshman Ncube) accused of treason and put on trial, allegedly set up by the CIO.
2003	September – First family of bearer cheques introduced; they became legal tender in Zimbabwe and are a form of promissory notes. Denominations of ZW$5 000, ZW$10 000 and ZW$20 000. December – Gideon Gono (ZANU-PF) appointed Reserve Bank Governor.
2003	December – Inflation at 455% Invitation for Zimbabwe to attend Commonwealth-Heads-of-Government meeting withdrawn. Mugabe announces Zimbabwe's pull out from the Commonwealth.
2004	The appeals by the MDC against the 2002 election results still not taken to court. USA, European Union and other European countries impose travel bans on selected ZANU-PF top brass and freeze their assets. Arms embargo also instituted.
2004	January – Gono places all foreign exchange under direct control of the Reserve Bank and introduces an auction system to allocate the scarce commodity.
2004 - 2005	Various banks placed under curatorship or closed by Gono. Banks accused of abusing foreign currency system and of various other misdemeanours.
2005	March – Parliamentary elections ZANU – PF 78 seats MDC – 41 seats Independent – 1 seat.
2005	May to June – Government launches "Operation Murambatsvina" – "clear out the filth". Thousands left homeless in mid-winter after illegal structures, vendors' stalls and other buildings are demolished. UN condemns destruction of property and issues damning report. Government embarks on rebuilding exercise, but runs out of money.

2006	August – Reserve Bank Governor Gono launches "Sunrise 1". New "bearer cheque" notes issued. Three zeros removed from currency. He calls it "Operation Zero to Hero". 1 cent, 5 cent, 10 cent, 50 cent, ZW$10, ZW$20, ZW$50, ZW$100, ZW$500, ZW$1 000, ZW$10 000 and ZW$100 000 notes introduced, i.e. 12 new notes. Business and civil society given 21 days to deposit old currency. £1=ZW$1 million on parallel market.
2007	June – Government introduces nationwide 50%-off price slash – all prices to revert to those of 18 June or reduced by 50%. Thousands of CEOs arrested and jailed for refusing to implement the ruling.
2007	December – New ZW$250 000, ZW$500 000 and ZW$750 000 "bearer cheques" introduced.
2008	January – ZW$1 million, ZW$5 million and ZW$10 million "bearer cheques" introduced. Daily withdrawal limit increased to ZW$500 million up from ZW$50 million.
2008	March – Harmonised parliamentary and presidential elections held for first time. Results delayed for four weeks amid mounting fears of rigging. MDC secures majority in parliament. Presidential vote: 47% Tsvangirai, 42% Mugabe. Second-round runoff to be held between the two. Tsvangirai pulls out, citing violence against MDC supporters. Mugabe declared President.
2008	April – ZW$25 million and ZW$50 million "bearer cheques" introduced. Parallel market rate US$1 = ZW$42 million. One loaf of bread costs ZW$30 million.
2008	April – Banks' computer systems no longer able to handle more than ZW$1 trillion – clients forced to open multiple accounts.
2008	May – Special ZW$5 billion, ZW$25 billion and ZW$50 billion "Agro-Cheques" introduced.
2008	June – German firm bows to international pressure and cancels 50-year-old contract to supply Zimbabwe Reserve Bank with currency-printing paper, ink and spares to print more money. Official inflation level given as 231 million percent but believed to be much higher.
2008	June – Daily withdrawal limit increased to ZW$10 billion from ZW$5 billion.

TIMELINE

2008 — August – Taxi trip to town costs ZW$10 billion. Ten zeros removed from currency. ZW$1 billion becomes 10 cents. Gono remonetises old obsolete coins of 10, 20 and 50 cents, ZW$1, ZW$2 and ZW$5, and introduces new ZW$10 and ZW$25 coins. New ZW$1, ZW$5, ZW$10, ZW$20, ZW$100 and ZW$500 notes introduced. No longer "bearer cheques". This time proper money!

2008 — October – Foreign exchange licences introduced for shops to trade in foreign currency. Fee US$20 000 per shop.

2009 — 2nd February – Twelve zeros removed and new notes introduced. A total of 25 zeros removed in two years from August 2006, three in August 2006, ten in August 2008 and 12 in February 2009.

2009 — 29 January – Licence to trade in forex scrapped. All allowed to trade in foreign currency. Zimbabwe dollar for all intents and purposes dead.

2009 — April – New Finance Minister Biti (MDC) suspends Zimbabwe dollar for at least a year. Trading in US$, Pound, Euro, Rand and Pula allowed.

ZIMBABWE **WARM HEART** UGLY FACE

1
OUR FAMILY
[1993 – 1997]

*Each new day is an opportunity to start all over again...
to clarify your vision* Jo Petty

I met Jane in November 1993 on a beautiful summer's day, filled with the promise of a new beginning for both of us.

Jane's closest friend Linda introduced us, when I arrived to fetch my children after school one day, outside Beaumont Primary school in Somerset West, in the Western Cape, South Africa. Named after Lord Charles Somerset, Somerset West, with an old-world charm, lies in a beautiful valley protected by the majestic Hottentots-Holland mountain range. Located about 50 kilometres east of Cape Town, it is close to both the sea and the magnificent, towering, breathtakingly beautiful Helderberg Mountains. It is one of the loveliest towns of the Western Cape, with tall, stately, lush green trees, scenic drives and nature reserves that provide a home to thousands of flowering plants that saturate the mountains with colour.

I was newly single, my divorce finalised only two months previously. Still feeling totally fragmented, I was trying to get some order back into my life.

I thought the company of a gorgeous blonde could only help in my endeavours to regain my sanity, after the shock of a divorce after 13 years of what I believed had been a happy marriage. Because in Linda's words she was just "perfect" for me, I agreed to meet this fun-loving ex-Zimbabwean.

Jane's husband had run off with his secretary, and my wife Caren had fallen out of love with me and in love with a provincial cricketer. Jane and I were both 39. Although the divorce had come as a terrible blow to me, Caren was a good mother to our children and we parted company on amicable terms.

I was a born and raised in Somerset West and Jane had moved down from Zimbabwe with her husband in 1980. It is my firm belief that we were destined to meet.

Jane had four wonderful children.

Tracy, aged 21, was warm and conscientious, with gorgeous freckles that were the bane of her life, but which we all loved. Brett, aged 19, was the great adventurer. He was constantly seizing the moment to do something extraordinary, like climbing Mount Kilimanjaro to raise funds for "Reach for a Dream". Nicola, aged 12, had such a loving and outgoing personality that she was forever hugging everyone, while Bronwyn, aged ten, was the shy tomboy who loved animals.

I too had fathered three great children. Jason, aged 14, was the clown of the three, always goading the two little ones to break Dad's rules. Candice, aged 11, was the outgoing blue-eyed daddy's girl, while Jonathan, aged nine, was the fun, sporty type, always up for a ball game, no matter what.

Jane and I were attracted to one another from the start and for two years we played the dating game. I just loved her warm, generous nature and friendly smile. Her beauty was an added bonus. As for me, Jane always described me as being a "go-getter" with a mind of his own, strong-willed and yet extremely generous. Jane, being the cautious type, turned me down twice before agreeing to marry me in 1995.

Our wedding was a quiet affair with family and friends in the Methodist Church, and the reception in my sister Bernice's garden.

I never regretted marrying Jane, for little did I realise that one day I would need a strong compassionate woman like her by my side, to support me through that which was yet to come.

We settled down in Somerset West and suddenly… we had seven children, demanding a huge adjustment from Jane. I had no problem with this, since I grew up in a family of six, but Jane came from a small unit of three.

Jane and her two daughters, Nicola and Bronwyn, moved in with me into the house I had kept after the divorce. It was a big face brick, double-storey home, which I had designed and built on the Helderberg mountainside, with a swimming pool at the back. It had panoramic views of the most distinctive and stunning of all African landscapes, overlooking Strand and Gordon's Bay, the two most popular resorts of the False Bay Coast.

Jane's son Brett had just finished his BSc Hons in Biochemistry and was living in Johannesburg, working for an office machine company, selling photocopiers and the like. Typical of Brett, he did this for nine months to generate money needed to pay back his study loans. Only then did he move into the pharmaceutical industry to apply his marketing skills.

Tracy, her daughter, was married to Jacques, a game ranger, and both of them worked for a safari lodge near the Kruger Park.

My children, Jason, Candice and Jonathan lived with their mother Caren, who was now renting a townhouse in Somerset West.

Jane was happily employed by the old Allied Bank, which later became part of ABSA Bank in Somerset West. I was a Human Resource Director for a national retail company in Cape Town, after completing my Masters Degree in Industrial Psychology at Stellenbosch, Unisa and Rand Afrikaans University respectively over a period of seven years, until finally completing my internship in 1980.

Weekend visits from my children went smoothly without any major hassles and after a few months we became what we called "a great blended family". Jonathan was the youngest and fortunately for us, each of the children was a year apart.

We had family holidays in Knysna, Sun City, Maduma, Boma in the Eastern Transvaal and at the Wild Coast, and spent days creating many happy memories of the joy of being together as a family.

Yet Another Beginning!

In October 1996, I was offered a position as Managing Director of a Company in Zimbabwe that had a chain of retail stores nationwide. My career at the time was at a stalemate and so Jane and I decided we would take the plunge, leave South Africa and move to Bulawayo, Zimbabwe.

Although people living overseas may think we were moving to "deepest darkest Africa", Bulawayo is actually a modern, spacious, sunny city with a colourful history. It is Zimbabwe's second largest city, and is famous for streets laid out like a giant matrix, wide enough to accommodate eight cars side by side. These wide streets were necessary in the 1800s to allow wagons, drawn by eight oxen, to turn around. The name Bulawayo means "Place of slaughter", thought to refer to the time when there was a civil war between groups of Ndebele warriors – although historians differ on its origins.

I was looking forward to the move because, being in a subtropical zone, Bulawayo has the most amazing array of flowering shrubs like the bougainvillea, which in winter flowers prolifically in many shades – from purple to bright reds and oranges. From September through to November, before the start of the rains, the beautiful lilac-flowered Jacaranda trees that line many streets, burst into full bloom. Soon after this, the fiery flamboyant trees, with their heavy masses of red and orange flowers, take over the landscape.

I was also comforted by the fact that Bulawayo was only about three hours drive from Beitbridge, the border post with South Africa, making travelling by road to South Africa easy.

Moving to Bulawayo was going to be a big adjustment for the family. Even though it was a beautiful city, life there was totally different from that in Somerset West.

The children were devastated when we broke the news to them one Friday night in November 1996. Jane's children Bronwyn and Nicola would come with us, but my ex wouldn't hear of my children leaving with us for Bulawayo.

Moving away from my children was probably the hardest thing I had to do, knowing that I would only see them once or maybe twice a year. It was, however, a once-in-a-lifetime opportunity for me.

2 BULAWAYO

Do not follow where the path may lead, Go instead, where there is no path and leave a trail. AUTHOR UNKNOWN

On the 17th of February 1997 we crossed the border at Beitbridge to begin our lives in Zimbabwe. Travelling to our future home by car in February was a very "warm" experience, to say the least. Temperatures at Beitbridge reach over 45 degrees Celsius and the day we crossed was no different. Only the air conditioner in the car got us through. Even then, each time we stepped out of the car, it was like stepping out into a furnace.

Beitbridge is situated 500 kilometres north of Johannesburg, the capital of Gauteng, South Africa, and is the busiest border crossing in Africa and perhaps also the most disorganised.

We became bogged down in a quagmire of humanity. The queues were long and service was very slow. Perhaps it was due to the terrible heat, or maybe to the pure incompetence, but our patience was sorely tested.

We had to wait endless hours in a long line of trucks and cars in the blazing hot sun, while our passports and papers were checked and checked again, our car was searched, every item had to be accounted for, until at long last, we were cleared by customs, allowed to leave and head for Bulawayo.

Interestingly the Zimbabwe dollar had been stable three years prior to our arrival in 1997 at around ZW$2 to R1. The Zimbabwe Stock Exchange had grown over 90% in US$ terms the previous year, and the business I was to take over, was poised for massive growth.

With already 120 stores nationwide, the aim was to double the company's size within five years. All things considered, this seemed like a golden opportunity. Little did I know that by November of that year, a mere nine months after our arrival, the so-called "War Veterans" would rise up and storm parliament, demanding gratuities, leading to President Mugabe's ZW$50 000 handout to each of them. This would convert to about R25 000 for around 50 000 people. Every one of them also received ZW$2 000 or R1 000 pension per month for life.

This one political move, devoid of any economic principle, was to be the catalyst, which, I believe, led to the slow collapse of the Zimbabwe Economy. On that "Black Friday", 14th November 1997, the Zimbabwe dollar, which had been so resilient, collapsed from ZW$14: US$1 to ZW$26: US$1, or from ZW$3: R1 to ZW$5,5: R1, effectively losing half its value in one day. The Zimbabwe Stock Exchange lost 40% of its value that same Friday. This was the start of the eventual total crash of the Zimbabwe economy and its currency.

In March 1997 we moved into a beautiful house, set on an acre of ground, in Burnside, Bulawayo. The garden sold the house. It had giant Natal mahogany trees, with lush lawns and a swimming pool for the kids. Jane was pretty chuffed with the big back garden, ample space for the bantam hens, which she had always wanted to keep, and a cool shade-cloth-covered area where she could grow her orchids. To crown it all, there was a huge birdcage where she could start an aviary, something she had always dreamed of doing. Birds were, and still are, her passion.

Of course, having a permanent gardener and a live-in domestic house keeper wasn't too bad either!

Despite living in such an exquisite home, as expected our first two years in Zimbabwe were the most difficult. They say, it can take up to five years to settle and make new friends when changing countries, and should therefore not be undertaken lightly. As expatriates, we found Bulawayo people a pretty tight-knit community, who had lived there all their lives. Return invites after a braai at our home were few and far between, but luckily we got to meet the parents of the kids' school friends, as well as other folks, when attending the odd social at schools.

I decided to join the Golf Club, having been Captain of the Somerset Club three years previously. Golf was my passion and it introduced me to a large cross-section of the Bulawayo community, which was very useful for developing business contacts.

While I was kept busy, especially with work and golf, Jane decided to study alternative healing methods. She found a lady who was a qualified reflexology teacher and after a year of hard studying, she opened her own practice at home. Reflexology is a form of massage where pressure is applied to parts of the feet and hands to promote relaxation and healing elsewhere in the body.

Her interest grew and she went on to complete Reiki and Shiatsu courses. Reiki is a treatment in which healing energy is channelled from the practitioner to the patient to enhance energy and reduce stress and fatigue. Shiatsu is a form of healing massage, in which the hands are used to apply pressure at acupuncture points on the body, in order to stimulate and redistribute energy. Now Jane became a qualified Complementary Health Care Practitioner, and her practice kept her really busy, giving her the opportunity to meet a lot of very nice people. Although many now have left Zimbabwe, they still maintain regular contact via e-mail.

We decided to explore our new home country with visits to Milibizi or Kariba, Victoria Falls, Great Zimbabwe ruins in Masvingo and Nyanga in the Eastern Highlands.

Of all of these, Victoria Falls was our favourite. The famous falls stretch over a width of more than 1 700 metres. We loved to stop in a clearing overlooking the Main Falls, and to watch the sun rising, its golden brilliance etching the mist that billowed up from the chasm below. We just never got tired of watching the water fall, as if it was hypnotised by the power of the Zambezi as it thundered into its self-made gorge. We often forgot to take our raincoats, so when a breeze blew the massive sprays of water up from the thunderous falls, it would drench our hair and T-shirts. The local name for the mighty Victoria Falls is "Mosi-oa-Tunya", in English "The smoke that thunders".

Another favourite was the huge Victoria Falls Safari Lodge Hotel, built entirely out of logs, and which pre-2001 was a bustling hive of tourists. We loved visiting the crocodile farm, playing golf on the magnificent Elephant Hills Hotel golf course, where impala and warthog were permanent, and stray elephant occasional residents.

Curio sellers with the famous Nyami Nyami river god necklaces and bracelets, beautifully fashioned out of stone, were a great hit at Safari Lodge. We would sit on their veranda, overlooking the waterhole, sipping an ice-cold "Pilsner" or "Bollinger", gin and tonic or just a rock shandy, watching vast herds of buffalo, various smaller buck, and on one occasion, a herd of over 50 elephant emerge silently from the bush, also anxious to quench *their* thirst. We were convinced this was the specially-protected Presidential Herd, about which we had heard so much, despite the fact that they were normally found in the Hwange reserve, 200 kilometres south of Victoria Falls.

When my children came up from Cape Town, we would take the five "little" ones on holiday around Zimbabwe. The brilliant climate made the whole vacation even more memorable. Hot in summer, approaching 36 degrees Celsius, with late afternoon thunderstorms from November through to April. Winters in Bulawayo could hardly be described as cold, with clear blue skies and only the very occasional frost in the early morning. Little did I realise just how important those happy memories would become, like a treasure chest for me to delve into in the years to come.

Bird life in our Burnside garden was prolific. We had our resident brown-hooded shrieking kingfishers, kestrels and Heuglin robins – olive brown above, white eye-stripe, and dull orange underparts – that would captivate us with their melodious voices at dawn and dusk. Other exotic residents were the brightly-coloured crested barbets, hopping around the trees or foraging on the lawn, sounding like an alarm clock with the bells removed.

Sometimes there was quite a symphony of sound when the Cape turtledoves joined in with their ubiquitous call that sounds rather like "where's FA-ther, where's FA-ther".

The family of hoopoes resident in our roof, delighted us each year by raising their little families of two or three chicks. These beautiful birds with rufous, black and white feathers, are about 20 centimetres tall, use long petite beaks for probing the ground for worms, and display distinctive brown feathery crests, which stand up straight when the bird is alert.

Jane developed an early-morning ritual of feeding these wild birds with breadcrumbs and wild-bird seeds, ensuring a steady stream of feathered friends in the garden. Their vibrant colours and different calls were like a glamorous and wonderfully melodious avian orchestra, performing throughout the day, in and around our home.

Schools in Zimbabwe were renowned for their high academic and disciplinary standards. This prompted me to bring my youngest, 12-year-old Jonathan, to Zimbabwe to complete his high school years at Christian Brothers College in Bulawayo in 1998.

Breaking up the family unit of my three children and their mom was not a simple decision to make. My eldest son Jason was doing Matric, so he could not join us, and Candice wanted to stay with her mom and close circle of friends.

I remember Jonathan's first days at a predominantly black school. It was a tremendous change for him, and adjusting to the new culture was not easy. Adapting was even more difficult because he came from the just-out-of-apartheid South Africa, where all his classmates were white and acted and reacted as he did, whereas now, for the first time in his life, his class was filled mainly with black pupils, who did not speak English as fluently as he did.

Jonathan went on to become senior prefect, even though he was not Catholic, and captained CBC's First Rugby Team. The highlight of his school sporting years was when he played lock, representing Zimbabwe at the South African schools Craven Week in Wellington in the Cape. His team-mates included the present Springbok Tighthead prop "Beast" Matawarira who, in the Craven week, played eighth-man.

On Jonathan's own admission, he loves Zimbabwe and, after graduating from

Stellenbosch University with a sports science and teaching degree, I believe, if it were not for the current situation in the country, he would be teaching in Zimbabwe now.

Life in Bulawayo for Nicola, Bronwyn and Jonathan was a lot different from their lives in Somerset West. There were no malls like the ones in South Africa, where the teenagers can hang out over weekends, perhaps go to movies with friends, have coffee or just browse through the latest fashions. No bookshops where the teenage publications fill three or four shelves, from health to the latest celebrity gossip magazines.

In Bulawayo there was school, school sports on a Saturday and maybe a Sunday spent at Ncema dam for a braai with friends. Teenagers tended to spend a lot of time at each other's houses, watching pirated DVDs or playing pool, if a table was on hand. Our swimming pool was also well used, as was our DVD player.

Socialising was a big part of the children's growing up. I like to believe that, although drugs were available, but because Bulawayo was a small white community, our young people were saved the peer pressure and exposure to the more seedy and negative aspects of teenage life, whilst enjoying the outdoors to a greater extent than the youngsters "down South".

ZIMBABWE **WARM HEART** UGLY FACE

3

THE GOOD TIMES
[1997 – 2000]

All your dreams can come true if you have the courage to pursue them. WALT DISNEY

Despite the depreciation of the Zimbabwe dollar during this period, our business grew steadily. Foreign currency was readily available from banks and we could import products from all over the world. Over the Christmas period our shops were filled with children's toys imported from Hong Kong.

The devaluation of the Zimbabwe dollar against other currencies was slow and manageable at the time, with an annual inflation rate in 1997 of 20%, rising to only 56% by the year 2000.

Our business grew from 120 shops to over one hundred and seventy. Life in Zimbabwe during this period – 1997 to 2000 – was really great. Products were the cheapest in the region. Biltong and cigarettes were the most popular items on visiting business associates' lists, at almost half the price of the same items in South Africa. The country's infrastructure was sound and well maintained, hotels offered quality service, tourism was still a big income earner and farmers were producing most of the country's food and beverage needs. The kids' favourite drink was Schweppes cherry plum. Of course mine was an ice-cold Pilsner or Bollinger beer, all produced and bottled locally. Bottles still carried a deposit, so there was an incentive to return them, unlike today when empty beer and soft-drink cans litter the countryside.

We managed to buy a second-hand car for Nicola when she turned 16, the legal driving age in Zimbabwe, to ferry herself, Bronwyn and Jonathan (Jonny) to and from school and sports' meets.

Everything was available, cross-border shopping wasn't heard of, except for a unique engine part or some other more specialised items.

Plumbers, electricians and other service providers would be around within a few hours if you needed them. There were no such things as power and water cuts. Garbage was collected once a week, and when a pothole appeared in the road, it was repaired within days. All roads had white lines, whereas today we wait for April to come around.

That is the time of the ZITF, the international exhibition, which runs concurrently with the agricultural show at the enormous showgrounds near the centre of town. The Bulawayo City Council patches the potholes and paints the white lines on the road from the airport through town to the exhibition centre, so that when President Mugabe arrives, he is not hit by the state of the roads around town.

Ten years ago we could not have imagined the decay that we would be facing.

Up until 2000, I was convinced that our decision to move to Zimbabwe was definitely the right one. As a family we were happy, the youngsters loved the schools and we had made a number of friends, so weekends were taken up with school sports days, braais with friends, trips to tourist sites and other family entertainment. Life was fantastic.

The Best Kept Secret in the World?

The Zimbabwean shareholders of the company I worked for owned a houseboat on Kariba, and we were privileged to use it. Pete, the patriarch, Clive, his brother John, Everett and Thano, had started the company in 1976. They had worked tirelessly to build a big family-owned business. By 1996, however, they realised that they had to review the ownership of the company and move to a corporate entity if they wanted to survive and grow. This prompted their decision to sell a majority stake to the Cape Town based international company, the first move that led to my arrival in Zimbabwe.

As shareholders, they had built a magnificent 20-metre (65-foot) single-hull steel boat with two inboard motors for their holidays on Lake Kariba. Pete had designed it and watched its construction in Zimbabwe. With two cabins in the front and one double cabin in the rear, the boat could comfortably accommodate eight people. It was air conditioned throughout for those 40-degree-plus days on Kariba, came complete with a captain, chef and deckhand, was fitted with a dining room and lounge, with a covered upper deck open to the lake. This certainly was the best kept holiday secret in the world!

We would drive up to Kariba from Bulawayo with the kids plus some of their friends or some of our visiting family. The journey itself took seven hours, broken by a lunch stop and a visit to the awesome caves at Chinhoyi with their spectacular indigo-coloured pools of water.

The last 70 kilometres of the journey are along a winding road down into the Zambezi Valley. The humidity in October is almost unbearable for outsiders, hence the air conditioning on the boat. Arriving for the first time at Kariba is quite breathtaking. A drive up to the Heights, a mountain overlooking Kariba town and nestled on the lake's edge, reveals a panoramic view of the lake.

I will never forget my first sighting of this vast expanse of water. For me, a Cape Town boy whose experience of dams was limited to the farm dams where as boy scouts we used to build wooden rafts, the size of Kariba was hard to comprehend. You could not see the end and the two sides were only just visible through a shimmering heat haze. Below, the houseboats were mere specks on the water.

In the early 1940s a study was carried out on the possibility of building a hydroelectric power plant on the Zambezi River. This scheme would supply power to the growing colonies of Southern and Northern Rhodesia, now Zimbabwe and Zambia.

Lake Kariba, until recently the largest man-made lake in the world, is located on the Zambezi River, about 1 300 kilometres upstream from the Indian Ocean. Building of the dam wall started in 1950. The name "Kariba" is derived from the local Shona word "Kariva", which means "trap" and refers to a giant rock jutting out from the gorge where the dam wall was to be built. Between 1958 and 1963 the dam filled up, flooding the Kariba Gorge and the Zambezi Valley, displacing thousands of the local Ba Tonga people in the process. In 1957, with the dam wall almost complete, the worst floods ever recorded on the Zambezi River struck. Much of the dam wall was destroyed and many workers were killed, including many Italian artisans involved in the construction. A memorial church was built on the Heights, the highest hill overlooking Kariba town. In the church, plaques with the names of those who died during the construction of the dam commemorate this sacrifice.

The local Ba Tonga people believe the river god Nyami Nyami, who lives in the river, was angry at the construction of the dam and took revenge with the flooding. In spite of the god's anger, in 1960 the generators were switched on, supplying hydroelectric power to Zimbabwe and Zambia for the first time.

We would arrive at about three in the afternoon, check into the Carribea Bay Hotel, a Sardinian-style complex built right on the lake's high-water mark, and immediately jump into the shimmering coolness of the swimming pool. The kids would be occupied on the waterslides, while we adults started to unwind with ice-cold refreshments.

Next morning we would drive the short distance to Marineland Harbour after a hearty Carribea Bay Hotel breakfast. All our food and drinks for the trip were ordered through the harbour staff, who offered this as a service. All you had to do was get onto the boat, sit back and relax. Of course all this changed over the years, and by the time we went on our trip ten years later in 2008, we had to bring everything with us, from meat to toilet rolls and beer, purchased across the border in Botswana, necessitating at least two cars and trailers loaded to the brim.

The houseboat holidays followed a simple routine. We would travel for about four hours down the lake to well-known spots like Bumi, Gordon's Bay, Tiger Bay or Elephant Point. We would arrive at about 2.30 in the afternoon. The captain would "beach" the boat on the shore very skilfully, and tightly fasten two ropes onto tree stumps to anchor the boat overnight.

At about three we would jump into the tender boats, two four-metre (14-foot) speed boats, together with our fishing rods, our bait of earthworms for the bream – tilapia, a very nice eating fish – and kapenta, a small sardine-like fish as bait for the famous Zambezi tiger fish.

Kapenta were introduced into Lake Kariba in the 60s from Lake Tanganyika. They multiplied at a phenomenal rate and now form the staple diet of many locals. Kapenta fishing rigs are no more than two pontoons with a derrick, the latter holding a bowl-shaped net the size of a small swimming pool. At night this net is lowered into the water, just beneath the surface, and a massive bright light is hung above it, attracting the small fish. The net is raised, emptied into containers and lowered again. This process is repeated until the crew of two have filled the boat. Kapenta fishing has become a huge industry in Zimbabwe, supporting thousands of families.

It is not hard to imagine, when watching the flickering kapenta rig lights dance across the water, that you are on a lake bordering a popular beach resort and not in the middle of Africa.

The captain and deckhand, who knew all the good fishing areas, piloted the tender boats. Once in the chosen spot, we would "worm up" our fishing rod hooks and simply dangle the line overboard. Within minutes we would be pulling up the bream. Average bream size is about one kilo, with rare records of four-kilo bream and above. So confident were we of catching fish, that Jane always left two evening meals open when drawing up the menu. Luckily we have never gone hungry on the boat!

Tiger fishing on the other hand is proper fishing. The tiger fish is a game fish and a predator of the Zambezi. Some specimens grow as huge as 16 kilos, but anything around one kilo and upwards will give you the fight of your life. Catching tiger is the ultimate ambition of any fishing trip to the lake. It is a sleek silver fish with black stripes and a big orange tail, razor-like interlocking teeth and jaws that open and shut with an audible snap. They fight madly to escape, leaping high out of the water.

The adrenalin rush when a tiger hits your line is indescribable. You cast far from the boat, preferably moored against Kariba's landmark and unique trees, and reel in quite fast. The predator tiger chases your bait aggressively, making for incredibly exciting fishing.

When Kariba filled in 1956, many trees were submerged. As a result, all along the lake's shoreline there are now forests of tree trunks sticking out of the water, resembling a world war battlefield of bare stumps, as if the trees were destroyed by explosions and fire. That these trees have survived and not simply rotted away, is a mystery to me. The unmistakable haunting call of the majestic fish eagle, nesting high in these bare trees, brings goosebumps to your whole body. Its distinctive dark brown wings and white breast, neck and cheeks make it easily recognisable.

Normally we would fish until about six in the evening, then head back to the boat for sundowners and snacks.

Watching the sun set on Kariba has to be the most impressive show nature produces! That huge blood red and orange ball, its colour intensified by the smoke from veld fires and dust, slowly sinking, highlighting the haunting dead trees in the water and silhouetting the hulks of elephants strolling down to the water to drink. I always said that everyone, once in their lifetime, has to experience a Kariba sunset, or risk dying having missed what life is really all about.

Sitting on the open upper deck watching the stars, while the kids take bets on who spots the first shooting star, is a uniquely enriching experience. The nighttime echoing bellow of the huge hippo, which sounds like a power boat starting its engine, the roar of distant lion or an angry trumpeting elephant, are all part of the deeply moving encounter with the magic of Kariba.

After a huge supper prepared by Aron the chef, in a kitchen no bigger than one and a half square metres and served in the dining room/lounge, we would clear away the dishes and break open a pack of cards or play Trivial Pursuit. By about nine everyone would be ready for bed. The kids would all opt to sleep under the mosquito nets on the upper deck because of the heat, which even at that time has not quite subsided, with temperatures still in the late teens and early 20s.

Next morning at six, after rusks, biscuits and coffee, we would once again set out fishing, returning at nine for a full English breakfast of crispy bacon, pork bangers, sweet-corn fritters, fried eggs, toast and marmalade, rounded off with steaming hot coffee or tea.

After breakfast or brunch everyone would do their own thing, some preferring to read, some snooze in the shade on the upper deck with the constant breeze, as we would push away from the shore and travel for another three or four hours up the lake to our next spot, while Jane would be scouring the shore watching the buffalo, lion or elephant herds as we drifted slowly along.

It really is difficult to describe the relaxation one experiences on a houseboat trip.

No news, no TV, just nature at its best. I recall one morning we had to delay our push off from the shore, as two big bull elephant blocked the pathway of the boat crew who went to untie the mooring ropes attached to trees on the shoreline. Whilst the one jumbo rubbed his back against the tree we were using as a mooring anchor, the other one was pulling muddy water grass from the shallows with its trunk, gently swishing it back and forth in the water to get rid of the mud. For over an hour we took photos and just quietly watched this gigantic creature behave so gently.

After four or five days on the houseboat, with our human batteries totally recharged, we are woken at five and set off for the harbour, travelling the last one hour from the nearest island Sampakaruma.

The trip back to Bulawayo was most times quiet. I am sure everyone was replaying in their minds the experiences of the last few days or just listening to their favourite artists on their iPods.

Tiger Fishing at Its Best

In 2000 Brett, who was now married and living in Johannesburg with his wife Nicky, organised a fishing trip with his father-in-law and two friends to the Zambezi river, at a fishing camp on the Zimbabwean side, just five kilometres from the Zimbabwe-Zambia border post of Chirundu. The camp consisted of four thatched rondavels surrounded with lawns that stretched down to the mighty Zambezi River's edge.

This was a tiger fisherman's paradise. Hiring small speed boats and drivers, who knew where all the sandbanks in the river were, we would push off from the bank and drift lazily downstream, all the while casting toward the bank in search of the elusive tiger fish. I drove up from Bulawayo, a similar distance to Kariba on each of the three trips we made.

The remoteness of the area was brought home on a number of occasions. Once we were prevented from pulling our speed boat from the river by a small herd of elephant that had decided to come down to our slipway for a drink. On another occasion, two of Brett's friends, who were both PHs from South Africa, were surprised by a hippo as they innocently relieved themselves behind a tree on the river bank one night as we were about to put the meat on the braai.

All we saw was a flash of two bodies flying past us with a hippo in pursuit! Luckily the bulky animal only took a few paces and then retreated into the water. Both PHs lost their sandals, or rather *ran out* of their sandals that night! When there were lions in the area, the camp owner would come down early in the morning and warn us not to wander too far out of camp because of the presence of the big cats.

Floating down the mighty Zambezi, in some places over 200 metres wide, with a tiger line in the water, sipping ice-cold lagers, has got to be *the* most relaxing of fishing experiences. We would put the boats in the water and let the current take us downstream, past the Kafue river mouth where it meets the Zambezi, all the while trolling for that elusive tiger fish. Since the Zambian bank is more heavily populated, more game roams on the Zimbabwean side, adding to the sense of Eden.

One day, relaxing in our boat floating down the river, we were jolted out of our relax mode by hysterical screaming. Where minutes before we had seen a "mokorokoro" or wooden dugout canoe with two locals, there was now frantic splashing in the water. They were obviously returning from an early morning or overnight fishing trip, fighting against the current trying to get from the Zimbabwean to the Zambian side. We had remarked only a few minutes earlier how crazy these guys were to be paddling a narrow open boat in crocodile and hippo infested waters.

Shouting to Mannie, Eric and Brett to reel in their lines, I swung the motor into life and gunned it to get us to the middle of the river where the locals had capsized. One was splashing around and we managed to drag him into the boat, but the second fisherman had disappeared. Suddenly Mannie spotted him just below the surface, wide-eyed. Within a few seconds we had dragged him into the boat as well, coughing, spluttering and half drowned. All they could say was "Bless you, bless you!" We only managed to save the one guy's still-floating flip-flops; the other pair was gone. All this took about ten minutes. Neither man was able to swim – as we discovered through excited sign language and gesticulation. They were Zambians, so we steered to their side of the river, about two kilometres upstream.

By the time we got to the drop-off place, a crowd of about fifty singing, wailing and praise-singing villagers had gathered. An elder stepped forward, thanked and blessed us for saving their children. How they had known that the two were in trouble, we never did find out. Mannie had the last word. In measured tones he spoke directly to the one guy he had pulled from below the water. "One day, when you become President of Zambia, just remember me and how I saved your life!"

That night while sitting around the fire, enjoying Mannie's five-star supper, we speculated what the fate of those two young men would have been, had we not been fishing for tiger!

These were wonderful days, when getting fuel for a trip of this nature was not a problem, as any garage on the road up to Chirundu was well stocked.

Brett's last trip with his father-in-law Mannie and brother-in-law Eric was in 2002, when obtaining fuel had become a serious problem and the state's paranoia was reaching fever pitch. After clearing the Beitbridge border, complete with fishing gear and foodstuffs, as well as 60 litres of fuel, they were stopped at one of the numerous roadblocks, which had sprung up all over the country. At this roadblock, about 80 kilometres from the border, they were asked to produce customs clearance forms for all their goods. No amount of explaining or reasoning could persuade these policemen that they were holidaymakers and had stamped passports and car papers to prove it. After making them unpack everything, down to their suitcases of clothes, these policemen ordered them back to the border to get a customs-stamped form listing all their imports. It was obvious they were looking for a bribe from what they assumed to be unsuspecting tourists. We suppose that, on discovering that the visitors were instead seasoned travellers to Zimbabwe and that the bribe would not be forthcoming, the police sent them back to the border so that the "forces of law and order" could save face.

This one experience cured them of ever coming to Zimbabwe again.

4. THE BEGINNING OF THE END
[2000 – 2005]

Our legacy should be that you made it better than it was when you got it. LEE IACOCCA

This period, which I have called "The Beginning of the End", was characterised by tremendous violence in the country, almost entirely directed at the white farmers.

From 2000, when the farm invasions were at their height, until 2007 – the years that are the main focus of my book – the country and its economy fell deeper and deeper into despair and ruin. By 2007 over 1 500 people per day were crossing the border at Beitbridge into South Africa. This started as a trickle in 2001/2002, but grew to a thunderous roaring river of people by June 2007. It was a direct result of falling standards, lack of products on the shelves and the worthlessness of the Zimbabwe dollar.

By 2002 the black market for foreign currency was flourishing. To catch the little amount that was on offer, Government maintained a totally ridiculous "official rate" of the US$ versus the ZW$, which was in fact up to ten times less than the more realistic parallel or black-market rate. For instance, if you were a visitor and had US dollars, you would receive ZW$1 000 for each US dollar at the bank. Should you, however, be brave enough to arrange to buy Zimbabwe dollars on the black or parallel market, you would receive up to ZW$10 000. All products and services were priced according to the parallel rate, by businesses that had to buy their raw materials using US$ sourced on the black market. In practice, this meant that a tourist coming to Zimbabwe would stay in a hotel in Victoria Falls for ZW$2.8 million. Using the black-market or parallel rate, it would cost R350 a night or about US$35 bought at ZW$8 000 to R1 or ZW$80 000 to US$1, which was a fair price.

An additional public-relations fiasco was the government-promulgated law stating that all foreigners had to pay their hotel bills, drinks, meals and all other consumables at hotels in foreign currency. To avoid cheating, it was compulsory for all Zimbabweans or Zimbabwe residents to show their passport or Zimbabwean ID when settling their hotel bills in ZW$. Therefore, tourists staying at the same hotel, who exchanged their US dollars at the bank, would pay US$350 or about R3 500 instead of R350 (or US$35) for the same accommodation, because all hotels had to use the bank rate when exchanging foreign currency.

No rocket science is necessary to deduce that with this dual currency rate operating in the country, tourism plummeted. Zimbabwe became the most expensive tourist destination in the world, with beer costing up to US$12 at hotels. Tourism, the second-highest income earner prior to 2000, simply collapsed.

Fuel – A Serious Problem!

This collapse was exacerbated by chronic fuel shortages. The lack of foreign currency prevented the government-owned and sole supplier of fuel from importing this vital commodity.

Fuel queues at service stations first surfaced in 2000/2001 and sitting in one was a novelty at first. They became longer and longer as the fuel dried up and imports dwindled. Our drivers worked shifts to fill the company vehicles, or simply left the cars locked in a queue overnight or for however long it took for the fuel to arrive – sometimes up to five days.

These queues became real social occasions. Wives would pack a basket of goodies and meet each other at a particular fuel station, which somebody had assured them would receive fuel in the late afternoon.

At the crack of dawn they would get into line, then spend the day socialising and chatting. Sometimes the fuel didn't arrive and ladies went home disappointed, only to start queuing again the next morning.

If you pulled your car out to go home, your place in the queue could be secured by any number of items – from dustbins to empty beer crates or a pile of bricks.

Of course as time went on, we made a plan and started sending our three-ton truck across the border to Botswana, an hour's drive away, with five 200-litre steel drums, which were filled with either petrol or diesel in Botswana and driven back to Bulawayo.

Because of these shortages, the government of Zimbabwe levied only a minimal import tax on fuel. The upshot of this was that Jane's and the kids' days of sitting in fuel queues were over.

These years also honed the smuggling skills of many Zimbabweans, especially in foreign currency. Obviously it was illegal to be caught with even the smallest amount of foreign currency if you did not have proof that it was drawn from a registered bank, which naturally did not have any to give you anyway! To simply survive, everyone had to buy foreign currency illegally on the street and for holidays or business trips out of the country, people needed the precious stuff for all their purchases, from clothing and tyres to calculators for the business.

I am sure the government was aware of what was going on, but turned a semi-blind eye to ensure the economy ticked over. Every now and then a businessman or private individual was caught and jailed for the possession of foreign currency.

Coupled with this was also the capital flight from the country. Everybody was trying to convert their Zimbabwe dollars into hard currency, usually Rands or US dollars, and then take it out of the country.

Smuggling of foreign currency took place on a huge scale. When flying out of the country, notes would be rolled up in balls of socks in suitcases, hidden in books, in shoes, on your person, in your underpants, wherever the traveller thought they would be safe. If you were driving it was much easier, since the same technique could be used in a motor vehicle.

Roadblock searches always covered dashboard cubby holes, sun visors, seat pockets and other easily-accessible places, but ignored CD shuttles, tool kits and spare wheels!

The Start of the Brain Drain

The year 2001, with the farms in chaos, and the government's vigorous persecution of everyone perceived to be disagreeing with its policies, the brain drain at our company started. "Brain drain" simply means that some senior well-qualified members of staff leave the company without notice and without telling their boss.

I will never forget our first case of brain drain. Victor was our Operations Manager. His wife and mother-in-law were heavily involved in the formation of the opposition party MDC. They had to flee the country and seek asylum in the UK, ending up in Birmingham, leaving Victor on his own in Bulawayo. One morning, about four months after Victor's wife had left Zimbabwe, I got a call in my office from someone identifying himself as Mr. So-and-So from immigration at Heathrow airport. He wanted to know if Victor, who was presently in his office at Heathrow, worked for us and whether he had been granted leave for a three-week stay in the UK. Not able to speak to Victor, but at the same time not wishing him any harm, I answered both questions in the affirmative. I asked around at head office whether anyone had known of Victor's plans to go to the UK on holiday, but no one knew anything. Needless to say, that was the last I ever saw of my Operations Manager!

Over the years we lost staff in various disciplines, from cleaners to senior bookkeepers, who would phone from down south or send a fax from Australia, informing us that they were not coming back. When I asked Fanuel, then our Personnel Manager, why they hadn't come and discussed their departure with us, his only comment was, "It's a cultural thing."

This brain drain wasn't limited to business only. Jonny's one teacher, Mr. Phiri, who was a real 1.45m (4ft 6in) bundle of energy, and whom Jonny and his mates really enjoyed, accompanied the first team as the team manager on a rugby tour to Boksburg near Johannesburg in South Africa. Within a month of returning to Bulawayo, he was gone. He had accepted a position at a private school in Johannesburg. About two years later he came bouncing into my office in Bulawayo, bypassing reception and my secretary, to let me know how he was doing in Johannesburg. He now owned a flat, drove a smart car, which he was paying off, was married and very happy. He reminded me of how he used to have to bum lifts to and from work from some of the senior boys or parents at CBC. Now he owned his own car, something he never would have been able to achieve in Bulawayo.

2003 – Health And Safety Issues

The year 2003 proved to be full of unique experiences for me. Inflation had now surpassed the 385% mark. This effectively meant that everything you bought last year now cost four times more. A dress selling for the equivalent of R100 last year, would now cost you R400. The stresses of replacement costing, government regulations, elections in 2002 and the accompanying violence and intimidation our staff were exposed to, were starting to take their toll on me.

I was trying to navigate a huge organisation through uncharted waters. There were no textbooks on how to trade in hyperinflationary conditions. Double-digit inflation was enough of a challenge, but we were in the triple-digit inflation phase. Pressure from staff for salary increases, landlords expecting their rent to keep pace with inflation, suppliers refusing to commit to prices until the product was delivered into our warehouse, were just some of the issues and pressures on me and the team.

Sitting in our monthly property meeting early in 2003, discussing the demand by more and more landlords to switch from annual lease negotiations to quarterly or monthly renegotiations of rentals, necessitated by the fast-depreciating value of the currency, I picked up a biscuit and took a bite. I swallowed and suddenly I had this tremendous tightness across my chest. Thinking it might just be gas, and never having experienced a heart attack before, I waited for the tightness to pass.

It didn't! Elana glanced at me and asked if I was feeling ok, since I had gone quite pale. I admitted I was feeling a bit queasy and that there was a tightness about my chest.

Within ten minutes I was in our local doctor Geoff's surgery with a tablet under my tongue. An ECG was what he felt I needed. Within another hour I found myself in the local Catholic hospital's Intensive Care Unit, with heart monitors attached to various parts of my body.

Jane was overseas in the UK visiting Bronwyn, who had decided to take a gap year. Jonny and I were alone at home, with him finishing his A levels. I phoned Jonny, told him not to panic, but that he should bring me pyjamas as I was in ICU. Within ten minutes he was there, obviously very concerned for my welfare. After two days I was discharged, instructed to take it easy and recommended to see a specialist down south.

A week after Jane got back from the UK, we were off to Somerset West to see the specialists. The angiogram showed my heart was great and free from blocked arteries. Then came a visit to the stomach specialist. He stood me in front of a machine to scan my abdomen and asked me to drink the vile paste-like barium meal, which if it had been a bit thicker, I would have had to chew. No wonder they call it a "meal"!

As this substance passed through my stomach, it was clearly visible on the screen and highlighted my stomach. The specialist asked me if I was under any stress. As usual I replied that I was not aware of any. He then requested me to look at the screen. There was my stomach, flapping around like a fish out of water. He then requested me to close my eyes and think of the most beautiful idyllic spot I had ever visited, and imagine myself there. I did as asked and after about a minute he said, "Look at the screen."

I was amazed. My stomach was as quiet as a soundly-sleeping baby. Absolutely still. Stress apparently causes the stomach to react this way and ultimately goes into a spasm, imitating the tight-chest feeling of a heart attack.

The specialist's advice to me, with Jane very keen to hear his diagnosis, was unequivocal: change your job or prepare for major problems up ahead. The stress, as he pointed out very candidly, was going to kill me!

Obviously the whole episode was a wake-up call. Living day by day in Zimbabwe, one tends to accept the situation as stress free, because every day one makes plans and solves problems, so that there seem to be no huge lingering unsolved and worrying issues. The specialist did highlight the difference between stress and worry, with stress not for nothing called "the silent killer".

On the specialist's advice, strongly supported by Jane, we decided that at least every six weeks we needed to escape the stresses of Zimbabwe and slip away, just to get out of the environment.

We decided to do shopping trips to Polokwane over a weekend, where I could have a game of golf and Jane could undergo some retail therapy. Although it entailed going through Beitbridge border post and driving a further two hours, it was worth it. After golf on the Saturday, we would go out for a nice meal in a good restaurant with a nice bottle of red wine.

Whenever Jane felt things were really hectic, she would suggest a flight to Cape Town for me to unwind for a few days. These trips certainly did the trick, and occasionally we would drive from Somerset West to Knysna on the east coast, about four hours away. At other times we would drive the one and a half hours to visit my dad Jack and his wife Val in the beautiful little village Bonnievale, on the east coast, on the same road as Knysna. He and I would have nine holes of "golf therapy" – as we referred to our time together. I would bounce all sorts of ideas and tales off him, and he would supply the wise answers that only an 80-year-old retired businessman and father could give.

Knysna was simply our best and most relaxing getaway. Good friends, Charles and his wife Libby, moved there many years ago and own a few fantastic restaurants and delis. Our favourite is "34 Degrees South". This is an eatery, deli and Knysna souvenir shop all rolled into one. Jane could choose her fresh prawns and calamari virtually straight from the seawater. I could enjoy traditional Cape Bobotie, a sort of South African curried sweet and sour cottage pie, without the mashed potatoes on top, served with yellow rice and chutney.

Staying with Charles and Libby would be a real break. Knysna exudes a much more laid-back lifestyle. We spent evenings at their home drinking lots of red wine, meeting modern-day hippies and reminiscing. These breaks helped us through the trying times in Zimbabwe, but more importantly, helped us maintain a perspective on what life is all about. One could so easily get sucked up by events and happenings in Zimbabwe that one could begin to believe one's own theories about how a business should operate.

Attempted Hijack!

Later that year, in September 2003, I was invited to the United States of America, together with colleagues who were based at our mother company in Cape Town, to attend a strategic retail management course, which was run by Babson School of Excellence in conjunction with The College of William and Mary in Williamsburg, South Carolina.

The course ran over eight days and was reputedly very intensive. I flew from Bulawayo via Johannesburg to Cape Town, where I met up with my five colleagues, most of whom I had worked with before leaving Cape Town. Not only was it great to see the guys again, but to be travelling to the States was a huge bonus. Leon, Louis, Paul, John and I had worked with or known each other before, but this was our first meeting with Graham.

The flight from Cape Town to the USA takes about 11 hours. Unfortunately, having boarded in Johannesburg, I was not seated with my colleagues, but was upstairs in the economy section of the old Jumbo Jet, also known as the bubble section. The flight itself was pretty uneventful, and I was battling to go to sleep. As I had seen the movies available, I decided to play some poker on the on-board entertainment console, really enjoying the challenge and stimulation it offered. I was up about US$300 000 – unfortunately only a computer game – at about four o'clock in the morning, about three hours out of Atlanta in the USA, when all of a sudden there was a loud shout, "Back off! Back off!"

Unsurprisingly, even concentrating as hard as I was, I almost jumped out of my seat. There, with his back to the cockpit door, about five metres in front of me, stood a wild-eyed gentleman with a weapon of sorts in his hand. I couldn't make out what it was, but within a few seconds the passengers in the front three or four rows were crowded around our seats because they were further back. In front of this potential hijacker stood the man at whom the calls to back off were made, a great hulk off a man, at least two metres tall and built like a front-row rugby forward.

I later found out he was the undercover air marshal, at least one of which travels on all planes flying into the States. After what seemed like an hour, the air marshal managed to talk this irate fellow into the front row of seats and handcuff him.

All this time the passengers in the upper deck with me were swapping animated theories of what was happening. Luckily, about two hours later, after breakfast, we landed in Atlanta. We were ordered to remain seated, and then these heavily-armed guys stormed down the aisle, trussed the would-be hijacker up even more, and lead him past us out of the plane. All he kept on muttering as he passed us was, "Sorry, folks, real sorry, folks!" It turned out that the alleged hijacker was mentally unstable and on medication, which he later admitted he had forgotten to take on this flight.

Of course all six of us were pretty high after I explained the exciting incident to my colleagues, who were seated downstairs and had missed all the action.

John insisted that instead of wasting the afternoon, as tired as we were, we should visit CNN television studios, which are based in Atlanta. This, he assured us, was his lifetime dream. So after checking into our hotel, not wanting to disappoint him, and being mildly interested ourselves, we headed off to the CNN headquarters.

To our utter amazement there was our attempted "hijacking", making headline world news, while we observed through the news studio glass window! Jane had watched the report on the news back home in Zimbabwe, not knowing that it was our flight, although she admitted afterwards, that knowing my luck, she had guessed it probably would be!

The course itself, as well as the ensuing visits to Florida, Washington and New York, were great and filled me with renewed enthusiasm.

Gideon Gono – "A Saviour of The Country" is Appointed

In December of the same year 2003, President Mugabe appointed Gideon Gono as the new Governor of the Reserve Bank. The state newspapers crowed and sang his praises, as he promised to lead Zimbabwe out of the wilderness and bring an end to public enemy number one, inflation.

Our Management Team consisted of Elana (Financial Director), Richard (Buying Manager), Larry (Operations Manager), Fanuel (Human Resources Manager) and I as Managing Director. Randall was our Factory Manager. At this stage we traded across the country with 185 branches or shops, ranging in size from 70 to 650 square metres. At our factory we employed just under 500 people, who produced about 120 000 garments a month or five to six thousand per day, spanning from ladies' dresses, men's trousers and shirts to kiddies' wear. Traditionally we purchased most of our fabric from manufacturers in Zimbabwe. Sometimes we imported polyester in its raw state on behalf of the manufacturer, who did not have access to foreign currency but who supplied us the polycotton material for our shirts and blouses. As the economy slowed down, we found ourselves relying more and more on direct fabric imports. Four years later, by 27th June 2007, we were totally dependent on imports. More about that later.

In 2000, three years previously, after the crash of the Zimbabwe dollar and the drying up of foreign currency, we took a strategic decision as a team to expand our retail arm into Zambia and to start exporting from our factory to neighbouring South Africa.

At our strategic planning session in 2000, we set our long-term objective to become self-sufficient in our foreign currency needs for imports. Our factory supplied about 15% of our total required units. By 2007, this had grown to 35% as many other manufacturers had closed and we had to rely more on our own production.

Gono had promised in 2004, at his Holiday Inn meeting with businessmen, that anyone caught with forex would be held over the weekend "at the state's hospitality" and the foreign currency would be confiscated, making it clear that holding hard cash was a criminal offence. *The Chronicle* headlines regularly screamed "White businessman caught with forex" or "Roadblock nabs hundreds in forex". It belonged in an FCA controlled directly by the Reserve Bank! There was no reason, according to Gono, for anyone to be walking around with foreign currency. After all we were a sovereign country and had our own currency, of which each and every citizen of Zimbabwe should be proud. "Zimbabwe would never, never, never be a colony again," we were told ad nauseam.

Imagine what the prohibition days in the US must have been like if you were caught with a bottle of "moonshine" or whiskey. Well, in Zimbabwe, being caught with forex was probably ten times worse!

"Outlawing" the possession of foreign currency, not surprisingly, lead to some hilarious and sometimes trying stories, as many Bulawayo businessmen kept their forex in a safe in their offices or at their work places.

Initially this heroism was an ego-enhancing act and was the stuff of good stories to tell at the pub. But as time went by, and raids on companies led to a number of Bulawayo businessman jailed for the weekend and fined double the amount of forex recovered, this bravery waned. These businessmen also attracted the attention of ZIMRA, who would then descend in their numbers on the suspect's company premises, and sometimes their homes, to conduct forensic audits of every transaction carried out over the last five years. Eventually this lead to the uncovering of numerous other "illegal" foreign currency dealings, which they had conducted just to stay in business.

Elana and I agreed that the prudent thing was not to have forex on our premises.

Many other businessmen applied the same strategy. One such businessman relates the story of how a false ceiling in his bar area served as his forex hiding place. Every now and then he would climb up into the ceiling to retrieve and audit his stash. One night-time the audit revealed to his horror that the rats had taken a liking to his wealth. Luckily they only went for his Botswana Pula, snubbing the Pounds and US dollars!

The crazy part of all this was that everyone wanted or needed foreign currency. In fact most service providers, like plumbers and mechanics, were demanding to be paid in forex, quite understandably. Obviously everyone needed a certain amount to slip across the border for groceries, car tyres, calculators, batteries and virtually everything else. There was nowhere to get the much-needed hard cash other than illegally from the "street". The banks had none and the Reserve Bank needed everything the economy was producing, however little, to implement its land distribution policy and to placate the newly resettled farmers, who had no capital of their own for farming.

Rabbits, Petunias and Uncle Abe

From 2002, right up until January 2009, there were a number of critical cash shortages. That is to say, Zimbabwe-dollar cash shortages in the banking sector. There just weren't enough banknotes being printed or in circulation to keep pace with galloping inflation. Simply put, if you had bought something for ZW$20 a month ago, using one ZW$20 note, after 30 days the price was ZW$40 and you needed two ZW$20 notes. No complicated maths necessary to work out that if inflation was at X million percent, then there needed to be ZW$X million in circulation. The government printers had to work overtime to keep up with the demand for banknotes.

When a cash shortage hit, some amazing deals could be done. If a businessman needed Zimbabwe dollars to pay staff or buy foreign currency on the street, cash could be offered from any of the following sources.

"Offshore-Offshore" deal. A US dollar, Pound or Rand transfer would be made from an offshore bank account to your bank account outside the country – hence offshore-offshore – in exchange for Zimbabwe dollars cash. Of course you had to be in a business that was generating cash in Zimbabwe dollars in order to participate in these kinds of deals. NGOs and churches, for example, were all ready to transfer money into your offshore account in exchange for Zimbabwe dollars necessary to buy the tyres for the priest's vehicle or paint for the rectory.

Money donated by parishioners in England, would end up in some Zimbabwean individual's bank account offshore, in exchange for the Zimbabwe dollars in Zimbabwe. Phone calls were received daily, asking if you were interested in any "Rabbits", the code name for the South African Rand, or " Petunias" for UK pounds, or simply the "Abe" or "green ones" for the US dollar.

If you were lucky enough to get an offshore-offshore deal, which people believed was the most difficult to detect, you then had to manufacture an invoice for the recipient of the Zimbabwe dollars to justify why your company had parted with X million or billion Zimbabwe dollars.

These invoices were easy to manufacture on the PC and, after being stamped on and crumpled, looked like a legitimate invoice from a bona fide company. Because so many goods were brought in by runners, it wasn't too difficult to dream up an imaginary company name, fictitious phone numbers and other details. Good luck to the authorities if they ever queried who this person or company was!

Or so I was told.

The response to the inspectors, I was assured, would be that this gentleman arrived with goods, issued an invoice and was paid in cash. One didn't bother to confirm his ID, address or telephone number as one had the goods and he had been paid. No one was at risk. That was the theory!

Of course you could always obtain your foreign currency from the "World Bank".

Before you start accusing that august body of double standards, let me explain. In Bulawayo there is a group of women, who belong to a religious order called the "Vapostori". These ladies are always clad in white outfits from head to toe, complete with a white embroidered headscarf.

They were also the money changers. They operated with relative impunity between 2nd and 6th Avenue and Fort Street in Bulawayo, thanks to their astute business skills involving bribery and other practices. *That* area of town was known as the "World Bank". Even Gono, the Governor of the Reserve Bank, visited it a couple of times, allegedly in disguise, to see what was going on. If ever you needed to know the street rate or parallel rate, you simply called by cellphone or visited one of these ladies, who would tell you exactly, on any day, what the going rate was for the US$, Rand or Pound to the Zimbabwe dollar. In fact, before we made *any* payments, we would phone Mrs. X, who served for five years as our "World Bank" agent.

If you were not able to offer forex for the Zimbabwe dollars that you so desperately needed, then you could also buy the cash using a cheque, but at a huge premium. This premium could be as high as 30% in exchange for a cheque payment into your account.

Only after the cheque was cleared, would the customer receive his/her Zimbabwe dollars less 30%.

Obviously during this period we still required more *forex* than we were producing. The source of this forex could be twofold. Either you applied to the Reserve Bank for excess forex they might have, or you bought it "illegally", according to the laws in place at that time, from another exporter who had excess and was prepared to sell it to you for an agreed Zimbabwe dollar price.

In 2003, Gono had just been appointed RBZ Governor and was beginning to take firm control of the whole economy. Farms had been taken from white commercial farmers and "new farmers" had been given this land. Gono needed lots of forex to buy them their tractors, seed, fertiliser and other inputs. It must be appreciated that on top of this, he also needed to import fuel for the whole country. For a company to get foreign currency from the Reserve Bank was therefore almost impossible.

It is important to remember, that up to 40% of export proceeds received from overseas customers, had to be surrendered to the Reserve Bank for a nominal Zimbabwe-dollar exchange rate. The problem with this was that one was either buying US$ from a friendly FCA holder "illegally" at a premium of up to ten times the "official" bank exchange rate, or at the rate paid for export proceeds by the Reserve Bank. So you imported fabric with FCA money – ten times the bank rate – exported the finished product, and received ten times less than you paid for the US$ on 40% of your export receipts.

There was another troubling catch. Any money paid to you by export customers, had to be used up within 30 days from the day the funds hit your bank account in Bulawayo. If you did not utilise these funds within the set period, the Reserve Bank would convert them at the official bank rate into Zimbabwe dollars. Coupled with all this was the fact that you had to acquit your CD1 export document in 30 days as well. For an exporter it meant that you had 30 days to get your export customer to pay you, before you were hit with penalties. Once you received the money, you had 30 days to use it to pay your importer. Of course this period was far too short to obtain proforma invoices and apply to the Reserve Bank for permission to import.

To make the whole situation even more frustrating, *they* decided whether you could use *your* hard-earned forex to import what *you* really needed. Often they rejected applications without giving any reason. All this took time, more than the allocated 30 days, so we had to forfeit a lot of foreign currency to the Reserve Bank, and in its place were given pretty worthless Zimbabwe dollars.

Exporters realised they were on a hiding to nothing and industry shrank even more as exporters, who were naturally relying on their export money to import raw materials, parts and other essentials, lost their hard-earned forex to the Reserve Bank as their 30-day period expired.

Money Auctions

In order to alleviate the lack of foreign currency for industry, Gono in January 2004, a month after his appointment as Reserve Bank Governor, introduced the ingenious foreign currency auction system. Importers could bid for foreign currency held by the Reserve Bank. This was the way to get to some sort of market value for the US dollar and at the same time make the distribution of scarce foreign currency fairer. Effectively we had to submit bids to buy foreign currency that we had earned for *our* exports from the Reserve Bank, which took 40% of it and gave us Zimbabwe dollars in exchange!

A percentage of the currency, which the Reserve Bank was auctioning, was made available for medical and study applications, sports bodies, schools and other deserving causes. At the Bulawayo Golf Club we managed to secure R18 000 for new green mowers through this scheme.

The process, however, was laborious:
1. Obtain a pro-forma invoice from the external supplier.
2. Submit this invoice and a letter of application with the necessary forms to your bank.
3. After about 14 days your bank would let you know whether the Reserve Bank had approved your application for importation. In principle, they were supposed to prioritise imports in terms of the nation's needs.
4. You would then submit a written bid in Zimbabwe dollars to your bank on every Monday as the auction was held each Tuesday.
5. By Thursday the bank would let you know if your bid was successful or not.

This bidding process provided many hours of mirth to our team. Every Monday we would gather in Richard's office and guess the rate for Tuesday. We normally submitted four or five bids, of course taking side bets with each other as to who could predict the winning bid. Companies were allowed to give a bid range e.g. ZW$250 – ZW$280 for US$1. As time went by, of course, the range got narrower and narrower as the forex available dried up. By May 2004, four months after the introduction of the foreign currency auction system, the range was denominated in decimal points, e.g. ZW$360.94 – ZW$360.96 for US$1.

As 2004 progressed, so the auction system fizzled out, as less and less people were getting forex, therefore less production, less exports, less forex generation and so on, as the domino effect increased and the circle got smaller.

This lack of official forex obviously just sent inflation soaring as our good economic friends "supply" and "demand" drove prices through the roof.

The Inevitable Economic Collapse

Coupled with the lack of forex to drive commercial activities, was the collapse of the broader economy. Zimbabwe was a big agricultural country. Tons of maize, cotton, citrus, tea and other produce were harvested annually, most of this for export.

As a big cotton-growing country, Zimbabwe was blessed with huge cotton fabric producers, such as David Whitehead textiles in Chegutu and Kadoma Textiles just outside Kadoma, to which cotton farmers, both rural and commercial, would sell their crop. These mills were in turn producing the fabric, which was sold to factories producing the fantastic brand names of clothing like "Julie Whyte" among many others. Zimbabwe was known for its good-quality cotton sheets and linen. By 2007, these producers had either collapsed or were producing very limited stock.

Many other raw materials were turned into end products, the wish of any major raw material producer. So for instance citrus farms produced and sold to factories which manufactured the "Mazoe" range of drinks. Vegetable farmers supplied local and export markets and you could find the baby mealie, asparagus and petit pois peas for sale in Sainsbury's in London with the label "Grown and Packaged in Zimbabwe". Tea and coffee plantations produced and packaged "Tanganda Tea" for local and export use.

As mentioned earlier, the pluses and minuses, rights and often violent wrongs of the farm takeovers are not the theme of this book. I mention them simply to illustrate how the economy was systematically strangled and starved.

Take away the raw materials, when the farms stopped producing after 2001, and your downstream economies just shrivelled up.

Any small rural town had in its centre the Farmers' Co-op, which sold everything you could think of, from groceries to fertiliser, nails or tractors. This Co-op was the farmer's lifeblood to keep his windmills turning, boreholes pumping and tractors running. It was also the central point where farm workers could buy their groceries and even some clothes. Once the farmers' land was taken away and divided up into small plots, the Co-op just slowly died. No more commercial travellers from the tractor manufacturers visiting weekly to see if any orders could be written up. No more Friday afternoon or Saturday morning visits by hundreds of farm labourers to town to buy their food, clothing and other necessities. No more guesthouses where the commercial travellers would stay. I could go on and on. The bottom line was that we lost thousands of customers and the economy, especially in the smaller towns, simply perished.

A New Phenomenon – Replacement Costing

Back in June 2002, I was sitting at my desk, analysing the income statement and wondering why our operating profit was climbing steadily month by month but our cash flow was getting tighter. As is my way, I took out a piece of paper and did a simple cash flow and profit sum. Cost + mark-up = selling price.

Using a six-month period for one product on its actual cost, I soon realised that we were paying more for replacement products than we were charging for existing products. This was the first time I had come across replacement costing.

Not being a financial whiz I took this to our then Finance Director and to my horror discovered he had never heard of the phenomenon. As a result of inflation the cost price was increasing with a greater percentage each month than the factor by which we were marking up our stock. Because we were buying product monthly, and because not all product was sold within the month, we needed to protect our cash flow by marking up existing leftover stock to at least the new cost price. This gave us a higher operating profit and to a degree protected our cash flow.

Once I understood this economic principle, I realised how elementary it was, but it seemed that Government never did. One morning the editor of the Bulawayo Government newspaper, *The Chronicle*, phoned to ask me why I was marking up my prices in-store unnecessarily. I tried to explain the principle of replacement costing – to no avail. When explaining that I had to sell a product with a full mark-up for ZW$200 but a new one would cost me ZW$210, I asked where I would get the extra ZW$10 to buy the new product if I didn't mark-up the leftover stock to try and protect my business. The trite answer after 40 minutes of discussion and persuasion was, *"Why don't you use the profits you have made all these years?"*

The above situation illustrates how the businesses in Zimbabwe, who were not aware of or hadn't cottoned on to this principle, eventually just shrivelled up. The rural shop owner couldn't understand why he was able to buy less stock each month. The outcome of this period was that companies were announcing super profits. This pleased the taxman, as the income from this revenue base was increasing exponentially, both from VAT and company tax. The problem was that companies didn't have the cash flow to pay for the tax. Nevertheless, the companies registered on the stock exchange were obliged to publish these super-profit results. Government, of course, used the publication of these figures to explain why prices were too high and kept on doubling. The words "economic saboteurs" and "regime-change agents" were becoming more prominent in the newspapers. The fact that companies did not have cash to restock, never mind pay the taxes on these super profits, was lost on the powers that be.

As a result of these increasing prices and galloping inflation the government had to introduce new banknotes of bigger denomination. The President had been on TV stating emphatically, *"Devaluation is dead. We will not devalue."* This policy continued and I think, in desperation, the Reserve Bank started issuing so-called Bearer Cheques in 2003, which were legal tender and were of higher paper value. At first Bearer Cheques were issued with an expiry date a year from date of issue. Then a SI was issued extending their validity indefinitely.

2004 – A New Corporate Culture

In June 2004 we had introduced a new corporate culture, intended to give an identity to our company, ensure staff commitment and generally improve motivation levels. Our mother company in Cape Town had introduced a similar strategy a few years earlier with great success. The strategy was what we called the "Red and Yellow Giant Concept". The colours referred to our company, whose corporate colours were red and yellow. The baobab tree became our company symbol.

The size of the giant baobab, also called the upside-down tree, found in dry areas below 1 000 metres (3 300 feet) above sea level, represented what we wanted to become as a company. As the baobab can be seen from miles away across the bushveld, so we wanted to be noticed on the business landscape. The baobab is also one of the tree species that lives for hundreds of years. Its core is very porous and soft, symbolising our values as individuals to stand tall and strong with a soft inner soul, epitomising the concept of "Ubuntu" or care for our fellow man. The closest English term to describe "Ubuntu" is probably "empathy".

Induction ceremonies were held with all staff at the conferences in Harare and Bulawayo. Each staff member was issued with a paper leaf, which they pasted onto a giant painting of a baobab tree, pledging to uphold the values of "Ubuntu" and commitment to grow our company to the biggest in Zimbabwe.

At the launch of this programme in Harare in July 2004, we had an interesting visitor. We had decided to hold the event at the beautiful Crown Plaza hotel in central Harare. In attendance were about ninety Shop Managers, ten Area Managers, ten internal auditors plus about eight head office staff. On the first morning of our two-day launch programme, our Regional Manager and one of our internal auditors approached me. They reported that we had, sitting in the audience, a smartly-dressed gentleman whom they did not recognise. Obviously my first thought was that this could be a relief manager from one of our deep rural shops, whom few people would know.

During tea-time we decided to confront this individual. With a cup of tea and cake in his hand, he calmly told us that he was from the CIO, even producing his badge, and had been sent to monitor our meeting. I was of course incensed by this. He, however, said he was happy that our meeting was non-political and that he would leave after lunch. In a most unusually calm way – for me – I told him that we would not tolerate his attendance any longer. We called hotel security, as well as the police. They eventually came and removed the gentleman.

What happened to him I do not know, but it was another reminder to us that the government was watching every move and that their informants were everywhere. Luckily we had not said anything disparaging about the authorities or their economic policies.

All staff were now called "Giants" and our greeting of each other was not a handshake but a "high five", symbolising the excitement and joy similar to soccer fans whose side is winning. We were winners, all of us.

This bond and team spirit no doubt helped us through the darkest days. We followed this up with a card and a telephone call from one of the management team to all Giants on their birthday. Newsletters, which were not only geared to excite but also gave the company's performance, were sent out under my signature on a monthly basis.

All Giants participated in a monthly bonus scheme, under which up to 1% of net sales was paid out, coupled with certain shrinkage conditions, such as stock theft or shortages. As a rule, 65% of shop Giants' net pay was made up of this bonus. This enabled us to limit our shrinkage factor to less than 0.5%, a phenomenally low percentage in retail terms.

Clear out the Trash!

The extent of government's knee-jerk reaction to any perceived threat to its power is best illustrated by the now infamous 2005 "Operation Murambatsvina" or "Clear out the Trash".

It was rumoured that this hare-brained, yet devastating operation, was based on the government's fear that the MDC was gaining in popularity, especially in the urban areas and bigger towns. In essence, the operation consisted of State Officials, CIO, police and army destroying any structure, whether permanent or temporary, which was not deemed to have been officially sanctioned, either by municipal or government authorities.

Thousands of urban dwellings, even some elaborate double-storeyed brick houses, were bulldozed. Shacks, backyard rooms and even informal vendor stalls were just destroyed, together with the contents if you were not quick enough. This led to a mad scramble to find house plans, shop plans, additions or alterations to houses and other buildings. Luckily Jane is a fantastic administrator and so found the plans for our house with the improvements, which had been officially sanctioned.

The curio sellers in the front of Bulawayo City Hall and vegetable vendors in 8th Avenue were not so lucky. Their shelters were simply torn down. I remember travelling to Kariba and Victoria Falls, and seeing the curio sellers' stalls on the side of the road reduced to rubble, thus robbing the traders of their meagre livelihood. No mercy was shown to anyone.

Rural landlords inundated our company property department, requesting we quickly have plans drawn up for their shops, which we were renting, to prevent them from being bulldozed. There were a few draftsmen and local council officials, who made an absolute fortune by drawing plans and getting them stamped by the local official for a small fee. Another operation, another crackdown. No planning, no thought as to the implications, just ensuring the populace are cowed into submission by fear.

The United Nations sent an envoy to investigate the situation and issued a damning report. But as usual, it was like water off a duck's back to Government, just: *"Western forces trying to reverse the land-reform programme."*

Property – Always a Good Investment!

While the government was destroying property, I had more by chance than design started buying property for the company. One of our senior staff, Ted, had decided to relocate to the United States at very short notice. In order to do this he needed quite a bit of forex within a few days. He came to see me and asked for my help. He had put his house on the market, but had no response from buyers. Nobody was really prepared to invest in property in Zimbabwe in 2005. I spoke to Elana. We did a few sums and decided that the company could do with a guesthouse in Bulawayo. This would save on hotel costs for visiting personnel. Besides, we were building up a small cash reserve and it was losing value daily.

We bought the house on half an acre of land for ZW$65 million, probably equivalent to R250 000 on the day of transfer, and R200 000 a month later. A year later, in August 2006, Gono removed three zeros from the currency, making the purchase price of a year earlier worth ZW$65 000.

I remember clearly the MD or Chief Executive Officer of our Head Office in Cape Town, to whom I reported, berating me and reminding me that we were not into property. No matter how much I tried to explain my reason that it was prudent to invest in assets that would hold value, he proceeded to lecture me on business and investment decisions, implying that I was a moron when it came to these matters, this despite the fact that he had spent perhaps no more than 48 hours over a period of five years in Zimbabwe. Anyone not living and working in the economic turmoil that was Zimbabwe, would not have understood my thinking, so I forgave him. When he left the organisation a few months later, I was not too upset. We purchased a few more retail properties, which in hindsight, I believe turned out to be one of my better business decisions.

5. IT CAN'T GET ANY WORSE, CAN IT? [2006]

He who smiles rather than rages is always the stronger.
JAPANESE WISDOM

In February 2006 our management team held a strategic session at Kariba. One resolution, taken at this meeting, was that we needed to stay as close to the business as possible. This meant visiting probably all shops to "eyeball" the situation on the ground. With this in mind we purchased a six-seater Toyota minibus, second or third-hand in Harare. The five of us would pack our bags for three or four nights and head off for a trip around the country, helping us keep up to date with what was happening all over Zimbabwe. Most times, Randall, our Factory Manager, would accompany us.

Each trip would be a real adventure and brought back to me those school outings, which we all used to look forward to, just to break the monotony of the classroom. Elana was always responsible for the "padkos" or snacks for the road. This included biltong, boiled sweets, my chocolate-coated peanuts and jelly babies, as well as cans of drinks, Coke, Fanta or whatever was available. These were all sourced from Solomon's, a grocery shop in town, renowned for having articles on their shelves that were unavailable in the rest of the country – but at a price! The high cost was probably because runners would bring in the goods. In those years, 2001 to 2007, if you had access to foreign currency, you could really live like a king. A Zimbabwean king that is, which was fantastic in comparison with every one else's living standards in the country.

Like a group of excited school kids we would head out on our shop visits and stay overnight at various lodges, dotted around the country, as well as at some hotels, like the Orange Grove in Chinhoyi on the way to Kariba. These lodges and hotels had really borne the brunt of the dearth of foreign currency necessary to maintain them. Falling standards were something we were getting used to.

The vinyl-covered chair in the room would only have one armrest or hot water could only be enjoyed on request from the reception. Frequent power cuts made the stay at these places a little less comfortable as well, because the menu at night became limited and fried or boiled food became the evening fare. Ample supplies of local beer and whisky, however, made up for these shortcomings.

On one such trip, we left a lodge just outside Masvingo on the Harare-Beitbridge road, at about 7.45 one morning, after enjoying a great cooked breakfast facilitated by the availability of power and the fantastic cooking skills of Amos. At 62 he could still remember the good old days when he had served as a chef on hunting safaris in the real wild areas of Zimbabwe.

Richard was the designated driver for the day. About one hour into our trip we could hear a loud rumbling noise above the animated discussion that was taking place between Richard and Larry regarding some merchandise, which Richard's buyers had bought, but, according to Richard, Larry's ops guys weren't displaying properly. That was just one of the pluses of these trips: we got to discuss details of the business, which we never would have time for in the office. The rumbling got loud enough to attract Richard's attention.

Suddenly he jammed on the brakes and pulled over. The temperature gauge needle was bending towards "hot". Once we had come to a dead stop, the cab quickly filled with steam, as the engine of these minibuses sits directly below the driver and his passenger. Of course Richard immediately went into his technical, diagnostic mode, while the rest of us quietly waited for him to offer a solution.

We all piled out of the bus and immediately grabbed our cellphones. Disaster, no signal! Fanuel made off to the nearest koppie about 500 metres away, in the firm belief that any height would increase our chance of signal. We were on our way to Shurugwi, a small town really in the middle of nowhere, with not a dwelling in sight. The fact that we had not passed a car in either direction for the last 30 minutes of our drive, was not lost on us. On Fanuel's return, bad news: the theory of height for cellphone signal was on this occasion a fallacy.

We agreed that we would attempt to stop the first vehicle to come past in any direction. Larry volunteered to go into the nearest town and phone for backup. In the meantime, Fanuel and Richard would head off into the bush in search of water to refill the radiator. We had five 250-millilitre bottles of water, but decided to save those for later, as the temperature was already at 32 degrees Celsius and climbing. Elana and I would stay with the bus, while Larry awaited his lift. The bush was pretty sparse and there were one or two cows wandering about, which, we believed, indicated a homestead nearby.

After about 25 minutes a police pick-up came past. We flagged it down and Larry jumped on the back. About 45 minutes later, Fanuel and Richard appeared out of the bush, drenched in sweat, but carrying five litres of water, accompanied

IT CAN'T GET ANY WORSE, CAN IT?

PUBLIC NOTICE

BANKING SERVICES FOR CASH SWAPS ON SATURDAY 19 AUGUST 2006

1. The public is advised that banks and building societies will be open on Saturday, 19 August 2006, for the purpose of accepting deposits of old Bearer Cheques and exchanging old Bearer Cheques for new Bearer Cheques only.
2. Please note that no other banking services will be provided by banks and building societies on this day.
3. The deposit facility has been extended by financial institutions in the interest of offering the public ample opportunity to deposit old Bearer Cheques into the banking system, as we move closer to the change-over date of 21 August 2006.
4. The Reserve Bank of Zimbabwe appeals to banks and building societies to be flexible in their business hours, to ensure that the public wishing to deposit or swap old Bearer Cheques, are afforded the opportunity to do so.
5. The public is advised further, that they can continue to make deposits of old Bearer Cheques into the banks and building societies, until the close of business on 21 August 2006.
6. Please be guided accordingly.

RESERVE BANK OF ZIMBABWE
17 August, 2006

PUBLIC NOTICE

SPECIAL ANNOUNCEMENT

1. The Reserve Bank of Zimbabwe wishes to remind members of the public that the 21 days of expiration of the old Bearer Cheques is coming on Monday, the 21st of August, 2006.
2. All holders of the family of old Bearer Cheques are, therefore, called upon to go to their banks as well as the roving Reserve Bank Cash Swap Teams who are moving across all Provinces.
3. In the same vein, the Reserve Bank, once again, wishes to remind major cash movers, such as the GMB to please cease injecting old Bearer Cheques back into circulation as this is working to defeat the noble objectives of the Sunrise Project.
4. Members of the public are, therefore, asked to report any cases of non-compliance with this call to the Reserve Bank of Zimbabwe in the National interest.
5. The Governor of the Reserve Bank is also appealing to our Honourable Ministers, Honourable Senators, Honourable Members of the House of Assembly as well as our Rural Community Leaders to complement and support the current efforts by bringing to the attention of the Reserve Bank Teams any unattended cases in their areas.
6. This will ensure that by the 21st of August, 2006, our stakeholders will not be caught unaware with valueless old Bearer Cheques.

1.11 In this regard, we would like to once again thank the ZRP for their immense flexibility in allowing the Reserve Bank to concert some of their Police Station facilities into temporary secure cash vaults.

Procurement Logistics
1.12 Procurement planning and logistics started in earnest early June 2006, though involving a few members of staff, at that stage.

Fuel Logistics
13 Fuel was purchased in bulk, comprising 1,755,000 litres diesel and 695,000 litres petrol for access from designated Z.R.P. Stations nationwide.

14 Re-supply of both diesel and petrol continued as per request of provincial teams, throughout the period of the operation.

15 Some additional refueling locations had to be added onto the master list following specific requests from Provincial Leaders.

Access to R.B.Z. fuel by R.B.Z. Officials at Police Stations nationwide was controlled by a procedural document, personally carried by all R.B.Z. Officials.

Fuel collected at Police Stations nationwide was strictly monitored by daily returns submitted to the monitoring team.

Communication Logistics
A 24-hour 7-day national toll-fee line was opened at the Communication Center, established on level 17 of R.B.Z. Head Quarters, for the specific benefit of the public to phone in on all queries, comments and suggestions relating to the currency reform.

Technical Services Desk
The Desk was being manned by 2 people, coordinating all the works for the Technical, General and Transport Services, and compiling vehicle breakdown reports from the regions.

Engineering Services
The Engineering Services were manned by 17 Technicians, repairing and supporting Banking Operations functions, and ensuring that all electrical and mechanical equipment was functional.

by the owner of the water. After filling the radiator, we slowly made our way to Shurugwi, 85 kilometres away. Our water saviour was only too glad to receive four baseball caps, proudly displaying our company logo.

We had agreed that once Larry got to a phone or within signal, he would phone the office and arrange for a driver to bring my car to us and drive the bus back to Bulawayo, 160 kilometres away.

We made use of the few hours to visit our shop and after a couple of hours we were ready to leave again in my car, which the driver had brought through.

Richard had become somewhat of a jinx driver, as on our second country trip, he too was the driver when we hit a huge pot hole and the back suspension of the minibus collapsed. This time we had broken a shock absorber. Probably due to the weight, as we had six people in the minivan plus their luggage, but in the trailer we had six 20-litre jerry cans of diesel.

As the sun was setting, we decided to unhitch the trailer, leaving volunteers Larry and Fanuel to guard it, while we drove the 80 kilometres back to Masvingo. The slow journey took us over two hours and it was only after 11.30 at night that we were reunited with Larry and Fanuel after finding a tow truck willing to go and fetch them and the trailer. These trips were not only great fun, but kept us well informed about the intricacies of the business – and we got to know each other so much better!

From Zero to Hero, Or Was it Hero to Zero?

In July 2006 Gono announced his "Project Sunrise", i.e. the removal of three noughts from the currency. He launched his "Zero to Hero" marketing campaign. Border posts would be manned by ZRP and "youths" to investigate the "illegal" import and export of local currency. He claimed this was necessary because the authorities could only account for ZW$10 trillion of the ZW$43 trillion in circulation. The rest, he declared, were in "mini central banks" and apparently another ZW$20 trillion doing business in other countries. Anyone caught with currency in excess of ZW$5 million would be prosecuted. Gold deliveries had declined by 31% in the half year to June 2006. In this speech, he promised the following by December 2008, i.e. two years ahead:
- Single-digit inflation
- Secure and stable financial sector
- A strong currency, market-driven exchange rates
- Single-digit unemployment
- Food, fuel and power self-sufficiency, and export surpluses
- No more arrears to IMF
- Zimbabwe to be the most "attractive investment destination by December 2007"

IT CAN'T GET ANY WORSE, CAN IT?

Well that was July 2006. Dream on! As business people, we quietly giggled at this delusional thinking, not based on any economic theory but his own, with no halt to the printing of money. On 1st August, the new currency was introduced.

As per usual fanfare and egotistical slant, the "Operation From Zero To Hero" was launched. Dubbed "Operation Sunrise 1", a new currency was issued and a deadline for handing in old notes set.

Businesses had *48 hours* to change all their prices, and all goods had to display the old and newly denominated prices. This was a nightmare exercise and incredibly time-consuming. Never mind the cost to the companies in administration and updating all systems. Payrolls and tax tables had to be changed, stock systems rewritten and financial packages redone. Companies had to hold two sets of books. One set was to close off at the end of July 2006 and the new set had to start on 1st August 2006 with the new currency.

The new currency consisted of notes of one, five, ten and fifty cents. Also one, ten, twenty, fifty, one hundred, five hundred, one thousand, ten thousand and one hundred thousand dollar notes. All old Bearer Cheques expired at midnight on 21st August 2006. With the new currency, three zeros were removed. So ZW$1 000 dollar notes could be exchanged at the bank for ZW$1 notes.

Mozambique had the year before introduced a new currency and ran the new currency *for a year* in parallel. In chaotic Zimbabwe, we had *21 days* to switch over!

One of our major problems was that we were only banking twice a week at our shops in the rural areas. In most cases, the shop assistant had to travel by bus to bank the takings in a nearby town. The day's takings of 21st August still had to be banked the following day as well and we were obliged by law to accept any customers' old money up until close of business on the 21st. Well, it was obvious that this was going to lead to chaos if the old currency lost value on the 21st at midnight. At the last moment, the authorities at the Reserve Bank extended the deadline for banks to accept old money by 14 days to also allow the rural folk, who did not have access to radio or TV, to get the news and change their money.

This "Sunrise One" must have cost an absolute fortune. Teams of Reserve Bank officials travelled the country, acting as a bank to change the rural people's money. This exercise, Gono believed, was going to mean the end of inflation.

On 14th August 2006, Jane and I did a trip up to Kariba, 700 kilometres to the north, to visit friends over the long weekend. We went through *14* roadblocks where all our belongings and our car were thoroughly searched for money. The government believed that the rising exchange rate, and hence prices of goods, was being fuelled by people hoarding bank notes to purchase foreign currency. As the time drew near for the expiration of the old notes, of course the exchange rate shot

IT CAN'T GET ANY WORSE, CAN IT?

up as people tried to exchange the old notes for foreign currency.

So steep did the exchange rate climb, that the value of the first six denominated notes, from one cent to the ten dollars, had already been overtaken by inflation within the first week of their launch. The State's paranoia was further exhibited by the SI stating that, *"Any person who brings an amount exceeding one hundred million dollars, or within any period of seven consecutive working days, brings an amount of old Bearer Cheques of one hundred million dollars (to deposit in a bank) will be issued with a one year currency stabilisation bond."* This would lead to an investigation of the individual by the anti-money-laundering unit as to the source of the funds. In other words, kiss the money goodbye. You could not even bank your own money!

A really nauseating facet of this "Sunrise 1" was that Gono printed a 36-page glossy colour brochure, complete with photos of rural Reserve Bank teams, exchanging the old notes for new ones. The entire brochure was, in my opinion, an egotistical pat on the back by Gono himself and the whole team at the Reserve Bank, for the success of the whole exercise, complete with statistics of how many millions of litres of diesel and fuel had been consumed, how many generators and vehicles had been bought and details of the many other expenses incurred. Of course, this brochure was printed with tax payers' money.

Our company motor fleet was made up mostly of imported second-hand Japanese vehicles, such as Toyota Corollas and Nissan Sunnys. Since early 2006, locally-assembled cars, imported from Japan in kit form, became unavailable due to the foreign currency shortage. As a result, the market in imported used cars blossomed. Paying for a car in Zimbabwe dollars was still possible and obviously a very attractive option. These cars were ex-taxis or family cars, so we were told by the agents, but in reasonable condition and certainly affordable. After replacing the shock absorbers and one or two other minor parts, the vehicle would be relatively reliable.

One morning Jane arrived back from her walk with the girls and excitedly told me that her friend Pippa's husband had just bought a brand-new Volkswagen Citi Golf or Chico for the ridiculously low price of ZW$5 billion! Converted at the parallel rate, this equated to R65 000, the same price as in South Africa. This was on the 10th of June 2006.

I immediately saw an opportunity to replace a large portion of our aging fleet with brand-new cars. Elana did a few quick calculations and informed me that we could afford ten vehicles at ZW$50 billion by the following month.

Since the vehicles were available in Harare, there would be no import hassles, no customs duty or any of the other obstacles that needed to be overcome when bringing goods into the country. Within a month, we had concluded the deal. Of course we were unaware at the time that Gono was about to lop three zeros off our currency. A month later, when we took delivery, we only paid ZW$6.5 million for each vehicle, or a total of ZW$65 million. The price had gone up from ZW$5 billion to ZW$6.5 billion in one month, but the three noughts had gone, so we still only paid ZW$6.5 million! Very confusing I know, but the bottom line was that at the parallel rate, it was still R65 000!

A month later we bought another vehicle for ZW$8 million. In October we were in a position to buy two more, but the price had now doubled to ZW$16 million each. Despite the increase, our outlay was still R65 000 – the Rand equivalent of ZW$16 million on the parallel market.

The 13 shiny new vehicles, parked outside our Head Office, certainly drew a lot of attention, but, more importantly, allowed us to buy new assets using Zimbabwe dollars instead of precious foreign currency – a rare occurrence in 2006. Unfortunately our lucky streak came to an end when the company selling the cars either realised they were on the path to fast ruination or ran out of cars. Whatever the reasons, the October purchase was our last new vehicle acquisition!

ZIMBABWE **WARM HEART** UGLY FACE

Management road trip with our old bus: Randall, Richard, Fanuel and Larry
ABOVE AND BELOW:
A typical road scene on the way to Victoria Falls

ZIMBABWE **WARM HEART** UGLY FACE

LEFT: **Elephants at Kariba**
ABOVE: **Kariba 2007. Grant, Jonny, Nic, Jonno and Kevin**

Our blended family. Front left to right: Jason, Candice, Nicola; back left to right: Tracy, Jane, me, Jonny, Bronwyn and Brett

A stunning sunset on Kariba

Bron and baby Rhino at Chipangali in 2000

Jason proudly displaying his first Tiger fish. (Sneakily trying to make it look bigger than it was)

ABOVE: **Candi** and the lion cubs. Antelope park, Gweru
RIGHT: **Nicola** and lion cub

The beautiful Disa lily found in the Helderberg nature reserve and after which Disa Gorge is named

ZIMBABWE **WARM HEART** UGLY FACE

Lake Kariba dam wall LEFT: Mannie, Ntuli, Eric and me. Tiger fishing at Chirundu-Zambezi river

ABOVE: The mandatory photo stop on the way to Leopard Rock hotel, with the unique rock formation in the background. From left: Bill, John, Tony, Nige, Welly, me, Murray, Rus BELOW: Marineland Harbour, Kariba – looking down from the "Heights"

The Orange Grove Hotel Chinhoyi menu. March 2008 (Note the prices in millions)

ZIMBABWE **WARM HEART** UGLY FACE

ZANU-PF and MDC political party election adverts 2008

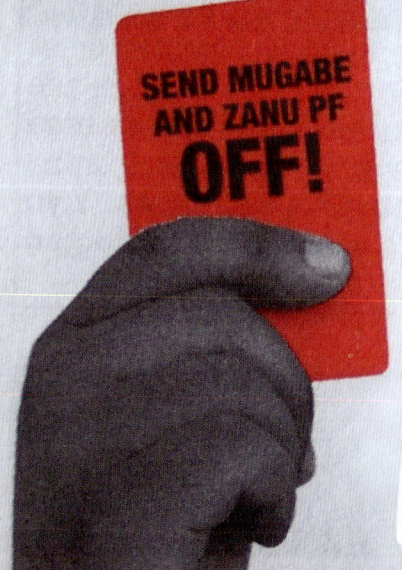

The magnificent Birchenough Bridge built in 1935

RIGHT: **A total of 84 banknotes issued from 1980 to 2009, 74 signed by Gono since 2003. Reproduced by kind permission of Jonathan Waters, ZFN Realtime Financial Intelligence**

Series 1 - 1980-1994 (4 notes, 6 coins)

Series 2 - 1994-2003 (8 notes, 8 coins)

Series 3 - Aug 1 2006-July 31 2008 (Bearer cheque series - 35 notes, 14 in initial issue)

Series 4 - Aug 1 2008-Feb 2 2009 series - 27 notes + 8 coins (includes new issue of $10 and $25 coins)

Series 5 - Feb 2 2009-Feb 9 2009 - 7 notes

Most Common Scene

Great Zimbabwe (12) | Victoria Falls (12) | Elephants (12) | Kariba (11)

Silos (7) | Village Scene | Miner | Inyangani | Eternal Flame | Aloe excelsa | Buffalo | Dairy | Hwange Power Station | Parliment | Ploughing

Doqufa | Bull | Coal Stack | Chilojo Cliffs | Tractor | Combine | Heroes

ZIMBABWE **WARM HEART** UGLY FACE

Balancing rocks – Matopos National Park Bulawayo

LEFT **The three generations December 2008, Jonny, me and my Dad Jack** BELOW **The Houseboat on Kariba – the best kept secret in the world**

Sunrise over the Hottentots Holland mountains from Strand beach

6

IT CAN GET WORSE!
[2007]

Chaos demands to be recognised and experienced, before letting itself be converted into a new order. HERMAN HESSE

The above very short summary of the goings on prior to the 2007 price blitz, gives some idea of the State's obsession with looking for saboteurs everywhere in the economy. The suspicion was that from businesses to individuals to banks, all were trying to undermine Zimbabwe's economy because the State had taken the farms from the white farmers. No real economic solutions were offered. No serious ongoing open-for-discussion type of interaction with the business community took place. All traditional economic theory was thrown out the window.

Gono made, in my opinion, the fatal mistake that anyone in the business or government sphere can make, ignore, underestimate and, worst of all, denigrate that amorphous thing called "the market". "The market will decide" concept clashed with the power-filled egos, who thought they knew better. Guess who won that contest?

This was the background that led to the price slashes, or as we jokingly called it *"the government's 50%-off closing-down sale"*.

In November 2006, we had ordered a new minibus, as we decided the old one was too unreliable. Elana did the research and came up with an eight-seater Mercedes Vito. Perfect for our needs. We had seen them at all the airports in South Africa, ferrying aircrews and other personnel. This we thought was evidence enough of their quality to justify importing one.

Importing any luxury item, such as vehicles or flat-screen TVs, was an absolute bargain. The duty was very high, 100% for motor vehicles, 65% for TVs and so on. The catch was that the Reserve Bank had the bank rate at which duty was calculated. So for instance, something costing R1 000 and having duty of 65% would cost R650 extra for the duty. However, the R650 was converted at the bank rate into a Zimbabwe dollar amount for duty purposes. Remember at this point in our history forex was outlawed, and only the Zimbabwe dollar was our sovereign currency. The economy on the other hand was being priced at the parallel rate. This meant, for instance, that you would source your R1 000 on the black market, which would cost you say, ZW$16 million at the rate of ZW$16 000 for R1. Technically the duty should have cost you ZW$10.4 million, if the customs people had been using the same rate.

However, the Reserve Bank rate was up to 40 times lower than the parallel rate. So the R650 converted by customs, using a rate of ZW$400 to R1, made the duty payable only ZW$260 000. This converted to the parallel rate of ZW$260 000 divided by ZW$16 000, worked out to only R16.25!

Of course this was a great saving, making for instance, the importation of second-hand cars from Japan big business!

In February, our brand-new imported Vito was waiting for clearance at Beitbridge customs. Within three weeks, it would be in Bulawayo and we would be smiling.

One week before it came through customs, Gono issued a SI that all duty for luxury items, including cars, must now be paid in foreign currency. No warning, no grace period, nothing. Obviously, his thirst for forex had overtaken his good judgement – again! Suddenly from R6 000 duty, converted at parallel rate, the duty payable shot up to R240 000.

We appealed the timing of the new regulations as our vehicle was partly cleared, but to no avail. Pay the R240 000 or lose the vehicle. Others caught in the same trap opted to go to court. We realised that fighting the revenue authorities in Zimbabwe at that time was a futile exercise. As a team, we now had the most expensive Mercedes Vito in Zimbabwe!

In March 2007, we awarded our staff a pay increase of 100%. Last month's pay was multiplied by two. Someone earning ZW$4 000 in February 2007, got ZW$8 000 in March. We had also resorted to paying our staff every two weeks, as inflation for expenses such as bus and taxi fares, was hitting every worker hard, doubling every week. Official figures published by the government put inflation at 24 000%.

On Thursday 26th April 2007, the RBZ Governor delivered his six-monthly interim monetary policy speech.

This was the follow-up to his January monetary policy speech. In this latest delivery individuals were allowed to withdraw ZW$1.5 million per day, up from ZW$500 000. Corporates were allowed ZW$3 million, up from ZW$1 million. Not even enough to cover our tea and sugar from petty cash!

Hundreds of tractors, thousands of animal-drawn ploughs and other farming equipment had been purchased for distribution to the newly-resettled farmers. Who would service the tractors, where were the spares?

50%-off Sale. Everything Half Price!!

On the morning of Friday the 6th of July 2007, the Heuglin robins were as always our alarm clock at 6.00am, give or take ten minutes. That day I was filled with excitement. I was off at 6.30 as soon as it was light enough, to fetch my youngest son Jonny and his three varsity pals, Jonno, Grant and Kevin from the Beitbridge border post. The four of them had driven up from Stellenbosch University near Somerset West and would leave their car in Musina, close to Beitbridge border post. I would cross, pick them up and escort them through the border and onto Bulawayo.

Little did I realise, as I climbed out of bed that morning, how my personal life, business life and that of thousands of businessmen and women in Zimbabwe, was to change traumatically for the worse later in the day.

I left our home in Burnside with a flask of coffee, a bottle of water, some rusks and a sliced apple for the 340-kilometre trip to Beitbridge. Unfortunately, the power on a Monday goes off in our area at half past four in the morning and comes back on at any time after two in the afternoon. However, these times are not guaranteed! This happens every week. Morning power cuts are bearable, but the evening ones from two to ten or eleven are the pits. Despite having a small generator, it's still painful to have to knock around the house with a torch and cook on a gas burner. The generator gives us quite a few lights in the driveway and lounge, but not in the whole house. It chews about two litres of precious petrol per hour.

Needless to say, the coffee was made on the gas stove, but no toast that day as the generator is too small to handle the toaster. It also means that my gorgeous wife, Jane, could not blow-dry her hair after her shower. Showering in itself is quite a process. Water cuts started in about May, two months earlier. March to November are the dry winter months and the last rainy season was a poor one. As a result, water cuts were now a daily routine, with some suburbs only getting water for six hours once a week. More about this later.

From Burnside, it is a short drive to the Beitbridge road, which via Esigodini, Gwanda, Colleen Bawn and West Nicholson takes the driver to the South African border. Bulawayo has four main arterial roads leading to and from the City. The Victoria Falls road leading north, Harare road going east, Plumtree road heading south to Botswana and the Beitbridge road going southeast. No fancy N1 or N2 or R36 numbered roads or highways here.

Getting to the Beitbridge road was and still is a bit of a nightmare, because of the number of potholes in the roads. Most of them are grouped around a hundred or two-hundred-metre radius – 600 metres apart, obviously a section of inferior quality road building. They are very difficult to dodge and make dealing with oncoming traffic pretty dangerous, with both of you swerving all over the road. A joke at the Golf Club went as follows. How do you tell a drunk driver from a sober one? The drunk drives in a straight line and the sober guy does not; he is trying to miss the potholes!

Having made it safely without any bent rims to the intersection of Cecil Avenue and the Beitbridge road, it was necessary to clear the last hurdle before the real journey started, the traffic-light-controlled [sic] intersection. At 99% of all intersections in Bulawayo traffic lights suffer from one or all of the following: a) all are out or broken; b) only one light of the four sets is working; c) one or more are flashing orange; d) two lights come on at once e.g. orange and green, red and green.

Obviously the least dangerous intersections are those where the orange or red is flashing or permanently on.

For some unknown reason, the previous powers that be decided that yield signs instead of stop signs were the way to go on subsidiary roads. Yield signs to the Bulawayo motorist mean slow down enough to take the corner. Giving way to traffic from the right does not feature in the driver's licence requirement curriculum!

The result is that approaching defective traffic lights require a wide-awake approach, lots of patience and a fair bit of luck to get through safety. It is also vital to find a position at the crossroads so that you can see as many of the traffic lights as possible to determine what action to take. If the ones facing you are out of order, you need to check if the cross lights are out as well, or else you could be edging through, only to be rammed by a car that screams through because it has very weak single green light in its favour.

Once I had negotiated the crossing with ease at that time of the morning, I proceeded towards Beitbridge. Just after the hills down to Esigodini, I hit the rumble strips. These are not designed to ensure drivers are still awake, but are remnants of Government's failed tollroad system. I can only imagine that some minister or bureaucrat in the Zimbabwe government had noticed the proliferation of toll gates in South Africa and had decided to introduce the same here. About two years ago with much fanfare, i.e. newspaper headlines, TV, radio interviews, the government announced the setting up of tollgates to collect revenue from motorists entering all big towns. This, we were told, would herald the end of poor roads in Zimbabwe. Eventually, with all the revenue collected, we too would have world-class highways of international standard.

Like most government-initiated endeavours, it was probably a good idea around the canteen at teatime, but lacked the planning and implementation assessment necessary to even get to roof height. Rumble strips were laid on both directions of the road. A slight gravel deviation was made so that the building of the toll gate, the size of a Wendy house or garden shed, could commence without traffic interruptions.

After about two months of feverish activity the brick shed, approximately two metres by two metres, in the centre of the road, straddling the white line, was about shoulder high. As suddenly as the project was started, it was stopped.

The brick shed was taken down first by a 30-ton rig travelling to Bulawayo from Beitbridge late at night, and finally by the people who erected it.

So died another bureaucratic brainwave. The rumble strips and indentation from the shed's foundations can still be clearly seen and felt. This same scenario played itself out on hundreds of roads around Zimbabwe.

About 20 kilometres outside Bulawayo, I pass Chipangali, an animal-rescue centre that has been run by the Wilson family for decades. Chipangali is well known for its rhino-breeding efforts. About three years ago, Jane and I visited a nine-week-old rhino calf born at the sanctuary. The Lady Diana Centre, built about ten years ago, contained goats, rabbits and small buck, and was designed as a touch-and-learn centre for the little kids. We supplied the wire mesh for the concrete sections from old shop fittings we no longer used. In return, Mr. Viv Wilson gave us life membership. Many a weekend was spent wandering through the lion cages, monkey enclosures, aviaries and enjoying refreshments and fresh chocolate cake.

Sadly, after almost ten years of decline, Chipangali is today a skeleton of its former self. The economic situation, poaching and lack of funds have robbed Zimbabwe of a fantastic wildlife, animal-rescue and education facility.

Monkeys, Donkeys, Cows and Goats!

During the day the trip to Beitbridge takes about three hours. Travelling at dusk or after dusk is suicidal because of the number of cattle next to and on the road. Some ten to twelve years ago most of the farms along the road were fenced. During the past eight years they have been taken over by Government, the former farmers chased off and new farmers resettled. The political pluses and minuses of this whole exercise would fill a library of books. Suffice it to say that many of the newly-resettled farmers lacked the financial power, and in many cases the skill and know-how, to maintain and erect new fences. The result is cattle, with huge square bells around their necks, wandering across the road or grazing next to the road. Goats and donkeys also abound. The goats are mostly well trained. When they hear a car hoot about a kilometre away, they will gap it off the road. If there is more than one and they split up, one to the left and one to the right, slow down. As sure as day follows night, the one will try and join the other, just as you are about to pass through.

Cows, on the other hand, are fine while their heads are down grazing. If the head is up and the cow has a faraway look in its eyes, slow down because it could be contemplating ambling across to greener pastures just as you arrive. In most instances, donkeys call for a complete stop of your vehicle if they are in the road. Even nudging one with your bumper won't guarantee it will move. Stubbornness personified!

Between Bulawayo and Beitbridge there are no rest places. To stop at an inviting lay-by, under a big baobab tree, is to invite trouble. Two of my friends have been badly beaten and robbed by groups of men, armed with pangas and mopani sticks, within the last six months. Each of them stopped for a nature break about 120 kilometres from the border. Luckily in both instances, passing truck drivers stopped and the attackers fled. Thankfully nobody was critically injured.

The drive to Beitbridge can be boring on your own. Intermittent radio reception on the two local government-controlled radio stations made switching on the car radio totally frustrating. In any case, five years ago, the infamous Minister of Information, Jonathan Moyo, had ordained that the government broadcaster could only play music with 100% local content. The local artists included the minister himself and one or two other cabinet ministers, who had released CDs of ZANU-PF propaganda songs! To be spared these creations, car satellite radios were the only option. South African *Jacaranda* or *East Coast Radio* were the stations of choice for most people, including for our staff, who requested a satellite radio in order to have music piped throughout the Head Office. Strangely enough, their favourite station was *Radio Jacaranda*. Even the locals didn't think the minister's *"local was lekker"*!

A few mental detours, evoked by some of the features on the Bulawayo-Beitbridge road. As will be clear throughout the ensuing pages, Government issues Statutory Instruments at will. I suppose "decree" is a more readily understood term and describes them better. Hence the 100% local music content. Coupled with this was the car-radio-licence SI. In order to fund their radio stations, Government introduced a SI on a Friday, and by Monday, roadblocks throughout the country were set up and drivers fined for not having a licence for their car radio.

After publication most Statutory Instruments [SI] were followed by "operations". These are so-called "crackdowns" on wrongdoers, all of course carried out "on orders from the top", clearly indicated Government's attitude to running the country.

Shortly after the SI regarding car radios, the SI controlling number plates was published. Our Zimbabwe car registration plate has three numbers, a hyphen, then three numbers followed by a letter of the alphabet e.g. 467-359B. For reasons best known only to the ones in charge, the new SI required all number plates to be changed to a three-letter four-number system e.g. AAQ 3468. This changeover, of course, had to be done within a certain period. Rumour had it that the Vice President was involved in producing the new number plates as a money-making venture.

Needless to say another "operation" was carried out, netting millions in fines. Like the radio-licence operation, this one eventually petered out, as not only had the producers of the number plates run out of materials, but the Zambian authorities were rumoured to have asked the Zimbabwe Government to call a halt to the exercise, as the number-plate-lettering system was the same as theirs, and they objected very strongly. Whatever the reasons, we now have two registration-plate systems running concurrently in Zimbabwe.

The route to Beitbridge takes you across five railway crossings. This is the path of the BBR, the Bulawayo Beitbridge Railway line, built eight years ago on a build-and-transfer basis – whatever that means – by a South African company. It was used at least once, because the famous Blue Train arrived in Bulawayo with President Thabo Mbeki of South Africa, who officially opened this new rail link. It was to be the start of a huge growth of unprecedented proportions for the Zimbabwean economy, or so the Government Information Minister predicted!

Between the fourth and fifth railway crossing lies Charles Davey's farm, demarcated with a 24-kilometre-long double game fence, along which giraffes, warthogs and other animals often stroll. Charles' daughter, Chelsea, was romantically linked to Prince Harry of the British Royal family.

On today's drive I pass a giraffe cow and her calf walking along the road outside the game fence. About two kilometres along, I stop to talk to a worker from the farm standing at the gate. He tells me the giraffes are not from this farm but from the "new" farmer across the road, who has not yet completed fixing his fence and so his game wanders. I can't but wonder what eventually happened to the two animals.

One hundred and twenty kilometres from Beitbridge is "Todds". Its official name is "Todd's Guest House and Watering Hole Bar", where in the past most visitors to Zimbabwe would have their first stop after passing through the border. Ice-cold beers, a warm welcome to Zimbabwe and a bite to eat were the order of the day. The owners also had a tame giraffe, their mascot. Tragically, it was killed two years back by "poachers". I will leave you to draw your own conclusions, but suffice it to say that the owners had resisted, by all legal means possible, the forced takeover of the guesthouse and land by a local councillor.

Having negotiated the gravel deviation ten kilometres from the border, which is where the road has been under construction for the past eight years, I arrive in the dusty, dry and hot town of Beitbridge, probably most famous in Zimbabwe for the number of Datsun 120Ys and 140Ys. These cars are really old, dating back to the late 70s. Their condition confirms their age!

Disorganised Chaos

To describe the border post as chaotic is truly an understatement. There are few directional signs and those that are in place are incorrect or outdated, or both. After paying the bridge toll – only payable on the Zimbabwe side, strangely enough – you have your passport stamped. Luckily we still don't have computer control for entry and exit, so this part is very quick.

Next a plain-clothes policeman stamps your gate pass at a table near the door. This he does only after he has checked the vehicle registration book and the vehicle-clearance form.

Every time one leaves the country, this form has to be obtained in Bulawayo at the Vehicle Inspection Depot, commonly called the VID, which sounds more sinister and invokes the fear that permeates every aspect of society, and that is generated by that other, more secretive, organisation known by its initials. The VID visit is a really painfully slow, time-wasting exercise, where licence, ID and registration book have to be produced. You queue up for your engine number to be checked against your registration book. No computers here, just big books where all details are laboriously written out. After that, your vehicle-clearance form is stamped, allowing you to take your vehicle out of the country.

Now back to the border. After the stamp of approval by the plain-clothes guy, who never leaves his table to verify the details checked in Bulawayo anyway, you proceed to a hut, where a Customs Official asks if you have any Zimbabwe dollars. After your reply in the negative, your gate pass is finally stamped. Why anyone would want to export Zimbabwe dollars, except for their collection value, I have never been able to work out.

Having collected all the necessary stamps, you may proceed to a boom leading to the bridge. Here the gatekeeper and gate-pass collector ask me to back up slightly as I have crossed the white line, painted on the road about 20 years ago and now barely visible. The last display of authoritative behaviour.

After crossing the bridge, you arrive at the South African border control, get out your car and walk through a metal tray with a damp hessian sack in the bottom, which is the foot-and-mouth-disease control dip.

Of course South Africa has computers, so the wait in line here is much longer than on the Zimbabwean side. Each passport is scanned and then stamped. Import papers and the cursory inspection at the gate for contraband is all that is now needed before you leave the border.

I meet the boys ten kilometres from the border in Musina, a bustling little town, bursting at its seams. Over the last six years, it has become a boomtown. Zimbabwe-registered cars outnumber those of the locals. Grocery shopping by families and cross-border purchases for resale in Zimbabwe, are what have created the boom. I suppose for the residents of Musina it must be much like the little towns in the gold-rush days: thousands of foreigners invading and taking over your town.

The boys were pretty excited about their trip to Zimbabwe and a houseboat trip on Kariba. Besides Jonny, who grew up and attended CBC in Bulawayo, the other three had never been to Zimbabwe.

We negotiated the border quite easily, going through the same process in reverse. Zimbabwe customs most of the time don't have any Customs Declaration forms so any scrap of paper will do, as long as your passport number, address and name appear on it as well as anything you would be foolish enough to declare. Normally groceries with an arbitrary amount in Rand will suffice to get the paper stamped.

You could be unlucky and be required to unpack the whole car and trailer. Whilst frustrating and time-consuming, it must be done! No backchat or discussion should take place. Should you be foolish enough to do so anyway, as punishment for daring to comment you may be required to pull over and wait for hours. I forget to mention that the temperature at Beitbridge reaches over 40 degrees Celsius most of the year, so it's a double whammy if you are delayed unnecessarily. No toilets – that you would want to use – or refreshment stalls around here!

The trip back to Bulawayo was pretty uneventful. The giraffes were gone, we hope retreated into the bush and to relative safety. We were stopped at three roadblocks by the ever-friendly police. Requests for your driver's licence and the same "Where are you going?" and "Where are you coming from?" at every barrier. Because we were on the Beitbridge-Bulawayo road, one could be forgiven for thinking these were rhetorical questions, but they required the answers "Bulawayo" and "Beitbridge" *every time!* Satisfied that five white males probably posed no threat to the security of the state, we were allowed to proceed. We kept the six loaves of bread well hidden, as no doubt the roadblock officials would have relieved us of a few had they spotted them.

Peggy and Rabson, our maid and gardener, were happy to see us return, excited at the prospect of the mealie meal, bread and few groceries I had time to purchase in Musina. Both have been with us since we arrived in Bulawayo, 13 years ago. They are part of the family. Peggy was especially happy to see Jonny, now a strapping young man, over 1.80m tall, who had left for varsity four years previously. Peggy's sons all work for the company and her youngest daughter, Bianca, has been schooled at a private school since Grade 0, thanks to Jane's generosity. Bianca is now 14 and has grown into a refined teenager.

Arrested!

After unpacking the car and since it was Friday, I decided to phone the office to see if there were any cheques that needed signing. The time was half past three in the afternoon. Little did I realise how the phone call would have such a profound impact on our personal and business lives!

I got through to Elana, my Financial Director, on her cellphone. I could hear by her tone and the sound of her voice that something bad was going down. The gist of her conversation was that Larry, our Operations Manager, had been arrested and that she was not in the office. She insisted that I should get out of town, but keep in contact with her. The events leading up to this were as follows.

We had been marking up our goods countrywide on a weekly basis by as much as 80%, in order to protect our stock from being overtaken by inflation. Suppliers were increasing their prices by up to 100% per week. Replacement costing of this nature had been going on for the past three years, but over the last six months, from January to June 2007, inflation had been rising and the value of the currency had been falling dramatically.

On Monday 18th June 2007, Larry, Elana, Richard, Fanuel and I had held our normal Monday "By-how-much-are-we-going-to-increase-our-price-this-week" meeting. We decided that doubling our prices would probably do the trick, taking into account the "black market" rate of the Zimbabwe dollar to the US dollar. A memo was drawn up and sent to all our shops, instructing them to mark-up all stock by 100% or double the price with immediate effect. It normally took up to ten days for this exercise to be completed in all our shops as it took a few days for the post to get to our deep rural shops. A further two or three days would be needed for the administrative tasks associated with the mark-up.

On Friday 29th of June the Minister of Industry and International Trade, Obert Mpofu, had come up with the bright idea that the prices of everything in Zimbabwe should, with immediate effect, be backdated to Monday the 18th of June.

The irony was that our memo instructing shop managers to double prices had probably only just been carried out by all our shops. Had we been instrumental in the minister's decision? Was our mark-up memo the proverbial straw that broke the camel's back as far as Government was concerned? We of course would never know.

With elections only a few months away, scheduled for March 2008, the Government was, it appeared, ready to do anything to win votes. Economic fundamentals and basic economic theory were thrown out the window as was clear from Mpofu's letter, which attributed the price increases to attempts at regime change by the business community (see appendix page 193 to 204).

IT CAN GET WORSE

The price slash was with immediate effect. The news of the price slash was as per usual carried on every news bulletin, with the normal propaganda slant blaming business for inflation and the country's woes. Obviously we wanted something in writing or at least something official. This we got on Monday 2nd of July. By Wednesday the 4th, our instruction memo to revert to our pre-18th June prices was on its way.

Little did we know that no time frame was allowed to carry out this excercise. With a government desperate for votes, we should have realised that this crack-down was going to be serious. With the markdown memos only being sent out on Wednesday the 4th, many of our shops would only receive them the following week Monday.

To markdown all stock with a price-marking gun in any one of our 196 shops, could take up to two or three days. Everything is then double-checked and the handwritten price reduction sheets are sent to Head Office. Unfortunately, this was not possible, as no shops were allowed to close. If you closed your doors to ensure accurate administration, the state regarded the company as its enemy, bent on regime change! Any state agent, e.g. traffic warden, policeman, soldier or administration clerk in a government office was either mandated or took the initiative to ensure compliance, while at the same time making use of the 50%-off Government-approved nationwide sale.

The markdown exercise in our shops was far from complete by Friday the 6th. In the meantime, since announcing the price cuts on TV and radio as well as in the government-controlled press, our shops were in chaos with every Tom, Dick and Harry demanding 50% off everything, whether it had been marked down or not.

Obviously, this feeling of absolute power now permeated every government official, and the poor shop manager had to agree to the price, whatever it was, or face instant arrest.

It was against this background that our Human Resource Manager, Fanuel, received the fateful call at about twelve noon from our Ops Manager, Larry, that eight of our Bulawayo shop managers had been arrested and detained at the "Drill Hall", which was the ZRP command centre. The Drill Hall is a beautiful colonial building in the centre of Bulawayo, which used to house the police riot unit. The crime of the shop managers was that they had *"not reduced prices in line with the government directive"* that ordered all prices to be reverted to the 18th June 2007-level.

Rumour reached our staff earlier in the day, that hundreds of Company Directors in Harare had been arrested for the same offence. Apparently, Comrade Mpofu wanted to send a strong message to all and sundry that prices had to stop increasing. This was typical of the intimidation and fear that absolute power generates. Panic and fear spread quickly throughout the country's business community.

IT CAN GET WORSE

Herald Reporter

NO ONE in private or public sectors can now raise salaries, wages, rents, service charges, prices and school fees on account of increases or anticipated increases in the consumer price index, the official and unofficial exchange rates, or valued added tax and duty.

The ban on indexing pay, prices, rents and fees to the CPI, an exchange rate or VAT — coupled with vastly increased powers for the National Incomes and Pricing Commission — was made by President Mugabe in regulations gazetted yesterday to temporarily amend two Acts: that setting up the Commission and the Education Act.

The regulations were made under the Presidential Powers (Temporary Measures) Act and fall away in six months unless Parliament amends the two affected Acts.

Under the regulations, all proposed fees, tariffs and charges by Government departments, State universities, statutory bodies, including statutory professional associations, and companies where the State is a majority or sole shareholder must be approved by the Commission in advance.

The Commission takes over the powers formerly possessed by ministers where ministerial approval was first required.

All fee increases by non-Government schools since June 18 are banned until the Commission gives approval. The Commission takes over the functions of the Secretary for Education, Sport and Culture in approving and setting fees at non-Government schools.

The Commission can only approve an increase if this is justified on some other grounds than the application of the CPI, killing the present link between fees and the CPI.

For all pay awards, and fee and price increases by the private sector, the Commission must now set standards after consultation.

When the rumours first surfaced, Elana had joked, that since I was out of the office, she as Financial Director was the next highest officer and she would be the one to get arrested. She declared she was going home early as it was a Friday and Fridays had become the favourite day for the government to enforce its will and intimidate the populace: if you were arrested on Friday, it meant a weekend in jail because Monday was the first time you would be able to appear in court.

The first such arrests were made three years earlier, when foreign currency was non-existent in the country through official channels like banks. To make the situation worse, the Reserve Bank had converted all FCAs (Foreign Currency Accounts) to Zimbabwe-dollar accounts, effectively stealing the forex holdings of companies. The Reserve Bank governor had on a Friday, three years ago, arrested many top businessmen for allegedly dealing in foreign currency illegally. This incident initiated the trend of starting the weekend at midday on Friday.

I remember a meeting held at the Bulawayo Holiday Inn, where the same Gono threatened the gathered business community that anyone thought to be buying currency through any other channel than the banks – who had none anyway – would face the *"hospitality of the state"*. This was said with a giggle and pompous arrogance. All companies were doing, was to stay viable whatever the cost. The fact that four years later they were still trading, bears testimony to their fortitude and initiative.

When private schools decided to increase their fees without Government approval, Headmasters, Governing Body Chairmen and others were locked up on a Friday. As a result, over the last four years, many businesses closed at one o'clock on the Friday and the directors "went away" for the weekend to avoid arrest. Many of my friends faced this horrific experience and preferred to leave for Australia, New Zealand and other safer places.

Larry, always the chauvinist, had offered jokingly that should Elana be arrested, he would go in her stead. Little did they realise that the joke was to become reality.

After a short discussion with Fanuel and Elana, Larry courageously decided to go to the Drill Hall and see what he could do to get his Shop Managers released. This trap, set by the authorities, worked. On his arrival at the Drill Hall he was greeted by gleeful policemen in charge of *"Operation Reduced Prices"*. The police were actually after the top managers and so, after introducing himself, Larry was promptly arrested and the eight managers released. At first they did not want to leave but instead wanted to "go inside" in solidarity with their boss. Larry managed to persuade them, especially the ladies involved, that their families needed them.

They reported back to Fanuel what had happened. By about four o'clock, after Fanuel's numerous phone calls to the Drill Hall, they still did not know Larry's fate.

Six weeks prior to those happenings, we had engaged the services of a Senior

Police Officer, Mr. X, who had resigned from the police force. He was disenchanted with the spurious orders they were routinely given, and became our security consultant instead. Fanuel phoned Mr. X to see if there was anything he could do to help. Thirty minutes later he reported back that the orders had come from the top and no one was prepared to help, fearing for their jobs and lives.

At around five o'clock, Fanuel decided to brave it down to the Drill Hall together with Mr. X, who still had serious connections and friends in the police force. There hundreds of people had been detained, some herded from office to office by heavily-armed soldiers and police. Deciding to first check out the lay of the land, Fanuel and Mr. X observed the ominous activities from across the road, fearing that they would be caught up in the mass of people and bundled into jail themselves. After about 30 minutes of observation, Mr. X spotted a very reliable ex-colleague whom he approached to find out Larry's whereabouts. He managed to get them through the throng of police and detained company directors. Larry was with a group, who had already lost their freedom. Fanuel and Mr. X were told that Larry's group included the "big wig" directors from all big and small companies in Bulawayo, such as Edgars, Jaggers, Makro and many other chain stores. These 15 were guarded by heavily-armed machine-gun-toting troops. Other groups were formed in and around the Drill Hall. Elderly men and women, young entrepreneurs, Indian, Coloured, White and Black – no one escaped this "crackdown".

Some administrative types were documenting all the particulars of each detainee. This in itself was a laborious task, as Fanuel estimates about three to four hundred businessmen and women had been detained. After a while, Fanuel and Mr. X managed to open informal negotiations with the police officers milling around. Somebody suggested slipping Larry out of the Drill Hall during the course of the evening. But this plan was ditched and Fanuel decided to go through the legal route.

Trying to get hold of a lawyer at eight o'clock on a Friday night was almost impossible. One could sense the frustration of the local police officers. Bulawayo is fervently MDC-orientated and very likely most of the policemen were not happy to have to carry out these orders, and probably the reason why our Mr. X had left the force. He had been unable to stomach the ludicrous actions initiated by some power-hungry bureaucrats who believe they have some God-given right to mess people around and intimidate them.

Around seven, Fanuel and Larry thought they had got lucky. The most senior police officer indicated that he had been on the phone to Harare HQ and that there was a meeting in progress, which was looking at the possibility of releasing all detainees for the night, provided they reported back on Saturday morning. This rumour spread fast through the masses. Even our Mr. X was convinced this rumour was true, as in his estimation there were too many detainees for the available holding cells in Bulawayo.

It's easy to imagine the chaos around the Drill Hall that night. Orders being shouted, people arguing, some women crying, pleading to be allowed to get back to their families. One single mother in particular was quite desperate as her child was at home with a domestic who knocked off at six o'clock. These pleadings fell on deaf ears, but it was clear that the police officers were not totally inhuman and is probably the reason why the senior officer indicated that he had asked HQ to release everyone.

Black Boots

Suddenly, out of nowhere, loud shouts materialised and instantly, as one, the whole crowd in the Drill Hall felt silent. In strode an extremely short senior police officer from the dreaded support unit, commonly called the "Black Boots". If the situation had not been so serious, it would have been very comical. "Black Boots" was dressed in his blue combat support-unit battledress, and from his hips dangled not one but two pistols. Fanuel reckoned it reminded him of a cowboy scene from a Wild West movie, when a deathly hush descends as the bad guys enter the saloon.

Immediate fear was tangible in all police present. Our Mr. X and Fanuel retreated to the back of the crowd to avoid being caught in any mad orders given out by "Black Boots". Then, with hands on hips, "Black Boots" announced triumphantly that everyone would be put in jail until Monday to teach everybody a lesson that prices should be reduced as ordered. Hearts sank, shoulders dropped and a few stifled wails rose from the female group.

What one needs to remember is that here was a group of law-abiding senior business people, who, for the last five years at least, had kept the economy going by all means possible. Their only crime was that they were slow, as in our case, or refused to commit economic suicide as ordered to by a demonic state. No other country would consider what they had done a criminal offence, or that they had broken any law. The state, using their favourite tools of fear and intimidation, was determined to win the election in a few months' time.

Prices had been skyrocketing, that is true, and were well out of reach for many wage earners. Basic commodities were available and affordable, but only just. A pair of jeans or a skirt, however, would cost about a month's pay. Bearing in mind that all civil servants received considerably less than workers in the private sector, one can understand the government's motives to win votes. The civil service was the biggest employer in Zimbabwe. Government's failed economic policies had civil servants over a barrel, since there just wasn't enough money to pay them a decent wage. Facile solution: make businessmen the evil scapegoats for putting up prices! Blame business for the hyperinflation, then turn the civil service against business. Blame business for wanting to effect regime change. Government could ignore basic Grade Eight economics of supply and demand, of inflation and its causes. Just continue printing money and keep blaming everyone else for the resulting chaos and misery. Like the story of the proud mom, watching her son's passing-out parade in the army. He was the only one out of step but, as a proud mom, she announced how good her son was as he was the only one in step!

Fanuel phoned Elana to inform her of the decision the police had taken. After some discussion it was agreed to try and persuade a very prominent lawyer, who had already been engaged by a few other detainees, to simply add another name to his list, whatever the cost. As he was on the scene, it would be easier to approach him than to find legal representation elsewhere.

The lawyer tried in vain to have Larry and his other clients released into his custody as no charges had been laid, citing the names of similar cases and precedents. To no avail. "Black Boots" was adamant. The word from the very top, according to him, was to detain everyone arrested. The atmosphere of fear was palpable.

After a number of frantic phone calls, our lawyer managed to secure the services of a judge who would hear the case on Saturday in an emergency sitting. The lawyer then persuaded "Black Boots" to agree to this solution. He was visibly disappointed he was not able to detain everyone till Monday. Those poor souls who had neither a representative, nor the necessary funds, would have to spend the weekend in jail. Our reprieve was extremely welcome, since we knew the conditions in the police holding cells. After we had been given the inevitable one night's incarceration, our Mr. X started negotiations to try and get our lawyer's group to an out-of-town jail, which he assured us, was not as lice-ridden and filthy as the ones in town. Surprisingly, his contacts seemed to bear fruit, as Larry and his co-accused were assigned to a small police station in the suburbs.

At about half past eleven that evening the convoy of police trucks loaded with the detainees, moved out from Drill Hall. Larry and the directors of Edgars, Jaggers, and other big concerns were loaded onto the back of an open 1600cc police bakkie. Not sure that the police drivers would stick to the negotiated destination, Mr. X and Fanuel followed at a distance. True to their word, Mr. X's ex-colleagues took them to the small, much cleaner police cells in the suburbs.

On arrival Larry was afforded two pieces of clothing. It was mid-winter, when night-time temperatures can drop to as low as three or four degrees, so this was a difficult choice. A year earlier, as part of our company uniform, we had supplied all staff with a fleecy jacket, complete with company logo. Larry chose this and his trousers. Fanuel arrived at the police station a short while later and was allowed to give Larry a blanket and some food. No one had received anything to eat or drink since lunchtime – 12 hours ago!

On Saturday morning our group and the lawyer were taken to court. At about midday the judge arrived, wearing sandals and a T-shirt. The public prosecutor was not sure of the charges, hence the judge remanded all the detainees out of custody until the charges had been formulated. At about two o'clock, Fanuel, who, as a good Human Resources Manager, had been following everybody's progress, managed to pick Larry up and drop him off at home. After a shower, which lasted considerably longer than normal, and a good meal, Larry went to bed and just passed out. In a police cell one doesn't get much sleep!

After receiving the news of Larry's arrest on my arrival from Beitbridge, I was struck by the fear that the CIO would come looking for me. The boys and Jane were also anxious for my safety, not knowing what the government was planning.

I set off immediately to the Golf Club, which I assumed was a safe haven from the dreaded CIO, because I knew they had my residential address. We had planned a homecoming braai for Jonny and the boys to celebrate their introduction to Zimbabwe. My idea was to go to the Club and from there coordinate a plan of action and find out how serious the situation was. Jane was left with strict instructions that, should anyone come to the house looking for me, she should claim I was out of town. She was the calmest of us all, having lived through the Rhodesian bush war. The boys, filled with youthful exuberance and testosterone, were prepared to make a stand should anyone threaten Jane whilst I was gone.

My first call from the Golf Club was to my good friend Billy, an upstanding member of the Muslim Council, but more than that with exceptional contacts in the CIO and police, which he had developed during his more than 30 years in Bulawayo and through his involvement in the community. Billy promised to make the necessary phone calls, but confirmed that the crackdown was serious and was being directed from State House in Harare. After about 30 minutes, in which time I had consumed three beers to calm my nerves on instructions from Ken, the Club Manager, Billy phoned. His contacts confirmed my worst fears. The authorities were out to arrest as many top executives as soon as possible, and he advised me not to stay at home. I relayed this news telephonically to Jane, who calmly said she would phone me back with a plan. Ten minutes later she phoned to say that our good friends Rob and Ally had insisted that I stay the night with them. They also insisted that the boys and Jane leave our house immediately and come to their house.

One remarkable trait typical of Zimbabweans, who have lived here all their lives, is their ability to expect the unexpected and to "make a plan". This is a fantastic characteristic and probably explains why the economy and country did not collapse years ago. Jane packed an overnight bag for me, loaded the boys and agreed to meet me at Rob's house.

I find it difficult to put into words the sheer terror I experienced in that situation. My biggest concern was not so much that I could be spending a weekend in prison, but more so that the boys would miss out on our planned Kariba boat trip. How disappointed they would be! My greatest worries were not knowing what the government was planning, the boys' safety and getting them back to varsity.

I snuck out of the Golf Club, watching every vehicle carefully all the way to Rob's. I decided to take a roundabout way to his house, just in case I was being tailed. In hindsight probably silly, but at the time I was filled will real fear and uncertainty. Reaching the sanctuary of Rob's, I found the boys and Rob had already introduced themselves and were having an ice-cold beer around the fire. All the while Fanuel had been in contact, enabling me to follow the proceedings at the Drill Hall intently.

The boys were pretty animated – probably a mixture of excitement to be caught up in the unfolding events and the underlying fear of the unknown. Needless to say, the evening's conversation centred on the happenings of the day, and much theorising about how the fiasco would end and the effect it would have on business. All through the evening, calls were coming in from many friends who were informing us of who had been arrested and enquiring after my safety.

At about half past midnight we all decided to go home. This decision was based on the assumption that enough MDs and senior people had been arrested by then to satisfy the rulers' gluttonous appetite for power.

On Saturday our daughter Nicola arrived and Jane and the boys fetched her from the airport. I elected to stay at home. My escape route, should the CIO arrive, would be over the back fence, through the neighbour's garden and on to Rob's, a short walk away. Thankfully this was not necessary. At about three I managed to speak to Larry who was now at home. I will be forever grateful to him for the sacrifice he made and to the one who plans our lives for ensuring that I was at the border, and not in the office, that fateful Friday.

On Sunday morning we travelled to Kariba and enjoyed four days of fishing with the kids on the houseboat. We decided not to travel too far up the lake, which allowed us to remain in cellphone contact with the office. As could be expected, the trip was interspersed with many long phone calls to and from Bulawayo to keep up to date with what was happening.

On Monday Larry again appeared in court and was once more remanded, this time until 6th August.

Over 1 850 Managing Directors or senior employees of companies in Zimbabwe were arrested and incarcerated over that weekend. The government press crowed about the success of the "crackdown", adding validity to Government's campaign of blaming business people for the country's woes.

On 6th August, the case was withdrawn after all those "accused" appeared in court. The SI, containing the instruction to cut prices back to those of the 18th June, had only been issued on that fateful Friday. The lawyer correctly argued, that the *Government Gazette* with the relevant SI only reached Bulawayo the next Tuesday by truck. The arrests were unfair, since the Bulawayo business community could not have had sight of the SI on the Friday in question.

Who says there is no law in Zimbabwe!

One of our more paranoid hindsight reactions to those threatening incidents, was to invest in four walkie-talkie radios for each of the management team. These were purchased legitimately in Harare and had a range of about two kilometres. We would each carry one so no matter where we were on the premises, we could be warned of impending visits by state agents. The action plan included Soneni, our receptionist and switchboard operator, who would establish the identity of any suspicious visitors. She would inform Richard, whose office was the closest to reception, who in turn would radio us, wherever we were on the premises, allowing us to make a safe getaway through the distribution centre or back entrances.

Thankfully we only used them once, and then with hilarious consequences.

One dreaded Friday afternoon, when all of us were as usual on our pre-weekend edge, three suited gentlemen arrived at reception. Richard had spotted them entering the building and proceeded to sound the alarm via walkie-talkie. Fanuel was at the far end of our distribution centre, when his radio burst into life. It was Richard, warning us all to take cover, until he had discovered who these chaps were. Poor Fanuel had not yet mastered the radio and couldn't reply to Richard's warning. In his desperation, he decided the most prudent thing was to gap it home through the back entrance, at speed.

The three gentlemen turned out to be pastors from Fanuel's church, wishing to discuss peaceful church matters! We managed to trace him on his mobile and urged him to return to the office that was holding no threat – at least not this Friday afternoon!

Appreciating the comedy, his comment was simply "Better safe, than sorry!"

Total Economic Destruction

By the end of July 2007, four weeks after the start of the government's 50%-off closing-down sale, business was in chaos. Shops selling TVs, fridges and other white goods were decimated. Top police, army, other government officials and anyone who had cash, simply cleared out any product they could lay their hands on. Shop owners were powerless to stop them. Within a month of this chaos, most shops had been "looted". Basic commodities were unavailable. Nobody could afford to restock.

We held a total average of between three to four million items in all our shops over the previous years at any one time. Almost 80% of our stock holding had been wiped out at a 50% discount in a two-month period. The end of September stock count showed that we had 800 000 items left. The administrative chaos is easy to imagine. Many shops simply were not able to reconcile the theoretical with the actual stock. Many items were not even rung up through the cash registers. In some shops, officials simply stood at the checkout counters, and after the customer's goods had been rung up, demanded they only pay half of what was rung up. Obviously we realised that amongst our own staff there may have been those who participated in order to enrich themselves. Whatever the reasons, our business was decimated as was the economy of Zimbabwe. Our mode of managing the business now changed from operating to surviving.

All shops in the country, not just ours, ran out of goods. Chemists had no more drugs; even a simple aspirin or Panado was unavailable!

Giant retailers like Edgars Clothing were cleaned out. Imagine a retail clothing shop, covering over 1 500 square metres, absolutely empty, except for an area in the front of the shop with two rails holding leftover stock of about 60 garments.

Bata Shoe shops had also been stripped. As a manufacturer of shoes in Gweru, with a huge factory employing over 3 000 people, Bata was the major footwear supplier in Zimbabwe. They did not have the forex to import the necessary raw materials and therefore were not able to restock even their own shops.

The situation was surreal. Shop assistants were just sitting on the counters with nothing to do.

Closing shops was not an option, as this would offer Government the ideal excuse to take over the business without compensation, as we were "enemies of the State"!

Our shops were not spared the ravages of the 50%-off sale. On a trip around the country in August 2007 we visited our shops, some of which with only a handful of products to sell, to encourage and motivate our staff into believing that things would come right.

Our saving grace was our shops in the rural areas where the money was not so freely available because there were few banks and zero income for ex-farm labourers. This protected our stock from being "looted", but it was not where it could sell. We were quite happy to leave it there, however, as we reckoned we would have something to trade with when the madness was over. It was estimated that over 300 000 farm labourers were chased off the farms since 2000, with no income and therefore no spending power.

The initial SI 142/2007 that informed us of the price freeze until 1st August 2007 was followed on the 31st July with SI 154/2007, which extended the price freeze to 31st December 2007. We could expect another five months of price blitzes.

SI 138/2007 prohibited the import and export of dozens of foodstuffs that were in short supply. On the 27th July, SI 153/2007 repealed the previous one, thus allowing people to import groceries. This flip-flopping by the Reserve Bank, which was assumed to be effectively in control of the whole country, gave credence to the stories that the government was in a tailspin and losing its absolute grip on every aspect of economic life.

SI 150/2007, published on the 27th July, extended the life of the Bearer Cheques, set to expire on 31st July 2007, by 12 months. At least someone somewhere was monitoring the situation. Not that it made much difference to the man in the street who, by this time, could not care less! The number of Statutory Instruments produced in the six months, from June to December 2007, was staggering. The only way we could keep track of any new laws having appeared was to get Fanuel to contact the Government Printers in Harare each Friday to find out what new law (SI) had been passed and printed.

BACOSSI Loans

In August 2007 ZANU-PF had drafted legislation, insisting that 51% of all foreign companies' shares should be held by local indigenous people, the same policy that had been responsible for the ruinous farm takeovers. Foreigners (i.e. whites) owned too much of the economy.

We spent hours with our lawyers going over the legislation and looking for ways to prevent this from happening to our business. The fear and hopelessness in the business community was tangible, causing feelings of deep depression and a wish to "give up". The legislation was passed by Government and is holding back investors to this day. As with all the laws and Statutory Instruments there was no public consultation, no matter how contentious the law may have been. This was probably the reason why so many SIs were amended or withdrawn, shortly after being implemented. We realised that this piece of legislation was primarily aimed at winning votes in the election only a few months away.

In order to get goods on the shelves Government realised it had to do something or face a major setback in the election due early 2008. Reserve Bank Governor Gono introduced the BACOSSI (Basic Commodity Supply Side Intervention) money. This in essence saw the RBZ lending any amount of money to a manufacturer at the interest rate of 25% a year. With inflation in the millions of percent, this was simply giving away money.

The move was intended to get all manufacturers up and running again, after the price slash decimation, and get goods back on the shelves. As was the case with all government initiatives, this loan facility was announced with much fanfare, with the usual arrogance promising the populace that, by the end of December 2007, our supermarket shelves would be full once more.

Nobody will be surprised to read that this miracle didn't happen. The only outcome was that a number of sharks saw this as an early Christmas present and proceeded to apply for huge loans in Zimbabwe dollars. They were converted into hard currency as soon as the loan money hit their bank accounts, either by using the cash on the street or simply by giving the currency peddlers a cheque.

Soon schools, one-man operations and, I am told, even some individuals were able to access the BACOSSI loans. To this day, if something in Zimbabwe is really cheap, it is nicknamed "BACOSSI".

Of course with no collateral in place, those loans would never be paid back, although Gono threatened with all sorts of reprisals. As a direct result of this ill-conceived "rescue plan", inflation gained even more momentum as more money chased fewer goods.

Traditionally, we would hold an August sale to clear any remaining winter stock in preparation for our summer season. In 2007 this was unnecessary. Our stock levels were so low, we now focused on protecting the limited stock that was left.

In May 2007 the National Incomes and Pricing Act [Chapter 14:32] was passed. This gave rise to the formation of the National Income and Pricing Commission or the NIPC, consisting of four people in Harare with a satellite office in Bulawayo.

The functions of this commission, amongst other things, were to:
A undertake research and maintain a national database to develop periodic pricing models
B monitor price trends and initiate corrective measures in cases of unscrupulous business practices
C consider, approve or determine as the case may be,
    i requests for price adjustments
    ii major cost drivers in the economy
    iii prices and industry mark-ups
D investigate pricing violations.

The act also provided for a five-year prison term for anyone "refusing to sell goods". This was spelt out and included:
A   falsely denying to an inspector that he/she has the goods in his/her possession
B   refusing or failing to supply to any customer the goods upon tender of immediate payment of the lawful maximum price
C   refusing or failing to expose or to offer for sale such goods continuously.

Penalties for failing to display prices and conditional selling – whatever that means – was also outlawed, with prison terms of two to five years for those found guilty of any of these offences.

It goes without saying, that they were aided by the usual security apparatus to ensure compliance. Unfortunately this commission was overshadowed by the feared "Cabinet Taskforce", headed by the Minister of Industry and International Trade, Obert Mpofu, which launched the price war against business on the 29th June 2007.

The NIPC and Salaries

As mentioned earlier, the purpose of this so-called National Income and Pricing Commission, now reporting to the Cabinet Taskforce, was to regulate all business activities in the country, the NIPC also forbade any company to increase salaries or wages without their permission. They thought they could arrest inflation by imposing these draconian and short-sighted measures.

We decided to ignore the salary directive and give our staff an increase in August 2007, as we had been doing every August for the past five years. Our argument would be, should we be arrested, that we had applied to the Commission in Harare, that this increase was planned for in June and as a result, since we had not received any response from the Commission, we had gone ahead with the pay rise. The letter, with the correct date was on file, just in case. We worked on the supposition that upsetting potential voters by making us retract the increase, would not be a very welcome prospect for the NIPC. This ploy worked, and we were never questioned or jailed for breaking this law.

Of course, there were a number of businesses who used this legislation to their advantage by not giving their employees an increase citing, quite rightly, that it would be against the law.

Our philosophy was different. We had a much longer-term view of our business, and of the positive relationship with our staff, realising it was critical to have motivated employees who are able to meet their basic needs.

Confusion reigned during those first four weeks after the price slash and Larry's sojourn in jail. Business throughout Zimbabwe was in turmoil. Not only shops, but also restaurants received visitations by police, who demanded to see the menu from before 18th June to check on potential price increases. Of course if there had been any, the manager was immediately arrested and imprisoned for a minimum of 14 days without bail.

Rent Freeze

Coupled with the price slash/salary freeze, the country had to endure the rent freeze. Landlords could not put up rents for the next six months until December 2007, as per presidential decree. This created indescribable chaos. Up until June, we had effectively been negotiating our rentals on a monthly basis, normally a fixed US-dollar figure, but paid in Zimbabwe dollars at the black market or parallel rate. This rate, not surprisingly, depended on where you were getting your exchange rate information from! A landlord in Mutare, the town bordering Mozambique in the north of the country, would have a totally different US-dollar versus Zimbabwe-dollar exchange rate from someone in Harare, Bulawayo or in some small rural town. For one week a month, every month, rentals for the more than 190 shops were individually negotiated. No new contracts, just a letter confirming the new rental. Administrating such a fluid system was a nightmare. In order to satisfy our landlords, we ended up paying many twice or three times a month to meet their demands and dodge the NIPC inspectors (see appendix page 199).

If the company wanted to increase prices, or price newly received stock at a higher price than the existing stock, e.g. something as mundane as a pair of jeans, you had to apply to the pricing commission for permission! Needless to say this was a fruitless exercise. Three weeks after submission of your application, approval would still be stuck somewhere in the bureaucratic pipeline. Elana and I set up a meeting with the Bulawayo NIPC officers on the 2nd of October to try and persuade them of the concept of replacement costing. Our in-shop prices were now all pre-June 18th. However, our suppliers were sending us the stock we had ordered before the price slash, but at higher prices than we were selling the same product for. Selling this new stock below what we paid for it, was a no-brainer. Hence the meeting with the NIPC Bulawayo office to persuade them to allow us to use replacement costing or in other words, allow us to mark-up our in-store stock to the selling price of our newly received stock.

In the meantime, to add insult to injury, the government had closed all abattoirs. The owners had to reapply for licences, enabling the state to impose more efficient price controls, and enforce greater indigenous shareholding in the businesses.

By mid-August 2007 no meat, milk, eggs, chicken or vegetables were available. Shops were *empty*, and I mean empty. Huge supermarkets had only bare shelves. If this exercise was to win votes, it had become clear that it had seriously backfired.

Eventually the government had to reverse its decision, shelve its lofty ideas and allow abattoirs to continue. Perhaps it realised its mistake or, probably and more likely, too many senior government officials owned abattoirs and were feeling the pinch!

At the meeting with the NIPC in Bulawayo we decided we would try everything to persuade the officials that replacement costing, i.e. marking up existing stock to the price of the newly received stock, was the only way forward if we were to survive. Our NIPC initiative, and the following "negotiations", need to be placed in the prevailing economic context, where literally *no* basic commodities were available, including the staple food mealie meal. Famine threatened the whole country.

With foresight we had been buying mealie meal on the black market. We sent our truck out at three in the morning to our contacts in the rural areas, where one of our staff members had an uncle who had access to mealie meal. At times the truck was intercepted by the "task force", consisting of war vets bent on stamping out "corruption". This "task force" was to ensure that the scarce commodity was channelled to the army and police. Needless to say, a few bags changed hands and we were able to bring our cargo, more precious than gold, to town. At this stage we were supplying all our staff with a free lunch. The mealie meal was critical to the continued functioning of our company, as in many cases, this was the only meal our staff would get each day.

In preparation for our NIPC meeting we strategically placed four bags of mealie meal next to our secretary's desk, in clear view of the arriving NIPC officials. The comments they shared on seeing the mealie meal made for a very productive meeting, and proved our ploy had been effective.

Elana's brilliant accounting methods and calculations were enough to confuse me, never mind the NIPC bureaucrats. On achieving our objective, the inevitable question was posed by the NIPC chief,

"Where can we get mealie meal?"

"No problem," says Elana. "We have a few extra bags."

This part was well rehearsed. Elana asked Marchelle to confirm the official Government Gazetted price of the mealie meal – though we had paid five times this price – but did not dare let this cat out of the bag. Once the price was confirmed, we gladly handed over the bags, insisting that we couldn't give the food to them without payment, as this would be tantamount to corruption. They enthusiastically paid the pittance. *We* were happy and *they* were happy.

Two days later, I received a call from the NIPC Chief, asking for a loan of ZW$2.4 trillion to pay his rent, since he had not yet been paid. I very courteously explained that, given our relationship, I would be loathe to do this as much as I wanted to help him out, because should he be found out, it could be considered a bribe and he could lose his job. Much to my surprise he understood and thanked me for being so honest. I didn't know what to make of that.

Having got the all clear to use replacement costing we could now trade.

The following week I accompanied my friend Rob, who ran a one-man business, to the same official's offices to get him to agree Rob could do the same costing calculations as we had. We had become good mates and without much fuss he agreed to Rob's proposals and he too could continue trading.

This was a major turning point after the price slash. It meant that we could start restocking and at the same time more effectively protect our cash flow.

By December 2007, cash was once again hard to come by. As indicated earlier, I am no economist, but a simple calculation told me that, in order for there to be enough cash with inflation at over 3 000%, the Reserve Bank needed to be printing money at a phenomenal rate to have enough notes in circulation. Already two of the noughts removed in August were back with prices spiralling once again thanks to good old market forces. Christmas 2007 was our worst on record. No cash for people to draw and long queues at the bank. It appeared as though Government had capitulated on its attempts to control all charges.

As a clothing retailer we were now operating again with a measure of normality. We had managed to import raw fabric from Mauritius, as most local manufacturers had no forex to import the content they needed to produce our goods. Our export to Zambia and South Africa, even after surrendering 45% to the Reserve Bank, gave us enough forex for the necessary imports. Clothing imports had been levied a 65% duty, payable in forex, with the aim to discourage imports and thus save the country's forex.

Look East

After the government's push to "look East" that saw it currying favour with China, there was a proliferation of cheap, below-standard Chinese goods shops, derogatorily referred to as "Zhing Zhong" when customers became aware of the low quality of products for sale. The government had promoted trade and tourism with China for the past three years since 2003. Chinese goods were coming in at such low prices that it begged the question whether importers were paying duty at all.

One must understand the absolute business chaos, confusion and corruption that this whole price slash and NIPC exercise generated. Dummy invoices and pro formas, cash deposit slips and other similarly doctored paperwork were the order of the day. NIPC inspectors wanted to see the original invoices of goods purchased to ensure you had not taken more than the prescribed mark-up. As a result people made up dummy invoices, pro-formas and other documents to hoodwink the NIPC inspectors and satisfy their requests.

On 21st August Mpofu issued another press release. In it he clarified, "retailers are allowed to put a maximum mark-up of 20% and charge value added tax of 15% on a commodity." As an example, a supplier charging a price of, say ZW$100 000, will see the product sold by the retailer at a maximum price of ZW$138 000.

This directive was issued in the form of a circular to the Chamber of Commerce, and through them to their members. There was utter confusion as to how to apply the 20%. Was it on the purchase price from the supplier? Was the manufacturer also allowed 20%? Where things became really confusing was when he also banned the indexing of prices, pay, rents and fees to the consumer-price index, or an exchange rate. When we imported fabric in US dollars for our factory, we had always used the bank exchange rate to pay the duty, and then priced the raw material about ten times higher using the black-market rate, or the rate we had paid for the foreign currency to buy the imported fabric in the first place. So what rate do we now use to price our imported fabric?

Trying to contact the NIPC for clarification was a nightmare. Their offices were totally flooded with price-increase applications and endless queries. While all this chaos was taking hold, shop managers were still being arrested around the country for supposedly not adhering to the directive of reverting to pre-June 18th prices!

A call would come through from a shop manager in Masvingo reporting that the police were in his shop and unless he produced the invoice for the cost of goods, proving that the price was pre-18th June, he would be locked up (see appendix page 205 and 211).

Although our central distribution centre was based in Bulawayo, all suppliers delivered there – from where the goods were chosen, invoiced and then sent out by transporter to the more than 190 shops throughout the country. No shop, therefore, would have an invoice from a supplier as it was held at Head Office (see appendix page 206).

So frequent were these calls from desperate shop managers, many of whom had already been jailed overnight, that we set up an office with our Mr. X, together with one staff member, who would pull the invoice of a particular supplier of the goods in question, and then fax this to the nearest police station. In many instances, long discussions and arguments would take place over the phone. The explanation that we had at head office, where all the paper work was kept, proved sometimes too difficult to comprehend for the price task force or for the policeman.

We decided to follow a 20% mark-up on the "after-all-costs" model, as we had not been able to get clarity from the local NIPC offices, who were staffed with policemen and women who obviously had no or very little accounting knowledge. We tried on various occasions to explain that a 20% mark-up, only on the cost from the supplier, was unworkable. How were we supposed to cover all our overhead costs like rentals, wages, salaries, fuel and insurance?

"The circular states clearly you can only mark-up 20% on cost," was the trite answer.

Almost a week later another circular appeared, allowing us to mark-up any goods a further 20% for transport, if they are sold outside a 40-kilometre radius of one's head office or manufacturing plant. This posed a huge problem for us, as not only was our factory in Bulawayo, but it meant that we would have to abandon our one-price-nationwide strategy, which we had applied for 35 years.

We decided to ignore this and take our chances. A two-pricing model would be unsuitable and impossible to implement, as so many of our trade principles would be prejudiced. For instance, our money-back guarantee. A smart customer would buy our stock in Bulawayo at 20% less than anywhere else, take it to Masvingo, 300 kilometres away, and ask for his money back, effectively costing us 20%, and making him a quick buck.

When a smart pricing commissioner raided our Bulawayo shop, querying the price of a pair of men's trousers, which cost the same as in his home town of Masvingo, we had to think quickly. Our now very efficient and resourceful price-dodging department produced an internal Stock Transfer Document, showing that this specific lot of trousers had been transferred to Bulawayo from a shop in Binga, over 400 kilometres away, thus justifying the extra 20% for transport.

In most of these incidents we managed to talk and bamboozle the price-task-force member. Where he appeared to be more stubborn and not willing to accept our ruse, it cost us a pair of trousers or some other piece of merchandise "required" by the officer.

In October, four months after the price slash, the NIPC had realised it was not winning. A new circular appeared, allowing a 40% overhead cost mark-up on the original cost. This included costs such as salaries, wages, insurance, fuel and rent, and then 20% could be added as a profit mark-up. Another 20% could be added for transport (see appendix page 210).

Well, we did the allowable mark-up calculations, and then fell about laughing. The legal mark-up now came to 110%, and our pre-June mark-up for our business model was up to 30% less than this! Bureaucrats – totally inept at running businesses! Despite these concessions, no price could be increased without it officially being approved by the NIPC. We, like many other businesses, decided to ignore the NIPC, as we still had applications for price increases sitting with them since August! This mark-up concession, of course, only served to drive inflation even higher. But there was light at the end of the tunnel: with elections only a few months away, Government had to ensure products started reappearing on the supermarket shelves!

As a result, teams of riot police, dubbed the "task force", the same guys who had ensured absolute compliance with the 50%-off price slash, were sent out to once again terrorise businesses that were hoarding, rather than distributing or selling, their goods. Inflation had not died down, it had in fact increased.

Government was convinced that business was the driver of high prices, with the specific aim of upsetting the population so much that they would bring down the government, either by riots or at the next election, a few months away. It was absolutely paranoid. In the meantime, all we wanted was to trade and make a fair return for our shareholders and give employment to our staff.

It seems surreal now to think back on the many meetings we had with the NIPC at our factory, clarifying how we were pricing, at the same time trying to explain to the Task Force what "Overheads" meant, the difference between profit and cash, or "replacement costing", aware all the time that at a whim they could lock us up for 14 days without the option of bail. Naturally we were always the sweetest and most generous to these gentlemen and women whenever they came knocking.

Another Cash Shortage

The cash shortage was really starting to bite now, so reluctantly we started to accept bank-guaranteed cheques. The customer would come into our shop, write down the prices of the goods he/she wanted to buy and then queue at the bank to get a cheque for the required amount.

On getting the cheque, sometimes after queuing for two days, the customer had to hope and pray we hadn't marked up the goods in the meantime. Sometimes, of course, the price increase would have taken effect and so one or two customers involved with the NIPC, which was still operational, would try to prosecute us. Most people were aware that prices were increasing, as the exchange rate they were getting for their foreign money sent from abroad was also increasing. It was an unwritten understanding as to how the economy kept going.

The involvement of the NIPC officials most of the time ended amicably with a few garments changing hands. Cheap price to pay for being able to continue trading.

Banks stopped printing personal cheque books for two reasons. Firstly, because of the shortage of foreign currency to import the paper, and secondly because of the exorbitant cost of a locally-produced cheque book. The inevitable happened: bank or counter cheques became scarce, thus increasing the waiting time for our customers in the bank queues and reducing the chance they would get the goods at their originally-quoted price. Customers moved between the shop and the bank until they managed to pay in full for their purchase!

Gono announces that the ZW$200 000 Bearer Cheque, the banknote with the highest denomination, would cease to be legal tender on 31st December 2007. He replaces it with a ZW$500 000 and ZW$750 000 note. At the last minute he reverses the withdrawal of the ZW$200 000 dollar note, realising that this would exacerbate the existing cash shortage and reduce the number of notes in circulation. This reversal does not help, as the queues at the banks are still kilometres long, with some people even sleeping in the line. Everyone is limited to withdrawing a maximum of ZW$5 million per person per day. With bread costing ZW$2 million and taxis at ZW$500 000 for one trip, the situation was becoming more than desperate.

After our December stocktake, our units were up to 1.1 million from the 800 000 in September, and down from our normal stock of over 3 million. We seemed to be winning!

Our cash flow was under huge strain and as a result we had to borrow ZW$350 billion in December 2007 for wages and creditors. At an interest rate of 500% per annum, we were keen to pay this back as soon as possible. However, we were not too concerned as we estimated inflation to be well over a few million percent. Once again, Elana was our top financial juggler, and by the end of January 2008, we were again flush with cash.

Home Shops

In Bulawayo we initially had three "home" shops: a "Woollies", "Pick n Pay" and "Spar". Enterprising individuals converted their garages, and in one case a lodge consisting of four Rondavels, into storage places for South African goods.

They were only open for a limited period during the week, and accepted Zimbabwe dollars or forex, but Zimbabwe dollars at the black-market rate. At least they had groceries. The charges were exorbitant, but as more home shops opened, so market forces drove prices down.

The "Woollies" shop stocked only Woolworths products and although with very limited choice, they were a treat. The "Spar" and "Pick n Pay" shops operated in much the same way, offering basic commodities like shampoo, peanut butter, rusks, breakfast cereal and other delicacies to a hungry and deprived consumer, prepared to pay up to a 80% premium.

The Saturday morning queues at these shops were long, but became Bulawayo social events and meeting places. Obviously they were illegal and would every so often get raided by Gono's Reserve Bank officials, and all the forex they had collected from sales would be confiscated.

In some instances R200 a week was the payment made to these officials – plus a few groceries – to make them turn a blind eye.

Parliamentary and Presidential Elections

By late January 2008, the election date had been announced. The 29th March 2008 would see harmonised Presidential and Parliamentary elections for the first time in Zimbabwean history, since normally the two ballots were held a year apart.

Since early 2007 the MDC and ZANU-PF had been involved in talks, facilitated by South African President Thabo Mbeki. They agreed on the harmonisation of the elections, but equally important was the decision that all election results had to be posted outside each polling station, thus eliminating – some thought! – the 2002 rigging.

Excitement was mounting in late 2007 when Simba Makoni, the ex-Finance Minister, threw his hat into the ring as a candidate for President and launched his new political party.

Amongst all the excitement, the deterioration of the infrastructure and economy was gaining momentum.

We decided to fix some potholes on the roads leading to our offices. We approached the City Council to ask permission to fill them ourselves. Our company vehicles were going through too many tyres and rims, all imported, and using up our scarce foreign currency. The council informed us that as the roads were so-called main arterial roads leading to the city, we could not repair them – only the council could. They had tar and stone to do the job, but no method of heating the materials. They could, however, send a team to do the job if we supplied them with broken bricks, which they would manually stamp and compact into the holes.

What about using the bitumen? If we supplied them with 20 litres of diesel for their truck and three tons of firewood to make a fire to heat the bitumen and stone, they could do the job. Fortunately one of our staff members had an uncle who was a newly settled farmer, with access to lots of firewood! We sent our three-ton truck out into the rural areas, past the airport, to purchase the wood. With the 20 litres of diesel and firewood in place, our potholes were repaired within two days. We had made a plan.

The traffic lights on the same main road were out, causing, in our opinion, a huge hazard. Some serious accidents had already occurred there. Once again we approached the City Council to see if we could fix the traffic lights – not personally – but by obtaining what they needed to fix them. No problem, but they did not have any transport. If we could collect their technicians, they would fix the traffic lights immediately. This we duly did. Suffice it to say, two weeks later they were out of order again, although this time two of the lights remained working. We gave up, and got used to watching out for the lights that were working when we approached the intersection.

Speaking of lights, we decided as a team that we needed to brighten up the lives of Bulawayo residents for December 2007, as everyone was pretty down after the price blitz and empty shelves. To that end we embarked on a project to clean up Centenary Park in the centre of the city and reintroduce Christmas lights. Centenary Park was the favourite spot for wedding photos and weekend picnics in days gone by. It even had a mini-railway system, run by the Rotary Club of Bulawayo, where the public could enjoy rides. The park now had waist-high grass and no visible lighting. We supplied the diesel and the council provided the machinery. We donated the paint for the swings, roundabouts and park benches, on top of that we purchased 3 000 coloured light bulbs to brighten up the park. The Rotary Club also got the mini-train running again. This was our contribution to bring a little cheer to the citizens of Bulawayo during the otherwise bleak Christmas of 2007.

As inflation spiralled out of control, more and more of our suppliers were moving to COD. Those that were prepared to give us terms, would simply factor in what they believed the value of the Zimbabwe dollar to the Rand or US dollar would be in 30 or 60 days time, and that then became their cost.

For instance, a pair of men's briefs would cost us US$1 from our supplier. Converted on the day of purchase it could be ZW$10 billion. If we wanted to pay in 30 days time, the price could be ZW$70 billion. Of course if you initially paid ZW$70 billion, it meant that the item after our mark-up would sell for about ZW$120 billion. However, if we had bought for cash, our customer could buy the same men's jocks for ZW$18 billion!

As you can imagine, the price distortions in the market were horrific. Jane and her girlfriends – the ones who used to sit in fuel queues all day – would do their "trawling" every day. This in essence involved going from shop to shop, trying to see who had the lowest price. In one day's shopping, they could save trillions of dollars!

The feeling of euphoria when they picked up a bargain was like winning at roulette. Even Gono in his 2009 book refers to the Zimbabwe business environment as a "Casino Economy".

A normal buying budget or "open to buy" – OTB in buyers' language – was non-existent. We had to centralise all buying decisions. The buyers would come to us with goods at a certain price. Elana would make a quick cash-flow prediction. We would discuss the exchange-rate movement and what we thought it would do over the next few weeks, taking into account any government actions that we felt could negatively influence the rate. Any positive actions by the Government, e.g. increasing the duty-free amount one could bring into the country monthly, only slowed the decline in the rate, never changing it to positive. One fact we could bank on, was that the rate was going to fall; the trick was to guess by how much! We would project our sales for the next month and, based on all these factors, make a decision on whether to buy the stock COD, in 14, 30 or 60 days time at the respective prices. Long-term planning was at the most 30 days. This was a really scary and nerve-racking time for all of us in the business. The situation was changing at a tremendous pace and decision-making had to be quick to avoid huge potential losses. Our retail business could not operate on a COD basis!

On average, we carried three months' forward cover of stock, which meant that at any one time we had enough stock to produce three months' worth of sales. Hence our previous 90-day terms with suppliers. Now we were effectively only buying with cash we had generated from our daily sales.

Suitcases Full of Money

Since early 2006, the daily cash-handling situation in our shops had become ridiculous. Imagine two normal suitcases, the ones that are designed to hold 20 to 30 kilograms of luggage, each filled to capacity with banknotes that needed to be counted each day. It was taking two of the Shop Giants between three and five hours a day just to do the counting. We decided to invest in 50 note counters for all our bigger shops, and bought them from a runner – no doubt called a smuggler in some countries – as the import duty would have doubled their cost. Shop managers were also authorised to employ a casual worker to cover for the staff member who was counting cash all day long. Of course, to count the cash in-store for administration and bank-deposit purposes was one thing, but the whole process had to be repeated at the bank when the deposit was made. Walking around with suitcases full of cash was an everyday occurrence. In any case, no one was going to mug you, since the hassle of counting all his ill-gotten gains would be enough to put off any mugger.

Overnight the cash had to be kept in a safe place in the shops. Obviously the safes we had were far too small. They were about knee high and as wide, designed to hold the cash takings as well as one or two administration books. For 25 years the company hadn't needed to increase the size of its safes, but two suitcases full of notes were not going to fit now.

Shop managers started using their own initiative, and notes were hidden overnight in all sorts of weird and wonderful places in the shop and storeroom. Thankfully we only had two overnight burglaries, in which all the cash was taken. Both, we believe, were inside jobs. Comforting was the thought that after only a week the stolen money would be worth only 25% of its "theft" value.

We were very chuffed when Gono slashed so many noughts in 2006, just when we were on the verge of buying 80 big new safes from Chubb, which would have set us back a fortune. It was the answer to our cash storage problem. ZW$200 000 became ZW$200, thus diminishing the number of notes taken a thousand-fold.

Administrative Nightmares

Stocktakes were done every three months wall to wall in every shop. Up until 2007 we had been carrying out the traditional financial stocktake by counting the value of all items physically in the shop and then comparing the result with the theoretical value of what *should* be in the shop. Opening stock plus inflows less sales gave one the theoretical stock. The difference between theoretical and physical was your percentage stock loss.

With inflation at millions of percent, the calculation of the stocktake, verification of all invoices sent to the shop, credit notes issued and mark-ups in-store processed into the HR system, took up to 14 days. Therefore stocktaking became completely meaningless. A 10% shrinkage at the time of the stocktake became 0.01% fourteen days later in real terms. Barely two months ago the price of one pair of trousers was equivalent to a whole month's sales. We realised our stock-take system wasn't going to work any longer as it had done for over 35 years. Instead we started basing our stocktakes on the number of units of stock in the shop, instead of on the value. This seemed to work for us and gave us a way to control our shrinkage.

ZIMBABWE **WARM HEART** UGLY FACE

7
HOPE AND SHATTERED DREAMS [2008]

Your biggest struggle will be your biggest victory
Louis Smith

As mentioned earlier, the NIPC's pointless persecution to gain votes for ZANU-PF seemed to be losing steam. We knew the risk of marking up prices without authorisation from the NIPC, but we still started aggressive mark-up and advertising campaigns in January 2008. They seemed to work for us, as our cash flow in January recovered nicely. We took the gamble as our competitors had little or no stock compared to us, and we were prepared to risk a lot to save the business and 1 500 families' monthly income. As Elana said, our propensity for risk was keeping pace with inflation!

On 18th January 2008, Gono issues ZW$1 million, ZW$5 million and ZW$10 million notes. Every time the RBZ issues new money, the forex rate jumps. So, for instance, on the 11th January, the rate was ZW$350 000 to the Rand. On the 19th, after the issue of new notes, it had shot up to ZW$700 000 to R1. We were now marking up goods every two weeks, hedging against what we believed the rate would be. In most cases prices were going up 200% every two weeks.

Diesel cost ZW$5 million a litre, with the cash-limit withdrawal still at ZW$5 million a day. The hardest part was that money in the bank was losing value by more than 100% per week.

Our December rainfall was the highest in a 100 years and so just maybe the country would reap the Mother of all harvests, which Gono had been predicting. In the run-up to the election in March 2008, thousands more tractors and agricultural implements had been imported for the newly resettled farmers.

Stolen Money?

In January 2008 we had applied to the Reserve Bank to make use of our R1.5 million, earned from export receipts, to import more fabric for our factory. Unfortunately the reply we got was that they had no forex to give us, the line all exporters received. In essence, they had stolen our hard-earned forex. Well, not technically stolen, just used it for what the government believed was more important purposes.

The frustration was everybody's inability to do anything about it. In a normal society one could, I suppose, have taken legal action against the Reserve Bank, but in Zimbabwe with elections two months away, an economy in free-fall, a government losing its grip on power and prepared to do virtually anything to cling to it, it would have been suicidal to even challenge the Reserve Bank on what happened to our funds.

It was only in February 2009, a year later, and fighting for his political life in the new unity government, that Gono admits in another 20-page newspaper insert to having taken all NGOs and private companies' forex, for the good of the nation!

We then had to ask ourselves, like many other export businesses did, whether it was worth exporting any more. Exports started to diminish, further destroying Gono's source of foreign currency. The mind boggles at what they were willing to do to satisfy their craving for power!

The thinking behind these shenanigans was that ZANU-PF's stronghold had always been the rural areas, and they reasoned that by giving out thousands of tractors and computers to rural folk and schools respectively, bought with our hard-earned forex, would ensure them victory in the upcoming elections. Of course the rural schools did not all have electricity, so some of the computers were pretty useless, but it was a good PR exercise!

Unfortunately, the December 2007 rains were virtually the only ones that fell, and many areas had none. Government admitted the harvest was a total failure.

By 1st March 2008, the forex rate was up to ZW$4.8 million, from ZW$700 000 in early January. A hotel room in Chinhoyi on the 25th February cost ZW$285 million. By the time I had booked for our family on 6th March, for our trip to Kariba on 27th March, the price was ZW$1.5 billion. An increase of 600% in less than two weeks!

The election date had been set for the 29th March. Excitement was mounting because there was a real chance that change was coming at last.

We were now paying all our 1 500 staff on a weekly basis. Our monthly salary increase for February 2008 was 2 000%. Someone earning ZW$4 000 in February, was paid ZW$88 000 in March. The situation was really desperate, with still nothing in the shops.

Morgan Tsvangirai of the MDC, Robert Gabriel Mugabe of ZANU-PF and Simba Makoni of the New Dawn party were pitted against each other for the Presidential

HOPE AND SHATTERED DREAMS

MDC election campaigns

election. Also running was Arthur Mutambara, a Zimbabwean professor of robotics who had studied in the United States, but had returned to Zimbabwe. Mutambara was part of Morgan's MDC party, but with a small faction broke away. Now there was MDC-T (for the Tsvangarai faction) and MDC-M (for the Mutambara faction).

Thanks to the South Africa mediated talks, opposition parties were allowed relatively free media access for advertising purposes. The level of political tolerance in the run up to the election was for us very unusual, and was probably because of world focus and the presence of SADC monitors.

Before the talks had started in 2007, there was absolutely no political tolerance. Anyone seen wearing an opposition T-shirt or any MDC emblem was at the very least quite savagely beaten. Everyone avoided being seen associating openly with anything but ZANU-PF. Many of our shop staff and area managers purchased ZANU-PF membership cards as protection.

Our staff in some rural shops had to catch buses to go to the nearest town to do the banking. Often the bus would be stopped at a roadblock and all passengers were requested to disembark and show their ZANU-PF membership cards. Failure to do so invited a beating or being refused permission to re-board the bus to continue their journey.

The campaigns of all parties were quite different in their approach. ZANU-PF was, in our opinion, backward-looking, still constantly referring to their hard-won independence in 1980 and campaigning on the slogans, "100% empowerment – we did it in 1980 let's do it again!" or "Never will we be a Colony again!" and others like it, appealing to its strong rural base. The MDC on the other hand, aiming at the struggling urban dweller, was focused on the economy and how far we had sunk. Adverts comparing the price of a loaf of bread in 1980 with its price today; promising a better future for all its citizens and other such inducements to vote!

The MDC was obviously gaining a lot of support because of its promises to correct injustices and free up society from oppressive laws and controls. Besides, many voters had never lived through the colonial era or they were not around at independence 28 years ago.

The atmosphere in the country leading up to these elections was not something we were used to. The two government daily newspapers, *The Chronicle* in Bulawayo and *The Herald* in Harare, carried some opposition MDC adverts, but were full of ZANU-PF propaganda with the liberation rhetoric mentioned earlier.

The president was flying by government helicopter from town to town, addressing so-called Star rallies, attended by school kids and rural folk, bussed in from far and wide to swell the numbers. Make no mistake, he still had huge support, especially outside the cities.

Zanu-PF election campaigns

Morgan Tsvangirai was travelling around the country in a huge red bus with his picture on the side proclaiming "Morgan for President". The red theme permeated the whole campaign. It started with a clever analogy to a soccer match, where the referee would brandish a red card when sending off an offending player. At Tsvangirai's rallies, people exuberantly flashed red MDC cards with the words "Mugabe must go" printed on them.

Interestingly, ZANU-PF members were always called "comrade", whereas the opposition representatives were referred to as "Mr." A clever nuance, I suppose, intended to indicate the important link of the "Comrades" to the liberation struggle, whilst the "Mr." distanced the others from the country's independence history, despite the fact that many of them had also fought the same battles against white rule.

Leading up to the election, it was common to find leaflets promoting the opposition strewn all around Bulawayo's streets, obviously distributed overnight for fear of the authorities.

After an early morning walk with the girls, Jane came home with hundreds of ZW$20 000 notes, found drifting all over the roads. Even I was initially excited, until we realised that, with the three zeros removed, the now ZW$20 notes were worthless, considering a box of matches cost ZW$2 million – 1 000 of these notes! Obviously an expressive ploy by an MDC organiser to illustrate the insignificance of our currency!

The much anticipated harmonised elections took place on Saturday 29th March 2008. There was great excitement, as all indications were that the MDC had made massive inroads and could possibly win the majority of seats in Parliament, but there also seemed to be a real chance that Morgan Tsvangirai would become the new president.

On Saturday 30th March 2008 we bade our farewells to our kids at the airport after a great week on the houseboat on Kariba.

Premature Celebrations

That Sunday afternoon, my good mate Rob called me, asking us to come over for a braai and celebrate what he believed was going to be an MDC victory. All afternoon, SMS's were flying back and forth from all over the country, from friends, family and others, giving updates on the election results posted on the door or tent flaps of the polling stations.

It is not hard to imagine the elation and expectancy everybody felt, that our lives were about to change for the better. Stories had been circulating of massive amounts of funding, which were going to flood into the country if the MDC won.

The money would not only kick-start the economy, but give those businesses who had stuck it out, the financial rewards everyone thought we so richly deserved.

There was absolute euphoria at the braai as SMS's came in fast with the news that many prominent ZANU-PF candidates had lost their seats, and numerous MDC candidates had won. It was difficult to tell the difference between fact and rumour, as many messages reflected second- or third-hand information. We awaited the results of the elections with bated breath.

On Monday morning, there were no doubt many serious hangovers throughout Zimbabwe. We were told by the state media that results were imminent. By Tuesday no results were forthcoming. The mood of excitement was starting to dampen a little. However, by Wednesday we received confirmation of definite gains by the MDC.

Another party was called for on Wednesday evening to celebrate confirmed wins, conveyed to us by very reliable sources. Again the mood had changed from one of damp squid on Tuesday to one of euphoria. Change was happening – or so we fervently hoped.

By the following Saturday it was clear that something was wrong. Still no official results. Stories of a replay of 2002 and vote-rigging started to surface. Why was the Electoral Commission being so secretive?

This went on for three weeks. Our only source of information was an MDC website, giving us figures, which they had collated from cellphone photos of the results posted outside the various polling stations. After four weeks the Electoral Commission finally started releasing results on TV and radio.

The end tally was Morgan 47% and Mugabe 43% of the presidential vote. The MDC, however, were no longer the opposition party, as they held a slim majority of seats in parliament. Because none of the three candidates won 50% plus one vote, a run-off for President was necessary.

The outcome was predictable: brutal violence and intimidation on a massive scale in the weeks before the June Presidential rerun. The MDC leader decided to pull out of the race. The only candidate, Robert Gabriel Mugabe, was declared the winner by default on 17th June 2008.

A huge depression descended over the whole country. Everything went back to square one! No huge inflows of capital with continuing hyperinflation and no end in sight. Only somebody who was in the country at the time could understand, feel, and accurately describe the utter personal and business despair that hung like heavy dark pollution over life in Zimbabwe.

We had been without a government since February 2008, a month before the election, when parliament was dissolved. The threat of this uncertainty was almost tangible. The business community went into a huge feeding frenzy. Our sales were skyrocketing as we increased our prices sometimes twice weekly. People were buying absolutely anything, knowing that the price could go up three, four or even ten times in one week.

As soon as salaries were paid, staff would ask for time off to go and draw what little they could. It would take someone two weeks to draw their whole salary because of the imposed withdrawal limits. Absenteeism at the factory was up to 60% on any given day. Production and our export orders were in jeopardy.

We decided to arrange with the banks that the company draw salaries for our staff on their behalf, just to get them to come to work. Our personnel department became a pay office, with staff lining up to receive their daily allowance, enough to catch a taxi to and from work the next day. The administration was a nightmare, with some employees off sick, others queuing in the bank to try and draw some money to supplement the cash we would be drawing for them. To describe the absurd situation as chaos would be an understatement!

We arranged with our banks to give us same-day clearance on customer cheques as apposed to the normal five-day waiting period. This allowed us to make purchases of local fabric from importers on a daily basis. Every cent we had we put into stock.

Banks were only too eager to lend us money at interest rates of up to 1 000% per annum. With inflation at millions of percent, we were winning all the way.

In April 2008, Elana came up with the brilliant idea to pay our staff weekly, and to add to this an advance on next month's salary. As long as the advance did not exceed their monthly pay, it was not taxable. Effectively, therefore, all staff was receiving double money. With increases of up to 2 000% each month, the advance from last month could be deducted the next month with a negligible impact on the take-home pay.

For example, if the person was paid ZW$2 billion a month, next month this could be ZW$120 billion, so we could pay the person ZW$4 billion and deduct the ZW$2 billion advance the following month. This gave the staff future time value of money and allowed them to hedge themselves to a degree against hyperinflation and soaring prices. This brilliant idea worked well for us and we applied it throughout the year.

Goodbye to More Zeros

As a result of our massive borrowings, our stock levels continued to increase, despite the huge sales. In August, Gono released new notes and allowed the old coins back in circulation. This he did by cutting ten zeros off the currency.

The following example illustrates the impact of hyperinflation up till the removal of ten zeros in August 2008. A ladies' skirt, which in February 2008 had a price tag of ZW$19.6 million, in August 2008 cost ZW$12.6 trillion or from ZW$19,600,000 to ZW$12,600,000,000,000. After dropping ten zeros, the same skirt now cost only ZW$ 1 260, still the equivalent of US$7 or R70 that the customer was paying in February.

I remember one day in our shop in Lupane, a rural area halfway between Bulawayo and Victoria Falls, a youngster came in with a rucksack full of old 20-cent coins, which had now regained their long-lost value and were now worth 20c again. This poor chap was struggling under the weight of the coins in the bag. He wanted to purchase a pair of trousers for ZW$510 dollars (ZW$5.1 trillion old currency). It took the staff almost the whole day to count out the coins, all 2 550 of them!

This scenario played itself out all over the country, as those who had been keeping their coins were suddenly rich. Under no normal circumstances could this poor rural boy have been able to amass the ZW$5.1 trillion needed to buy the pair of trousers. Why people had hoarded the old coins, no one will ever know, but the reasons were varied and colourful.

Of course this just put more strain on our business, as well as on the banks, which had to handle the deposits. A lot of shops refused the coins for the simple reason that the work involved in counting them was too great. We used their refusal as a great opportunity, and we advertised the fact that we accepted coins!

The mental adjustments everyone had to make, after talking in billions and trillions and now suddenly back to hundreds and thousands, was huge. In the beginning, with every transaction everybody added on ten noughts just to make sure there was no cheating.

By September 2008, after ensuring that all our stock had been re-marked, and our cash registers reprogrammed without the ten zeros, at least two zeros were back already!

On 8th September the same ladies' skirt, which on the 13th of August cost ZW$520 (ZW$5.2 trillion revalued less ten zeros) was selling for ZW$21 600. On 11th September, three days later, the skirt was selling for ZW$43 200! The following week, it was at ZW$86 400 and by the 2nd of October, barely two weeks later, it was ZW$1,728,000 (one million seven hundred and twenty-eight thousand). By the 20th of October 2008, the price had jumped to ZW$414 million (ZW$414,000,000).

Of course, over the year it had moved only slightly to ZW$414 million from its original price of ZW$19.6 million in February 2008. However, that is less the ten zeros, which had been removed from the currency. So add the zeros back on and the October 2008 price becomes ZW$4,140,000,000,000,000,000, or in hyperinflation speak ZW$4.140 quintillion. The mind boggles.

Payment Systems

Before things become even more complicated, it may be necessary to discuss the many different payment systems in Zimbabwe at this time and how they affected the forex rate on the street.

Cash payments. These are payments using cash notes, either Bearer Cheques, which were actually currency, or new banknotes as and when they were introduced. And of course those notes still in circulation.

Firstly, cash notes were untraceable when used in a forex deal on the street, and as a result attracted the best or lowest exchange rate for forex. Everybody wanted forex, therefore everybody wanted Zimbabwe dollars in cash. Whoever had access to cash notes was King.

The problem of course was that salaried employees received their salaries directly into their bank accounts and cash withdrawals were limited to the equivalent of a few loaves of bread. Regular shortages of banknotes only drove up their value, making them more precious. I think somewhere somebody called it a "catch 22 for the salaried guy".

As a result of the limit placed by the Reserve Bank on cash withdrawals, most people had more than one bank account, some had up to eight! This allowed them to draw the daily allowance, but from all their accounts all kept at different banks, spending most of the day in some bank queue or other.

In December 2008, Gono changed the withdrawal limits to a weekly amount, possibly after realising that most workers were spending everyday in a bank queue to draw their money – instead of contributing to the nation's economy. The weekly withdrawal certainly eased the absenteeism at our factory.

RTGS system. This system was introduced by the Reserve Bank to eliminate the ten-day clearance period for a traditional cheque, which meant that people were charging a premium to cheque payers. They knew that the prices would have increased by the time they could get the cheque validated. The RTGS system was the next best thing to cash payments, because amounts reflected initially after 12 hours, then immediately, in bank accounts. The downside was still that the money was stuck in the bank, your drawings per day were limited, and the amount of paperwork involved was enormous. Each RTGS had to be handwritten in quadruplicate, one copy for the seller, one for the buyer, and one each to their respective banks.

All RTGS payments had to be presented at the bank for processing before 10am each morning, for the next day's value. Just imagine the administrative nightmare.

Submit the RTGS a few minutes late, and the price would go up, necessitating cancellation of the RTGS and starting the application process all over again. The copy of the RTGS payment had to be faxed to the supplier, before he would deliver the goods. The overload on the RTGS system through the banks was inevitable.

The system, designed to give same-day value, got slower and slower, eventually also taking up to ten days, with the inevitable result that the rate increased. Knowing the payment value would only reflect in the account ten days later, necessitated an increase in the price of the goods being sold, driving the parallel rate even higher. The whole RTGS system and the associated paperwork gave the banks serious constipation. Eventually and inevitably the system collapsed and was withdrawn by Gono in late 2008. He also realised that the slowness of the overloaded system was driving prices up at an alarming rate, thus fuelling inflation, or as he called it "Public Enemy number 1".

Cheque payments. Either personal or bank-counter cheques were the most popular form of payment in Zimbabwe, before March 2008, when the situation really started to get out of hand. The only reason we were still accepting cheques up till October 2008, was because we had a deal with the banks for same-day clearance on all cheques issued by our customers in the shops. As mentioned before, cheques took up to ten days to clear, which in Zimbabwe's thousands of percent inflation, could cost you a lot of money. Besides the money was still stuck in the bank and withdrawals were limited. Up until 2008 nobody ever carried much cash and most payments were by cheque.

Credit cards. Never part of the Zimbabwe banking system, they were only used by tourists or those living in Zimbabwe with bank accounts outside the country. Tourists would come into the country with a Visa card and go to the few banks that had facilities to draw Zimbabwe dollars cash using the international credit card. The downside was that they would draw Zimbabwe dollars at the official rate, which could be up to ten times lower than the street or parallel rate at which all goods and services were priced, making a holiday in Zimbabwe exorbitantly expensive.

Debit cards. They were introduced in about 1998 by only two banks. Some supermarkets had a card-swiping system to facilitate payment, if there were funds in the card holder's account. The flip side of this system was that the links to the banks from the supermarket were via telephone lines, which at best were very unreliable. Often the teller would ring up a trolley of groceries, only to find the telephone was off-line and the transaction could not be completed. So the customer resorted again to paying by cheque.

Internet banking was first introduced in about 2002 by a bank, which was eventually closed down by Gono and amalgamated with other banks because it had been buying shares and property as a hedge against inflation, thus seriously hampering its liquid assets. Or so the nation was told. Only two other banks, of the 14 operating in Zimbabwe, offered this facility. Unfortunately telephone connectivity was critical to its smooth functioning. Internet cafés blossomed all over Zimbabwe for a short while, but eventually they were curtailed by two factors. Firstly, the bank systems simply could not handle the number of noughts. Secondly, in 2008 Gono started raiding internet cafés, as forex dealers were using them to do fast transfers of huge amounts, which could not be picked up by the banks until the deals had been concluded. This after Gono had ordered banks to notify the Central Bank and the CIO whenever their customers made deposits of or transferred large sums of money.

No More Trading

We stopped trading or selling goods in our shops on the 10th November 2008. We didn't close our shops, we simply stopped accepting cheques.

We were forced into this situation because our shops were being cleared out by so-called "burners". They would come into our shop, buy ten or twenty pairs of men's trousers and pay for them by cheque. This "burning" phenomenon first came to our attention in September 2008, but we never discovered where the phrase originated. The closest we got to its origins was the fact that you were giving away so many Zimbabwe dollars for so little forex, you might as well have set fire to them or "burnt" them. This reminds me of the first ZW$500 000 note: it was red, went out extremely fast and was affectionately called a "Ferrari". Yes, even amongst all this chaos, we Zimbos still maintained a sense of humour.

A brief summary why, in the hyperinflationary economy of Zimbabwe, this "burning" was a disaster.
1. Firstly our suppliers of merchandise in Zimbabwe had, in October 2008, stopped accepting cheques in payment of their goods.
2. The amount of cash one individual or company could draw from their bank account was limited to ZW$10 billion a day, enough for two loaves of bread.
3. Because nobody could draw more than ZW$10 billion per day, cash was locked up and depreciating in the bank at 65 and 100 noughts percent per year.

So if someone issued a cheque for ZW$100 billion, or 20 loaves of bread, it would take ten days to draw the money from the bank.

By the time the tenth day came around, the goods would have gone up by

Cash shortage worsens price distortions

CHRONICLE REPORTER

THE ongoing cash shortages, worsened by an unrealistic $1 000 withdrawal limit offered by banks, have resulted in unbelievable price distortions, with shops displaying dual prices for commodities.

When a customer buys goods for cheque, the price is often inflated up to 1 000 times the cash price.

Despite the historic agreement which has paved way for the establishment of an all-inclusive Government, prices have continued to go haywire, leaving ordinary people in a quandary. The shocking wave of profiteering has been attributed to bank transfers which have seen many people becoming millionaires overnight, although ordinary members of society have remained wallowing in poverty.

Changing US$100 on the blackmarket was giving one $70 000 yesterday while the transfer rate would give one $4,5 million. In a snap survey, Chronicle observed that some shops, especially those that accept cheques, had virtually pegged their prices on transfer rates, resulting in ridiculously high prices.

The prices in shops which accept cash only are significantly lower although people have been failing to buy the commodities because of the cash shortages.

However, it is the disparity in prices that has shocked many shoppers as some basic commodities, such as fruit juice, have a difference of more than $300 000 depending on the shop.

For example, a two-litre bottle of Mazoe Raspberry at Bellevue Spar, which accepts bank cheques, was selling for $360 000 on Sunday while at Greens Supermarket along Robert Mugabe Avenue in the city centre the same commodity was selling for $3 800.

A 150-gramme satchet of snacks was going for $5 000 at Bellevue while the same packet was going for $500 at Greens.

Some shops, including fast food outlets such as Innscor, are displaying dual prices, with a cash price and one for cheques and those who use debit cards. At the Pizza Inn outlet at Haefelis in the city centre a large Hawaiian pizza was selling for $8 000 cash while the same commodity was going for $400 000 if one used a bank cheque or "swiped" using a debit card. Varieties of pizza such as Avacado Delight, Banana Passion, Royal Chicken, Spicy Chicken and Meat Deluxe were selling for about $20 000 but for swiping or using a cheque, one was expected to fork out above $1 million.

Furniture outlets have not been left out of the price madness, with outlets such as Vision Wise Marketing selling 21-inch colour television sets for $70 000 yet the same sets are selling for between $35 million and $45 million at outlets such as TV Sales and Hire.

Most outlets that sell clothes are also using transfer rates to determine prices. Trousers and shirts are going for more than $50 000, at a time when most people earn about $15 000 per month.

"Most outlets are assuming that everyone is doing transfers hence their prices are determined by the transfer rates. It is unfortunate because ordinary members of the public are suffering because they do not know much about this spinning of cash. It has put us in a difficult position," said Mr Naison Mudzingwa, who was shopping at a retail outlet.

A shop employee revealed that most outlets resorted to pegging prices at the transfer rate after realising that those who were involved in the practice were literally looting their shops using cheques.

"It's unfortunate because some people who are affected by the prices are not involved in this transfer business but if you had seen how people were buying using cheques before we increased prices, you would appreciate that the prices were too cheap.

People were making huge profits using the bank transfers and because they couldn't withdraw their money, they resorted to bulk buying as a way to beat inflation. That's why the prices also went up," he said.

Some people said the bank transfers were justified, as they were the only way Zimbabweans could conduct transactions in an economy hit by critical cash shortages.

thousands of percent, because the money would have devalued by thousands of percent. Accepting cheque payments was a certain way to bankruptcy.

Because bank withdrawals were limited, it became more difficult to buy the much-needed foreign currency on the street, as the "Vapostori" insisted on cash. The "burner" bought foreign currency by cheque, obviously at a huge premium to himself e.g. 400 times the cash rate on the street.

This astronomically high rate evolved because the market was trying to predict what the Zimbabwe dollar would be worth after the time it took to draw the limited daily cash. With quadrillions of dollars stuck in bank accounts, and with fewer people willing to accept cheques, the cheque or "burning", also sometimes referred to as "Spinning" rate for forex skyrocketed.

The "burner" would sell US$10 cash in exchange for a cheque deposit into his bank account. He would go to our shop and buy the ten pairs of trousers, paying for them by cheque, then take the trousers down town and sell them for Rand, US dollars or Pula at a 30 to 50% discount, thus ensuring a quick sale. The hard currency generated, he would sell in exchange for another cheque deposited into his bank account, at 20 to 100 times the cash purchase price of the same US dollar or Rand on the street. He would then go back into our shops, buy 30 pairs of trousers with the money generated by this round tripping, once again paying by cheque. This "liberated" his Zimbabwe dollars, which would otherwise remain stuck in the bank.

I calculated that it was theoretically possible for someone, starting with just US$10, and burning at this rate, to become a US dollar millionaire after just six deals. Obviously this was not practical as it would require a few trucks by the time you got your third transaction, and you would need to have a guaranteed market for your product. There were many dealers who made obscene amounts of US dollars during this period of "burning".

We tried to outrun the "burners", who were virtually clearing us out, by 10 or 15 price increases each week. However, our average "non-burning" customer was really suffering since people, who were not involved in black market forex deals, were unable to buy anything.

That is why on the 10th of November the team and I took the decision to stop taking cheques, effectively putting an end to all trade.

This was not an easy decision, but by this time we had amassed over ZW$36 quadrillion in our bank accounts. We calculated that was enough cash to see us through December and January to pay all overheads. Enough certainly to pay our salaries, wages and rentals via bank transfer, and our utility bills to parastatals e.g.

telephone, electricity and rates by cheque, which by government decree, they had to accept.

Since October, when the burning had started, we had decided once again to stop sending stock of goods out to our shop, to thwart the "burners", in the belief that change was just around the corner. All our purchases we held in our Distribution Centre, exactly as we had a year previously with the price slash. We effectively, for the second time in a year, reached a stage where we didn't want to sell any stock, simply to protect our long-term survival.

To any businessman, and especially to a retailer, this must really sound crazy!

The devastation of the economy was now almost complete. For years we had thought often that we had reached absolute rock bottom. For the last four years we had been saying that it could not get any worse. This time it really appeared as though we had reached the bitter end.

On 19th September 2008, the two factions of MDC and ZANU-PF signed a "Global Political Agreement" in Harare, after months of hard negotiations facilitated by the then President of South Africa, Thabo Mbeki. We, like many others, were not too comfortable with the agreement, which gave Morgan Tsvangirai the position of Prime Minister, and his party members, control of parliament, but left Mugabe as President and his loyal followers in control of key ministries such as defence, police and home affairs. The economy and its resuscitation was handed to the MDC. At least after nine months in limbo, we finally had a government.

In November 2008, grocery shops were *really* empty. We started running trucks to Francistown in Botswana, a short two-hour drive away, initially once a week, later daily, to purchase mealie meal, toilet paper, soap and cooking oil for our Head Office staff and especially for our factory workers.

Our head office resembled a grocery store. Each morning I would arrive to see mountains of toilet rolls piled up in the passage, or boxes of powdered milk, hundreds of bottles of cooking oil, and walk past the scented boxes of bars of green soap. The guys must have got back from the border late after their shopping in Botswana, as the tell-tale white powder trail of mealie meal revealed, and it had been offloaded late at night.

Through contacts we managed to source cheap mealie meal at a group of Spar shops in Francistown. So on a daily basis Fashion or Nyathi, our drivers, together with Thembani or Edward of our Head Office staff, would journey through the Botswana border to procure the staples necessary to keep our work force at work.

We discovered that each person was entitled to bring 500kg of mealie meal per crossing, so a one-ton truck did very nicely, bringing 50 ten-kilo bags per day. After ten days we had enough mealie meal for each worker at our factory, which could last their family for about two weeks.

Every now and then we sent the three-ton truck with some guys in a car to accompany them to justify the allocation, allowing us to import a sufficient quantity on one trip, thus saving time.

During December 2008, households experienced horrific shortages. Cooking oil, mealie meal, salt and other essentials were to be had from some supermarkets that had stock, which, like our goods, was priced at the burning rate. Unfortunately salaries were still based on the cash rate for forex and workers still were not allowed to draw their whole salary in cash from the bank. So effectively, people could not buy anything, since their money was stuck.

This desperate situation created real panic throughout the population, unable to feed itself. Children would faint at school; parents were riddled with guilt.

The inability to feed themselves and their families was noticeably affecting our workers' attendance and output. Added to this was the time spent in bank queues, trying to draw the meagre amount of money, enough for a taxi fare and a loaf of bread.

The impact on our production was dramatic, with a drop from 6 500 to just over 2 000 units a day. We needed to get our export orders out in order to maintain our forex inflows, which would allow us to purchase coupons for 40 000 litres of fuel from Caltex South Africa. These coupons we now used to pay landlords their rent, city council rates, telephone bills, in fact virtually everything, because everybody had stopped accepting payment in Zimbabwe dollars and cheques.

As a result each factory worker received a ten kilo bag of mealie meal, a litre of cooking oil and a bar of soap every two weeks through November and December.

In order to increase the attendance at the factory, we also introduced a morning meal of porridge. Threatened strike action two weeks before our export deliveries were due to be dispatched, saw us giving each factory worker a ten-litre fuel coupon, so that they could travel home for the holidays. It was traditional for the factory workers to visit their rural homes over Christmas and take home lots of goodies for their families, but this year the bus fare to get there and back was all they had. The ten-litre fuel coupon worked. No strike. We had made a plan and our export order was completed on time (see appendix on page 207, 208 and 209).

Newspapers had also become unaffordable, but were state propaganda tools in any case and so really not worth buying.

Looking back now it all seems like a bad dream. We lived each day with whatever challenges came our way. It really was a case of "adapt or die". Through all of this, our senior factory and shop staff remained focused on our long-term survival. It would have been so easy for them to give up. I would like to believe that the climate and atmosphere of team work, initiated so many years ago, had paid off. Without their commitment, we could never have continued to exist.

Throughout 2008 there was never a dull moment with daily frenetic changes. Even the Golf Club wasn't spared the scarcity of product. One day we would be able to source a few cokes, enough for a week. The next week only lemonades or beers, our staple drink, were obtainable. Players started smuggling hip flasks and mixers into the Club. We knew it was happening, but Club Management had to turn a blind eye. "Captain Morgan" rum and coke was a popular drink at the Club, but "Captain Morgan" was imported and unavailable. The local dark rum, which was still in production, became affectionately known as "Captain Moyo" – a reference to one of the most common Ndebele surnames.

Going to the few remaining restaurants in town was no different. The smiling waiter would arrive at your table with the customary, "Good evening. Welcome. What can I get you to drink?", but would then proceed with the by-now-expected apology that he did not have cokes or lemonade, and that the beers would only arrive next week. We got used to pre-empting the waiters by asking what drinks were available, which saved them the embarrassment of having to say no to every request.

In June 2008, the infrastructure had collapsed to such an extent that cholera broke out in Harare's big satellite town Chitungwiza. Within weeks the disease had spread the width and breadth of the country. International news bulletins gave daily reports about the rising death toll. Thousands died and many more were infected.

By December, thanks to international NGOs and other donors, the cholera epidemic was under control. Our company was not spared the ravages of this outbreak. The situation was desperate, especially in the rural areas where a collapsed health system and infrastructure posed serious threats. At one stage we considered importing, for our affected staff, the 30-day course of tablets to combat cholera, but fortunately this was not necessary, because wherever our staff contracted cholera, we were able to source the necessary treatment.

By 15th December 2008 our cash reserves were running so low that to save the situation, we were forced to "burn" US$10, so that someone would transfer quadrillions of Zimbabwe dollars into our account.

In January we had to do the same. These "burnt" US$10 provided us with enough of a Zimbabwe-dollar bank balance to sustain the entire company for a month, covering all our expenses. Looking back now it seems not only unbelievable but totally ludicrous!

Obviously, we still needed Zimbabwe dollars for petty cash, to buy foreign currency, milk, tea and for general expenses. As a result we decided in early December 2008 to test one shop in Bulawayo as a "cash" shop. Remember we hadn't sold one item since 10th November.

The cash shop marked the goods at the cash rate for forex. For instance, if you had Zimbabwe-dollar cash notes, you could buy one South African Rand for ZW$1 billion cash. The "burning" or cheque rate would have been ZW$200 to ZW$300 billion. If a pair of trousers at a retail outlet in South Africa would cost around R100, we simply multiplied this by the cash rate for the day, marking the trousers ZW$100 billion for cash notes. The same trousers, if purchased by cheque, would be ZW$150 trillion. In fact all our merchandise was still quoted at "burner" prices, except the cash stock.

This trial brought us in a couple of billion dollars a day in cash notes, which enabled us to keep a reasonable level of petty cash and even more importantly, enough to purchase much-needed foreign currency. We eventually had five cash shops running in Bulawayo. Obviously the sales were low, but they helped us keep our heads above water.

Everyone's a Criminal

Every resident in Zimbabwe was a criminal. Hurtful as this may sound, it was true. With the plethora of petty laws governing every aspect of life, it was inevitable that everyone was breaking some law each day. Just possessing foreign currency was illegal, according to an SI gazetted in 2004. Having multiple bank accounts to beat the daily withdrawal limit was illegal. Not having the right number plates on your car, or no car radio licence or no generator permit, all were laws somebody somewhere was breaking.

This knowledge of having done wrong, changes everybody's psyche. The propensity to take risks becomes greater. Corruption now has fertile soil to grow and flourish. The feeling of power that now drove many government officials, was the perfect ingredient for fraud.

When leaving Zimbabwe, it was compulsory for everyone to declare all electronic instruments in their possession. Laptop and cellphone serial numbers and the like had to be written out and checked by the customs official and then stamped by him on your Customs Declaration form. On your return, this form had to be handed back to the customs official to ensure that you were not bringing these electronic goods into the country for the first time, since any newly imported electronic goods attracted a 100% duty charge. All this did, not surprisingly, was encourage "smuggling".

Smuggling, in normal circumstances, results in enriching the smuggler. In the case of Zimbabwean residents, it was a matter of survival. Cash slips from shops in South Africa and Botswana were probably the best way to get goods into the country. The once-a-calendar-month duty-free allowance for all Zimbabweans was the equivalent of US$250 or R1 800 per person. It was not a problem to ask the cashier to ring up the groceries up to a value of approximately R1500. This generated a cash slip for duty purposes. The rest of the groceries, and any other goodies you had bought, were rung up separately and the slip was immediately destroyed on leaving the shop.

The border crossing always caused much stress and anxiety, while everybody prayed that some power-hungry official would not want to unpack the car and check each item. Of course bread was very scarce, as were most other basics. The treasures were always placed in clear view on top of the other groceries when packing the car. This generated a much smoother passage through the border, of course arriving home with a few loaves less.

I suppose Gono would call that petty corruption, but a more cynical view would be that travellers were simply being philanthropic, helping people who were poorly paid and very hungry. Whatever one's view, this traffic managed to sustain many families, ourselves and the economy the last few years. Of course there were a variety of other ways of getting the necessary goods into the country. Suffice it to say that Zimbos always made a plan.

Corruption was not a recent development. I recall opening our second store in a rural town in 2001. In order to start trading we needed a shop licence from the local municipality, as well as a stamp of approval from the building and the health inspectors. One week before our intended opening, all the council employees embarked on a strike for higher pay. Two days before our opening, we still had not been able to obtain the necessary permit. I decided to visit the council offices myself. The town clerk was very helpful, but explained that we could not trade until we had the necessary stamps on our documents. As luck would have it, the building inspector was in his office, so I managed to obtain his seal of approval. The health officer was nowhere to be found.

One of our staff members happened to know where he lived, so off I went to find his house in the middle of the township. Once we were there, our staff member was informed that the inspector had gone to a braai with a friend. We eventually tracked him down at a shebeen, where he and some mates were enjoying a midday barbecue – while on strike! After about 15 minutes of animated discussion, we managed to persuade him to accompany us to the shop to carry out the inspection in order to obtain his all-important stamp.

We drove to the shop together with two of his mates, with all the car windows wide open to try and lessen the smell of alcohol. After a cursory walk through the shop, I was told that the walls needed another coat of paint, as in his opinion the paint job was not up to standard. I realised that arguing with him would be to no avail, seeing that he was about three beers away from falling over, and remained adamant. In the meantime, towards the back of the shop, his two mates were admiring our stock of men's trousers and shirts on offer at very good opening prices. We walked together to where his buddies were browsing. I summed up the situation very quickly. I was totally against any form of bribery and had resisted for the past four years. Realising that repainting would cost us a fortune and a lot of lost sales, I made a decision.

Three pairs of new trousers and three men's casual shirts later, we were on our way to the council offices, where we managed to obtain the vital stamp, indispensable if we wanted to open our shop the following day.

This was a tremendous blow to me. I had crossed the line. I had given in to the way of doing business, which I had fought so hard to resist and for which I had criticised many others. "Welcome to the real world," some acquaintances told me. I will, however, never forget that incident, which ultimately influenced me profoundly and made me see situations in a different way.

Somebody told me about another ingenious and cheeky incident involving a golf cart. On leaving Zimbabwe by road, this chap, I am told, had dutifully completed his Customs Declaration Form listing his golf clubs and golf cart. The golf cart was actually a three-wheeled trolley that most golfers use! He also declared his empty trailer, which he was taking for repairs to Johannesburg. On his return he arrived at the border with a four-wheeled electric "golf cart" – actually a golf cart used by most golf estates in South Africa, which seats two people and also accommodates their golf bags.

At the border he produced the stamped Customs Declaration Form stating the trailer and "golf cart". The customs official confirmed the details of the trailer, licence disk, chassis number but questioned the golf cart. Of course this was also clearly stated on the form. Without another word the official waved him through. Needless to say, the golfer was smiling from ear to ear!

Every time we successfully cleared through the border, whether with TV sets, hi-fis, toasters or kettles, all nicely surrounded by groceries with the bread on top, we could not help but give high fives all around. The stress and anxiety simply dissipated.

Another way to clear the border was to pay for it, so we are told. On reaching Musina on the South African side of the border, one would call "Mr. Y", a tout who had excellent connections with all departments at the border. For R250 you would not even have to get out of your car. Mr. Y would ensure your gate pass was stamped by the Bridge Toll guy (saying you had paid your R100), your passports by Immigration and your Road Tax slip, as well as your Customs Declaration Form by ZIMRA.

After reappearing with your passport, Mr. Y would get into the car with you, drive past the customs shed, where the customs officer received a folded newspaper, resulting in an immediate call to the gatekeeper, who would also smooth one's passage. After handing the gate pass to the gatekeeper, Mr. Y would get out of the car with the R250, plus the six loaves of bread he had asked for during the first phone call to him from Musina.

Another casualty of the debilitating economic and social situation was the further education of some of our staff. In 2006 we had enrolled 15 staff members at UNISA, a distance-learning South African university, to study for various economic and business degrees. After only 18 months of successful studying, it all came to nothing. I experienced a sense of acute loss at this development.

All 15 had stopped their studies. UNISA was now demanding all fees be paid in foreign currency. Up until then, they were paying in Zimbabwe dollars, and so could access a Zimbabwe dollar study loan from the company. We, however, were not in a position to give staff loans in foreign currency as repayment was impossible.

My favourite motivational saying to our staff was: "If you stop growing, you start dying." To me this was so true of daily, and not only of academic life. My disappointment at them for giving up was huge, but I could truly understand their decision.

Petrol Coupons – The New Zimbabwe Currency

By September 2008, the Zimbabwe dollar had become worthless as a form of payment, other than for buying the odd bag of mealie meal and some vegetables from the hawkers. The majority of our shops were rented both from individuals and institutions, such as Old Mutual Properties, Knight Frank and CB Richard Ellis. Individuals were now demanding rental payments in fuel coupons

Since 2005 the only way to obtain fuel was from one of the many black-market dealers, or from a provider such as Caltex. Obviously as a large organisation, we preferred to buy coupons in bulk from the recognised fuel provider. This entailed an offshore payment to Caltex in New York, then their notification to their counterparts in Zimbabwe, who in turn would issue us with the 20-litre vouchers.

Unfortunately there were only a limited number of Caltex garages dotted throughout the country, and they did not always have fuel. This further hampered our Area Managers travel to our shops. To overcome this we fitted long-range 120-litre tanks to all our Area Managers' and Auditors' trucks, thus enabling them to travel greater distances – when they did find fuel.

In order to avoid any problems or Government interference, landlords became very creative as the currency became more and more unattractive. Old Mutual would send out a statement for rentals due, based on Old Mutual Units. The OM unit was effectively another way of quoting in US dollars.

However, Gono's paranoid crusade against any form of foreign-currency dealing was still continuing, and business people had to be inventive so as not to fall foul of the Reserve Bank Governor, who was de facto running the country.

These so-called "Units" became the currency of the day. Golf clubs charged their members units for subscriptions and cellphone companies for recharge cards.

The units were linked to the US-dollar price of a litre of fuel. As a result fuel coupons effectively became our new currency. Of course, it was not as straightforward as paying, for instance, ten 20-litre coupons for rent, because the fuel price fluctuated weekly. The creditor would send a statement for a certain number of units, but by payment time the bottom line could be a few litres more or less. Since coupons were denominated in 20 litres, giving change of three or four litres was impossible. Arguments and correspondence with landlords regarding this issue took up a tremendous amount of time and wasted much energy.

Added to the above complication, was the value-added-tax dilemma. VAT was payable on all transactions, but not by using a book of fuel coupons! Companies would send out two invoices. The first a Zimbabwe-dollar invoice, of trillions of dollars plus the VAT, which would be submitted to ZIMRA and allowed everyone to stay within the law. The invoice was based on the parallel rate to the US dollar and equated to the units or litres payable. The second invoice would be quoted in the units the creditor expected to receive. The creditor was happy to get his coupons, the Receiver of Revenue was happy to get his VAT – albeit in worthless Zimbabwe dollars – and companies managed to stay in business.

Christmas 2008

On 19th December 2008, the RBZ allowed individuals to withdraw ZW$10 billion cash per week, or the equivalent of R200, up from the ZW$500 000 allowed before that date. Since the banks were computerised it was impossible to draw more cash. The obvious way around this was to open more bank accounts, so with five accounts, one could draw ZW$50 billion per week, which on the street could buy R1 000.

The banks were inundated with new account holders. As a result they increased their handling fees to try and discourage new account holders, and they raised the minimum account balance. This prevented most blue-collar workers from opening more than one account.

Because we had stopped taking cheques on 10th November, we had zero sales for November and December, and our staff was just sitting in the shop doing nothing. They had to pay ZW$10 billion per week just for transport to and from work, the equivalent of their weekly bank "allowance". This scenario influenced us to close our shops and factory on 23rd December, effectively sending all our staff on three weeks' paid leave. Our plan was to reopen again on 19th of January 2009. This was the first time in history, I would think, that a retailer had willingly closed down over Christmas.

Traditionally Christmas is the time all retailers make their money. Sales are two or three times more than what they would be in any other month of the year. When expenditure is fixed, it is not unusual to generate up to 30% of annual profits in December alone.

As a retailer, I was devastated that I could not trade. It was as if someone stole the Christmas tree and all the presents under it on Christmas Eve. The depression one would feel after that on Christmas morning, waking up to no Christmas tree and no presents, was pretty much how we as a team felt over Christmas and New Year of 2008/2009.

ZIMBABWE **WARM HEART** UGLY FACE

8 TRAGEDY

Never send to know for whom the bell tolls, it tolls for thee JOHN DONNE

Every year in June, an eight-ball team – two teams of four golfers – from our golf club in Bulawayo participated in a golf week at Leopard Rock, a magnificent hotel and golf course situated in the Eastern Highlands of Zimbabwe, very close to the Mozambique border.

Describing the golf course and its scenery is a tall order. Located in undulating terrain with phenomenal vistas of mountains, valleys and distant lakes, in an almost tropical climate with very lush vegetation of tree ferns, lianas and orchids, one could almost imagine being in Bangkok or some such exotic location. The golf course is very hilly to say the least, but in magnificent condition.

Each year this eight-ball would spend three days participating in a competition comprising about 150 golfers from as far afield as Malawi and Johannesburg. The emphasis, I had gathered, was not so much on winning the competition, but on the camaraderie – on the golf course and around the casino tables until late at night.

For a number of years I had indicated my interest in joining the tour as a reserve in the event someone pulled out. In June 2008 I was invited to join the team as Brett, who had been a regular on the tour, had left Zimbabwe for Johannesburg with his family.

I was pretty excited, not only to have made the team, but also for the welcome break that a week away from the chaos that was business in Zimbabwe would offer. Of course as one of the reserves, I would have to undergo a selection process. I am convinced that the fact I had an electric golf cart gave me the edge! Nevertheless I was more than happy to tow the cart up to Leopard Rock so that Nigel, the selection convener, could also partner me on the golf course and enjoy a ride!

Leopard Rock is a seven-hour journey from Bulawayo. The road winds through Zvishavane, an asbestos-mining town, and Masvingo, then through Birchenough Bridge and on to the Eastern Highlands. The crossing at Birchenough is over a huge suspension bridge, built in 1935 by the British. It is as imposing as it is majestic. It protrudes from the barren landscape and spans the Save river.

Here and there, all through the two-hour drive from Birchenough to the city of Mutare, people on the side of the road would jump up while gesticulating wildly, their two hands' thumbs and forefingers touching making the shape of a diamond.

In 2007, near Mutare, at a place called Marange, diamonds were discovered, setting off a diamond rush last seen in the Kimberley area of South Africa over a hundred years ago. Buying diamonds on the side of the road was still possible a year after their discovery. No doubt the peddlers had sold many a fake diamond to gullible travellers. After all, how many people know what a rough diamond really looks like?

During the bush war of the 70s, Mutare was on the receiving end of the devastating mortars, fired by "terrorists" from Mozambique. Thirty minutes drive from Mutare, up the mountain, lie the magnificent Leopard Rock Hotel and Golf Course.

On Sunday the 1st of June 2008, I arrived at Nigel's home in Bulawayo at 7:30am as planned. Nigel "Nunja" Murray, a.k.a. Meat Pie, Mick, the artist, and I were to drive in my car towing the golf cart.

The mood in our group was very sombre, however. Ian, one of our eight-ball had pulled out because his mom had passed away on Thursday. Tragically Marty, who really was the chief organiser, had heard on Friday night that his sister had been killed in a car accident in Mutare. She had been married to Brian, a white MDC candidate in the March 2008 elections, who had just been elected Mayor of Mutare. Obviously the conspiracy theory quickly surfaced that she had been "taken out" by the CIO, as a message to the MDC, to show who was in control.

Whatever the reason for or how the accident happened, it is not difficult to imagine how seriously the excitement for the week ahead had been dampened. We left Nigel's at about 8.00am in the direction of Mbalabala, where we turned off the main Beitbridge road on our way to Zvishavane, which we reached two hours and three roadblocks later.

As we were leaving Zvishavane, we came upon a roadblock manned by more than the usual policeman and his "May-I-see-your-licence?" roadblock. The number of plainclothes, AK47-wielding soldiers made this a serious roadblock. We dutifully stopped as requested.

"Please get out of your car," commanded the policeman.

As we alighted from the vehicle, they wanted to know where we were going and where we came from. I suppose four white males in the countryside, just after an MDC victory in the election, would increase the interest of the roadblock managers.

Leopard Rock was a hard-currency cash zone, as most if not all businesses, including hotels, were not accepting Zimbabwe dollar cheques, and Zimbabwe dollars cash was hard to come by. I knew that between the four of us we were travelling with at least US$2 000 in cash. Once the police and AK47 guys started searching our car and luggage, I realised they were after Gono's much prized foreign currency, and I anticipated that a body search would follow the fruitless search of the car.

I immediately started my normal "spiel".

"Sir, can I ask you to do some advertising for me?"

"What?" was the surprised response. I repeated the question while at the same time retrieving from the boot some golf caps emblazoned with our company logo. As usual the mood suddenly changed.

"How many are you?" was my next question.

"We are seven," they replied.

I always travelled with about twenty caps and a similar number of branded wall calendars in my car for just such eventualities.

Glancing across through the open doors, I saw Nigel with his arms outstretched, about to be body searched for the more than US$600 he had in the back pocket of his jeans. Once again the poverty and deprivation of the police force and of the population at large worked for me. No one could resist the temptation of receiving a brand-new bright-red cap for free, no matter what their station in life was.

It was as though someone had cast a magic spell. All of the officiators stopped what they were doing and rushed over to see what they could get for free. One minute later we drove away from the roadblock, smiling to ourselves at the ten or twelve recipients of vivid red golf caps, who were waving us joyously on our way.

As we drove away I received an SMS. Cellphone signal in Zimbabwe is only available in most big towns, so any messages sent or received will be transmitted if you are in or near a big town. The SMS read, "Hi dad, please phone urgently. It's about Jason." The time was 10:15am. It was from my youngest son Jonny in Stellenbosch. I pulled over and tried to send a reply, but no luck. We decided to press on to Masvingo, an hour away, where we knew there would be mobile signal.

Naturally, as we were driving, the guys started asking questions and I related how passionate Jason was about motorbikes. Mick, the artist, also rode a motorbike from his farm to the golf club, and all of us wondered how, after a great Thursday Club, he managed to wind his way home!

I was somewhat concerned, but went along with the flow of motorbike banter between the four of us, describing who had ridden what, when, the reaction of the folks and other delightful stories.

Back in Bulawayo, Jane was involved in the annual SPCA "Scruff's" day, held once a year on a Sunday in June, to raise funds for the SPCA. She too had received Jonny's SMS. Being in Bulawayo with good cellphone signal, she had managed, after the usual ten to fifteen attempts, to get through to Jonny.

By the time we got to Masvingo, I was extremely anxious to contact Jonny. I rang Jane's cell phone in Bulawayo. She indicated that she was still trying to find out what had happened, and that at this stage all she knew was that Jason had been in a motorbike accident. The guys and I realised that this could be serious.

I was ready to throw my cellphone in the nearest ditch, such was my frustration. Then Russell, who had been travelling with the other three players, arrived. He had international roaming with a South African cellphone SIM card.

Eventually Jane phoned me, and my worst nightmare came true. "Hi, my love, I'm so sorry, but Jason has died in a motorbike accident no more than two kilometres from his house on the Gordon's Bay road." All I wanted to know was whether they were positive that he had died – clinging to the last vestige of hope. I promised Jane that I would drive back immediately. Eventually, thanks to Russell's phone, I was able to get through to Jonny. He confirmed that he and Caren, Jason's mom, had been there when the paramedics pronounced Jay had gone when they placed him into the back of the ambulance.

I had moved away from the car to make the call, while the others had stayed huddled together next to the car, obviously waiting for some news. They were phenomenal.

When I howled, "Oh no!" and burst into tears, they all came over. Grown men crying together at my loss. The overwhelming empathy was amazing, even from one or two I did not believe were capable of showing any emotions. After all, except for Murray who was unmarried, we all had kids. So perhaps they were silently giving thanks that "There by the grace of God go I."

I was remarkably calm and rational. Within five minutes the trailer was unhitched and, together with a tuck box of goodies and drinks supplied by Murray, I was on my way back to Bulawayo.

I wouldn't have believed it was possible to cry continuously for three hours. Initially I felt consumed by guilt, then just by gut-wrenching grief. Jason's 28 years were replaying themselves over and over in my mind like some bizarre movie. Each time a vivid memory came to me, I would howl even harder. They undoubtedly were the longest three hours of my life.

When I arrived home, Jane was waiting for me at the garage. We just hugged each other and sobbed for about ten minutes.

During my return drive she had organised with Gay, a travel agent friend of ours in Durban, to get the Monday Air Zimbabwe flight from Bulawayo to Johannesburg and from there the connecting plane to Cape Town.

That Sunday evening we sat together on the veranda at home in Bulawayo, sending SMS's to family and friends, with a simple message, "My eldest son Jason has died this morning in a motorbike accident. Please pray for us."

The next week was characterised by an overindulgence in tranquilisers and sleeping pills. Jay's memorial service was held on Friday the 6th of June, and I was absolutely astounded and overwhelmed by the number of people, both from work and from his motorbike club, who turned out to pay their last respects.

For the first time in their 15 years of participation, the group of my Bulawayo mates back in Zimbabwe won the Leopard Rock tournament.

I bought the book *Grieving for Dummies* to help me recognise emotions that I would be going through, and to prepare myself for something no one can prepare you for – handling the death of your child. At 28, my eldest son Jason was dead. No wedding, no children, no grandchildren, no more asking for my advice. He would not be able to fulfil the prediction that I made in the foreword of my master's thesis, when he was only three years old and wanted my attention. "One day you will understand when daddy says, 'Not now, my boy, daddy's busy.'"

On 12th September 2008, Jay's birthday, Caren and her husband Ryk, Candi, Jonny, Mary (Jason's fiancée) and I went up Helderberg Mountain in Somerset West. We climbed along the Helderberg Nature Reserve paths up Disa Gorge, which Jay had loved so much. Disa Gorge is named after the rare Disa Lily, found in the damp undergrowth next to the river, high up at the top of Disa Gorge. The early morning smell of the pine forests we walked through filled the air. The clay paths were a little slippery from all the winter rain and from the damp forests. A wide array of beautiful proteas, one of Jay's favourite flowers, was in full bloom all over the mountain.

I carried Jay's ashes in a knapsack on my back. September in the Cape is pretty much middle or late winter, and still sees days of rain or drizzle. September 12th 2008 was a peach of a day. Cool, about 15 degrees Celsius, bright blue sky with not a cloud in sight and not a breath of wind.

We all said a few words and then took turns to scatter Jay's ashes in Disa Gorge, his final resting place.

Jane has been a real star and true soulmate; helping me work through the tremendous guilt as perceived by me of the things I should have, could have or would have done for Jason. To support the certainty that he is alive in my heart and mind, Jane had a beautiful verse printed for me with a photo of Jay, which she mounted and now hangs in my bar in Bulawayo. The words have special meaning;

> **I Have Not Gone**
> You think I've gone, that I am dead, and life has lost its will.
> But look around, I am right there, living with you still.
> I watch your tears, I feel your pain, I see the things you do.
> I weep as well, each time you cry, my soul it lives with you.
> It gives such joy to hear you laugh, and do the things you do.
> And when you smile o'er bygone days, I smile right with you too.
> For we're still one, just you and me, one mind, one soul, and in the
> Stillness of the night, when the pain it really starts,
> stretch out a little,
> With your mind and draw me to your heart.
> For I am always right in there, always by your side.
> For you have been, all my life's days, my joy, my love, my pride.

The saying that things happen in threes came chillingly true that fateful weekend: Ian's mom, Marty's sister and my son.

You can call it premonition, fate or whatever you will, but in November 2007, nine months earlier, we had been planning a houseboat trip on Kariba with all the kids. Logistically it never came off, but Jay was the one who insisted that we at least had to try again.

So it was that on the 19th March 2008, three months before he died, Jason, Mary, Candi, Jonny and Jonny's girlfriend Tori arrived at Bulawayo airport for our trip on the Kariba houseboat. We had a fantastic time with all the kids. Jonny, Jason and I spent at least nine hours alone in a speedboat, fishing and talking, reminiscing and confessing. It really was an awesome week, arriving back in Bulawayo on Friday 28th March, a day before the election, which we hoped was going to change the face of Zimbabwe politics, as well as our business and personal lives.

On the Saturday of the election, Jay made his famous potjie with beer. A potjie is probably best described as a stew made over a coal fire in a traditional African three-legged black cast-iron pot. Mary baked the potjie bread, and that night we all sat in the lounge and watched home videos of the children. Over the years I had been a bit of a nuisance recording memories, and by now had nine three-hour tapes of the kids from birth, through school, weddings, Christmases, Easters and many more family occasions. We laughed as one big family. It was awesome.

Even weirder was the fact that in April, a month after the boat trip, Brett, Nicky and their two boys came out to Cape Town from Bangkok. Jane and I flew down to Cape Town to see them.

It meant that for the first time, and for only a few days, since Jane and I got married 13 years earlier, our complete blended family was together, in Somerset West. Being the nostalgic, history-loving, sentimental person that I am, I insisted that we have a session with a professional photographer with all of us together, including grandchildren. Nic, our sunshine kid, decided we should all wear jeans and white shirts for fun. The hour-long photo session was tremendously amusing, with Jay the clown as usual. These are the last photographs taken of Jay, two months before he died. We truly are blessed to have these happy pictures to remind us of him and our last time together as a complete family.

Coping with all the stress, paranoia and fear under which we had been living, dealing with the price slashes, having missed going to jail by a whisker – I had to seek a philosophical approach to Jay's death amidst all this turmoil.

I sunk into a deep depression. Sure I wanted to give up my position. Definitely we had had enough of Zimbabwe, with the power cuts, the deteriorating infrastructure, the lack of goods in the shops. All that weighed heavily on me to make the decision that Jay's death was the last straw. We should leave Zimbabwe and move back to Cape Town to be closer to our kids and grandkids. At the time of emotional downs, I of all people know that nobody should take big decisions. Luckily sanity prevailed, and we decided to stay in Zimbabwe. As they say, "Why walk out of a horror movie ten minutes before the end?"

Christmas 2008 was our first without Jay and was celebrated with Caren and Ryk, Candi, Jonny and some of Caren's family. We had Jay's favourite meal, a braai and potjie at Caren's house. Easter 2009 was also an emotional milestone, as we reflected on the previous Easter, when we had all been together, all seven children and partners, with grandchildren, and had a picnic in the Helderberg Nature Reserve.

As 1st June 2009 approached, so did the golf trip to Leopard Rock. Obviously I was apprehensive, but realised I needed to make the trip, to put all of last year's memories to rest and to be able to move forward. Making the trip, Jane suggested, would help with the healing process. So a year to the day, we once again set off for the Leopard Rock golf tournament in the Vumba Mountains. This time Mick, the artist, couldn't make it, neither could John – who could hurl a putter further than Retief Goosen can hit a pitching wedge – so Nigel's brother Tony, the tennis player, and Wellie, the Bulls supporter, took their places.

On 1st June 2009, the morning of the anniversary of Jason's death, I spent on my own, high in the Vumba mountains about four kilometres from Leopard Rock Hotel. At about 6.30, as the sun was rising over the misty landscape, I drove from the hotel until I found a place where I could get cellphone signal. The breathtakingly beautiful Burma Valley stretched as far as the eye could see, with the magnificent mountains of Mozambique in the distance. I phoned Jane, Jonny, Candi and Caren, and then sat on my own in the car listening to a song Jay had played over and over at Kariba a year before, when we were all together on the houseboat, a real party song called "Leeu Loop" (Lion Walk) by an Afrikaans South African singer Robbie Wessels.

As Jane said, being so high up in the mountains put me close to my boy. I had a good, releasing cry and then drove back down to the hotel. The mist in the valleys and the crisp mountain air made the experience truly memorable.

As any parent who has lost a child will know, the emotional heartsore moments come in waves and are unpredictable. A song, a saying or a situation could bring back a flood of memories and, as if you are jumping off a cliff, drive you into a deep depression. These intensely painful moments can last a few hours, a few days or months, depending on the circumstances and on the individual.

Through all of this Jane was fantastic and incredibly sensitive, ready with the hug when I needed it, and avoiding those trite sayings, which are supposed to ease pain, but which, I felt, inflicted or exacerbated the emotional distress.

9 STARTING FROM SCRATCH [2009]

The greatest thing in this world is not so much where we are, but in what direction we are moving. OLIVER WENDELL HOLMES

The biggest challenge faced by all businesses after the minister's announcement in January 2009, that all could now trade in forex, was the recapitalisation of their businesses. As there were no savings, banks had no money to lend. The US$100 a month that government paid all civil servants, became the benchmark for all companies.

We were grappling with the questions about pricing our goods, remunerating our staff, products to sell and terms from our suppliers. Just to have a situation where you knew a price wasn't going to go up, was great. Mealie meal, the staple diet of all Zimbabweans, had dropped in price from the December 2008 black market price of R130 to R45 per 10kg bag by March 2009.

On 23rd January 2009 a loaf of bread cost ZW$50 trillion, four days later it cost ZW$150 trillion. The RBZ on the 16th of January had released new ZW$10, ZW$20, ZW$50 and ZW$100 trillion notes.

Headlines in *The Herald* on 16th January 2009 read, "*RBZ unveils ZW$100 trillion note.*" The article explained, "*In a statement yesterday, the Reserve Bank of Zimbabwe said the notes would ensure that those in formal employment withdraw their salaries with minimal hassle.*" With effect from January 12th 2009, workers could withdraw their entire January salary in cash as long as they produced their current pay slip.

We did *not* know that this development would be announced, when in December Elana and I had decided to bring forward the January pay date to the 12th, as opposed to the usual 25th. The concession was made due to pressure from our staff, who indicated that they would not have enough money to even come to work. After the RBZ made the announcement, our staff all pitched up on Monday 12th January 2009 at their various banks with their pay slips.

A flurry of phone calls ensued from the banks, wanting to know why we had paid our staff so early. They had not yet received official authorisation from their head offices to carry out the RBZ's directive. Nevertheless, by the Wednesday, we had a lot of happy staff who could obtain their cash in full, which of course was immediately exchanged for hard currency on the streets!

With the shortage of cash at the banks, and the fact that as from November, for obvious reasons, no one wanted to accept cheques, the government introduced SI 175/2008 on 12th December 2008 regarding payment by cheques. It read, *"The penalty for refusing payment by a cheque/bank card or other bank-mediated electronic payment method, will be a level 8 fine or imprisonment for a period of six months or both."*

Obviously we ignored the SI as it was totally at odds with reality. We can only assume that the RBZ with their 12th January announcement wanted to keep as much money in the banks as possible. Since we stopped accepting cheques on the 10th of November, effectively ceasing all sales, we knew that this new law that forced companies to accept cheques again opened up the possibility of a jail sentence for one of us at the office. We had dealt with so many disastrous and irresponsible Reserve Bank decisions in the past, that we were not going to give in to their threats any longer.

The scary part of this SI was that *"Every director or member of the governing body of the trader, practitioner, parastatal or institution shall be liable to the same penalty if institutions or parastatals flout the regulations."* The threat to business was still as evident as ever, no consultation, just intimidation.

On 29th January 2009, the Acting Minister of Finance presents his budget. Chinamasa lost his seat at the last election in 2008, but is a senior ZANU-PF member and was Minister of Justice in the previous government. He is the same fellow who had the scuffle in Parliament with the MDC's Roy Bennett, when Bennett was the MP for Chimanimani. He allegedly called Bennett's forefathers thieves and murderers. Bennett took exception and pushed him to the floor. A Parliamentary Committee of ZANU-PF sentenced Bennett to one year in Chikurubi, the feared High Security prison.

Anyway, this character is now Acting Minister of Finance. Bearing in mind that parliament was dissolved in February 2008, the mind boggles as to how people can be referred to as Ministers of Information, Finance or any other for that matter. I don't pretend to understand the machinations of governments or politicians!

Chinamasa announces the budget in US-dollar terms, despite the fact that we still trade with Zimbabwe dollars and a few shops have been issued with Foliwar licences. He announces that we will from now on be allowed to trade, using other currencies. All very confusing. Blow me down if at the end of his budget speech he does not mention a few other initiatives Government has taken to generate forex. I sense a déjà-vu situation.

- Rudimentary toll gates to be set up, initially on inner-city highways by 1st March with the following charges: Motorcycles US$1; passenger vehicles and light trucks US$2; minibuses US$3; business US$5; heavy duty trucks US$7 and haulage trucks US$10.
- The requirement to obtain new number plates upon change of ownership of a vehicle to be dropped.

Just as I did, you can only shake your head and laugh out loud to keep sane. Hadn't we tried the tollroads before at huge expense? Maybe this time they had another plan?

This budget was of course presented as a proposal, and in any functioning democracy, has to be debated in parliament and approved before implementation. Needless to say, this was not necessary in Zimbabwe! On Monday 2nd February, ZIMRA was already charging P50 road tax at the Botswana border. No amount of reasoning and arguing could persuade the officials otherwise. The minister had spoken and now his word was de facto law.

Financial comedy show Part 2. On 2nd February, four days after the Acting Minister's budget speech, which I may add was extra long owing to the many interjections and jeers from the parliamentary benches now packed with MDC members, the infamous Gideon Gono, Governor of the Reserve Bank, delivered his monetary policy speech.

Remember in October 2008, four months previously, he had pompously announced the introduction of the FOLIWAR shops that allowed licensed operators to charge forex for goods and services, the panacea for all our economic woes.

He withdraws a number of failed systems, with their endless bureaucratic red tape, such as the obligation to bank all the previous day's forex cash before 11.00am each day, to record on the deposit slip all serial numbers of US dollars or other currencies received, or to pay all suppliers within seven days.

FOLIWARS were out the window, though in this speech there was no reference to FOLIWARS or adjustments to that system, just a new system. No thanks for all the trouble the business community had been through, no apology that he botched that one. Nothing. Everyone could now trade in forex, be paid in forex, draw as much of your forex as you wanted. No more Central Bank control. On top of this he also announces that another 12 noughts are to be dropped, and new notes introduced. The largest value banknote in the world the 100 trillion dollar, introduced on 16th of January, two weeks before, is overtaken by new notes, less the 12 zeros.

There was a catch to this whole "cleansing-of-his-soul-and-opening-up-the-economy" scenario.

Firstly paragraph 5.18 on page 107 reads: *"All traders shall therefore, in addition to selling their goods in foreign currency, adopt a dual pricing framework where goods will also be quoted in local currency."* This means that prices can be in Rand or Zimbabwe dollars, US$ or Zimbabwe dollars.

5.19 reads further, *"The dual pricing framework to be adopted by all licensed entities shall be legally enforceable and the pricing formulae to be implemented shall be based on the interbank market determined exchange rate which shall be fixed at the mid-rate level and communicated to the market by the Reserve Bank of Zimbabwe on a regular basis and/or as appropriate."*

5.20 – *"This extended framework for foreign exchange licensed shops is expected to achieve the desired objective of increasing the number of participating outlets and covering a wide spectrum of the country's economic sectors to ultimately increase the availability of goods and services in the country."*

Helloooo!!! What planet do you come from Governor? For the past ten years the black market – no pun intended! – has ensured that the hunger for real money has seen the Zimbabwe dollar become worthless. Why, all of a sudden, after dropping 12 noughts – that is 25 noughts since August 2006 if you've been counting! – does the governor believe the Zimbabwe-dollar value will not keep falling?

So now not only are we forced to sell in Zimbabwe dollars, still devaluing daily and one can safely assume likely to continue doing so, but we also have to find the foreign currency to pay all our overheads, including our new licence fee to operate, payable into the RBZ coffers.

We decided to have a quick group think. This was 3rd February 2009. In approximately two weeks we would have to run our payrolls, pay our landlords and start paying all our utility bills in forex.

We decided to start trading on Tuesday the 10th of February, three months to the day since we stopped, with all our prices in Rand. All our shops would have to have three deposit accounts for their takings. One Zimbabwe dollar, one Rand and one US dollar. We decided we would not take the Pound or Botswana Pula at our shops, as this would worsen our headache. We also decided not to run a dual currency system, i.e. we would not price in Zimbabwe dollars. As Elana so defiantly put it, "We trade in Rand, if they come for us, then they come for us!"

The implications of dual currency trading, with one stable currency and one in free-fall, was just too horrific to contemplate. Until, with balance of payment support, the Zimbabwe dollar could stabilise, it was in fact a useless currency. Never mind the accounting systems and cash register nightmares, but also the potential fraud and overload on our stock-keeping systems, which are still all manual.

In any case, what was the point of selling in Zimbabwe dollars unless the currency was at least regionally acceptable? Even Peggy and Rabson, our house staff, were refusing monthly pay in Zimbabwe dollars, as they could not buy anything with them because even vegetable vendors wanted hard currency! And here was the Governor once again asserting his power and authority, going against economic practice and forcing us to sell our goods in Zimbabwe dollars. Mind-blowingly weak and unbalanced governance!

We had submitted our application for a FOLIWAR license on 26th January 2009, eventually capitulating because we couldn't continue any longer without an income from trade. We had been surviving on the "burners" money, which had come into our shops up till 10th November when we stopped accepting cheques. We had enough Zimbabwe dollars in the bank to sustain us till the end of February. We banked on the Government of National Unity coming into force and a new pragmatic Finance Minister getting real and opening up the economy.

Unfortunately, the SADC meetings on Zimbabwe's GNU delivered no substantial progress. As a follow-up, a special SADC meeting was held on Monday 26th January 2009. Coincidentally on the night of the full moon of Friday 30th, the MDC agreed to join ZANU-PF in a GNU – a Government of National Unity.

With Gono's new monetary policy speech came the new licensing arrangements for EFFELS – Extended Framework For Foreign Exchange Licenced Shops, which took the place of FOLIWARS. The US$20 000 licence fee required for a FOLIWAR licence was also dropped. As teenagers we used this word to describe condoms or French letters (FLs). It was therefore ironic that Gono should come up with this acronym. As if we hadn't been screwed enough!

We changed all our prices to Rand and now eagerly awaited our EFFELS licence. On Friday 6th February 2009, we found out that it was being printed, that we should only open on Tuesday 10th, and that our license would be faxed to us on Monday 9th. We decided we had waited so long to start trading, we might as well wait another day. By Friday the 6th February, we also found out that Gono's Zimbabwe dollar versus Rand interbank rate of 2:1 was already at 4:1.

Prices of goods were still horrifically high as everything was imported. Limited supply and high demand allowed traders to exploit the market for their own benefit, making a quick buck! In December, to feed our factory staff, we had been buying 10kg bags of mealie meal at P22 or R25 in Botswana, but it was now selling in Bulawayo for R120!

What was really positive about Chinamasa's budget speech and Gono's monetary policy statement was the freeing up of the economy. The pressure from SADC and others seemed to be showing results. Gold miners, who had been forced to sell their gold to the RBZ, had not been paid the forex since November 2007, 14 months ago. All miners in the country had as a result been starved of vital forex to sustain their operations and so had mothballed their businesses in 2008.

The budget now allowed them to freely sell their gold on the open market. The Reserve Bank retained only 7.5% or swapped it for Zimbabwe dollars.

The Grain Marketing Board lost its monopoly on the sale of maize and other small grains. Up until the budget, small rural farmers and the remaining few commercial farmers in the country had to sell all grain produced to the GMB. Now all producers could sell to anybody on a willing-buyer willing-seller basis.

Relinquishing their control must have been a huge bitter pill to swallow for the ZANU-PF stalwarts like Gono, who had thrived on this power. With immediate effect, the RBZ would stop printing money to fund its quasi-fiscal policies and would focus on its core function of stabilising the Zimbabwe dollar. No more loans of BACOSSI money, buying tractors, fertiliser or fuel for the party faithfuls. For the first time in 20 years, and after *fourteen* Monetary Policy speeches, the Acting Minister aimed to balance his budget. Wow! Though we were excited at all these new economic freedoms, we still remained pretty sceptical.

For the first time in over five years we retailers felt energised and really optimistic that we had reached the bottom and that now the only way was up! Only time would tell if our optimism was misplaced. Finally, on Tuesday 10th February, we started trading again. Our cash flow was non-existent.

Fortunately we had an export order, which had been paid and we held this money in our FC account. In the Monetary Policy speech, Gono had allowed banks to once again import cash notes through their NOSTROs accounts. In turn this enabled us to draw cash notes from our FC account at the bank. For importing the banknotes to the value of our export order, the bank charged us half a percent of the value.

Cheap at the price to get our hands on new crisp money. Who would have thought that the Zimbabwe dollar would become worthless? Even more amazing that we would only have US dollars and Rands in our wallets after the persecution and imprisonment of anybody found in possession of foreign currency only two years previously!

A New Government

It seemed almost an ironic coincidence that on the day we started trading again, heralding our new economic freedom, 18 years previously on 10th February 1990, Nelson Mandela obtained his freedom after 27 years imprisonment. F.W. De Klerk, then State President of South Africa, announced Mandela's release the following day, 11th February. Further irony was that Morgan Tsvangirai was sworn in as the Prime Minister of Zimbabwe in the new Unity Government on 11th February.

The mood in the country was exciting, upbeat, similar to the joy experienced after the first summer rains, after eight months of dry, dusty weather.

We decided to screen Morgan Tsvangirai's inauguration on the big screen in our entertainment room at Head Office, after a number of requests from staff who wanted to be part of the moment. Thembani and Tracey organised a "Wiztech" decoder and a big screen TV. The "Wiztech" is a decoder and satellite dish, which picks up SABC1, 2, 3 and ETV, 2 God channels and a sports channel. Once you have bought the decoder and dish for between R800 to R1 200, TV viewing is free. How long it will take for SABC to catch up on the number of free viewers I am not sure, but it has allowed Zimbabweans to watch South African channels for free for the past two years. Zimbabwe TV, ZBC, has intermittent breakdowns and only screens archive material from the bush war, extolling the virtues of the party, interspersed with local music videos. Really exciting!

There were shouts of jubilation when Morgan Tsvangirai took the oath of Prime Minister and also when Mrs. Thokozani Khupe took her oath as Deputy Prime Minister. She was a Bulawayo lady and so had great support. One must remember that the MDC had a strong base in Matabeleland, with Bulawayo as the main city.

It was interesting to note that Morgan never made eye contact with President Mugabe after his signing-in handshake, neither with the two ZANU-PF Vice Presidents when he shook their hands.

At last we were on a road to economic and, we hoped, to political freedom. The sense of relief after the swearing-in ceremony was almost tangible in every person in the room.

Three days previously, the interim President of South Africa, Mothlante, in a televised interview suggested that Zimbabwe take the Rand as its currency in order to bring a quick turnaround in the economy. This caused great excitement, as the majority of the two to three million people, who had left Zimbabwe over the last five years, were in South Africa.

Was our second-guessing of the government's economic policy on the way forward going to work in our favour?

Terror at the Airport

On Monday 16th February 2009, we were all filled with optimism as the new Government of National Unity promised to usher in a new era for all Zimbabweans. As if to remind us that we were still in a state governed by fear and intimidation, Jane and I had a nasty experience when returning from Cape Town at Bulawayo airport!

Bulawayo boasts its own regional airport. Until 2005 there were only three flights a week between Bulawayo and Johannesburg, on Tuesdays, Thursdays and Sundays. On any other day you had to travel the 440 kilometres to Harare from where there were daily flights. From 2005 *South African Airways Airlink* operated daily flights, much to the relief of people living in Matabeleland.

Bulawayo's old airport was a throwback to the 50s and 60s. It could probably hold a maximum of a hundred people. The lounge area upstairs opened out onto a balcony, where one could wave goodbye or welcome back family or friends. The lounge chairs were old wooden-framed ones with vinyl covering. In the upstairs dining room smiling waiters would serve a toasted-cheese sandwich or an egg-and-bacon breakfast, while diners used steel-legged panelite tables and chairs. Pictures adorning the walls were faded big posters of Hwange Safari Lodge and Victoria Falls. Baggage receipt was no modern carousel, but a wooden knee-high contraption with highly polished brass strips, which allowed the luggage to slide smoothly as it was offloaded from the old hand-pushed trolley. It was cosy and filled with memories of sad goodbyes and joyous welcomes.

We knew the lack of money was starting to bite when you had to pay ZW$5 to go upstairs and wave goodbye. If you were flying and had your ticket, there was no charge. Getting past the lady official sitting at the bottom of the stairs, selling the ticket to go upstairs, became a game. If you went in a group, all you did was start a highly animated discussion with much laughter and talk as you proceeded past her. The passenger flashed the boarding pass, while the others kept moving. I can't remember ever paying the ZW$5.

The Civil Aviation Authority of Zimbabwe then decided to build a new airport terminal building. Construction started in earnest in about 2001. To date this building is still incomplete. Of course every time an election came round, the local newspapers were full of promises that the construction would be complete by the

President's next birthday on 21st February 2002. This was extended to October for the grand opening to which, we were told, various Heads of State had been invited. Not surprisingly, as the economy slowed so did the building progress on the new terminal. A "temporary" terminal was opened in a big World War II hangar, with a high corrugated iron roof and a concrete floor.

Workmen erected partitioning for toilets, immigration and customs offices, lounges for arriving and departing passengers. You don't want to be caught in this "temporary" terminal if your flight is delayed. Temperatures in Bulawayo climb to over 40 degrees Celsius for four or five months of the year. The corrugated iron hangar becomes like a sauna.

The airport staff is very friendly, as almost all Zimbabweans are. Because Bulawayo is a small place, most of them know you by name. Every year I made a point of giving out company calendars to all who worked at the airport, obviously as an advertising exercise, but of course also to smooth our passage, especially through customs, on our way back into the country.

Every time we returned from a trip we were loaded with goods – as much as could fit into a suitcase, together with clothing for a week or two – which we regarded as essentials, but which customs officials often considered contraband. These included medical supplies for the SPCA, of which Jane was Vice Chairman, or for the few oldies at the old-age home, whom Jane also supplied with toiletries.

The bread shortage since 2005 had been quite acute. I really was missing my whole-wheat bread from Woolworths in South Africa. Local white bread only lasted two days and then would start falling apart when trying to slice it. Rumour had it that the flour was mixed with mealie meal to conform to the 700g weight, which the government was policing with a vengeance, to ensure that the *"bakers who were bent on regime-change"* did not do the customers down. Of course, the low bread price was state controlled, which made it unviable for the local bakers to produce. Hence the bread shortage.

I discovered that six loaves of Woollies whole-wheat bread fitted perfectly into a cardboard wine box. That is how the tradition started that each time one of us went to Cape Town to visit the kids, we would return with the precious six loaves. This served more than one purpose. It kept me smiling and regular, and it diverted the customs official's attention away from our suitcases containing the essentials.

Arriving inside the airport terminal, we would collect our cases, load them on the trolley and on top prominently display the cardboard box. Needless to say, it was solidly taped up with numerous bright red "Fragile" stickers.

It never ceased to amuse me how the customs official would rush off for a pair of scissors and tape when he saw us.

"What's in the box?"

"Bread."

"Aah, I must look inside!"

Then followed the ritual of cutting open the box, only to find I was telling the truth. By this time, feeling probably a touch embarrassed, and under pressure from the other 30 passengers waiting patiently behind me, he would wave us through. I thought it was a nice touch when he would offer to re-tape the box, I would reply "Don't worry, it will take too long and we will be using it soon." This distraction worked every time and we would be waved through, of course after he had asked whether we had been out of the country that same month.

The question was critical, because we are only allowed a US$250 duty-free allowance on the first trip of every calendar month, the date of which would be recorded in your passport, but the allowance only applied if we spent a minimum of 24 hours out of the country. Frequently either Jane or I had been out of the country during the month, but even if we had bought nothing on the previous visit, we had forfeited our duty-free chance and duty would be payable on the goods brought in during the second trip.

The whole journey required dedicated forward planning. Accommodation, meals, tollroad fees and the fuel, as well as the South African government's requirement of R1 000 every time you applied for the compulsory visa when travelling on a Zimbabwe passport, made grocery shopping in actual fact rather expensive.

In June 2008, when there was absolutely nothing on the shelves, the government dropped the requirement to be out of the country for over a day to qualify for monthly US$250 duty-free imports.

This made Francistown in Botswana our choice destination as it was only two and a half hours away from Bulawayo, including the time spent at the border – if you were lucky! At times the border crossing alone could take four hours because of the sheer numbers – of mainly shoppers – negotiating their passage.

On that Monday 16th February 2009 we followed the same procedure that had worked like clockwork for the past four years. All went well at first. We cleared customs with our box of bread and luggage, only to be met at the door by two gentlemen who were checking everyone's passport. This was strange, as we had already passed immigration.

Instantly, when we presented our passports, the two gentlemen in civilian clothes became animated and their eyes lit up. The shorter one composed himself and with a stiff official voice announced,

"Mr. Gardner, please would you come with us? We are from the Central Intelligence Organisation and would like to ask you a few questions."

Being interviewed by the feared CIO could not be good. Before I could respond, Jane took the words out of my mouth.

"What's this about?"

"Please sir, we don't want a fuss. We just need to interview you."

Because Bulawayo has a small white community, it ensured that most of us knew each other. This conversation took place in front of a few of our friends. I politely asked the CIO if I could load my luggage in the car.

"Yes sir, no problem."

Strangely enough there was none of that panic, which I had always imagined I would experience if ever confronted with this situation. I must admit that on the way to the car my mind was racing. *How did they know I was on the flight? Had I said something to someone about Bob or any of his fellow party members? Had the fact we had started trading without Gono's authority or licence come back to haunt me?*

As I followed the CIO officers across the parking area to the little shack, which served as their office, I have to admit that I felt the tension in me rise. A million things went through my mind, not least that on any myriad of spurious charges and for no logical reason, you could be incarcerated. After all many of my friends, as well as Larry, had spent a weekend or longer at the hospitality of the state, before the authorities dropped the charges.

Make no mistake, this intimidation tactic by the government of the day *did* instil fear into every citizen of the country.

I calmed down Jane and Bron, who had come to pick us up. Paranoia had flourished in all of us over the past ten years because of the oppressive police-state atmosphere we lived in.

I was lead into a corner office and told to sit.

"What is this all about?" I asked.

"Sorry sir, we are only acting on orders from Harare."

Of course he still had my passport and was proceeding to fill out a form with all my details. I had always told myself that if confronted with such a frightening state of affairs, I would do my little puppy act and remain timid and submissive, while they tickled my tummy. I reckon it would be ill-advised to become aggressive and on the offensive.

He fired his questions one after the other.

"What is your residential address?"

"What is your home telephone number?"

"Mobile number?"

"Sorry, but I don't give that to anybody," I replied.

To my surprise he accepted this, even joking "What about to your kids?" followed by a giggle. Was this the technique of cracking a joke to soften me up? He continued.

"Where have you been?"

"What was the purpose of your travel?"

After about ten minutes he asked me if I knew a John Peter Gardner?

"No," I replied, "never heard of him."

"Are you sure he is not family of yours?"

"Yes I am," I replied, "I don't know who he is."

From the office I could hear a woman's voice asking, "Where is Mr. Gardner?"

While I was inside the office a group of Jane's friends had been discussing the possible reasons for my demise, and decided to send a group to find me and see how they could help.

I wasn't alone in hearing the voices. All of a sudden "Shorty" decided the interview was over.

"Thank you for your cooperation, Mr. Gardner. You may go."

Apparently a Unity Government was not going to stop the harassment and intimidation. Obviously both Jane and I were concerned that despite the fact that they had let me go, there could be a follow-up to the whole episode.

Unfortunately, paranoia was part of life in Zimbabwe. Fear and lack of recourse to justice, I believe, were the causes of the general feeling of insecurity and the flight from the country by millions of people.

First Tentative Steps to Recovery

Our first days trading in Rand and US dollars fell just short of our expectations, but nevertheless gave us hope that in the 15 trading days left in January we would generate enough cash to cover all our costs for February.

Morgan's first speech as Prime Minister on 11th February at Harare Sports Stadium was quite impressive. For a politician, who had been horribly beaten up on numerous occasions, setup and tried for treason, survived an assassination attempt and got more votes than Mugabe in the 29th March 2008 election but still didn't have the power, he was incredibly magnanimous. His promise to pay all civil servants in foreign currency by the end of February was the point in his speech, which caught our attention.

I had resisted registering as a forex shop when the scheme was launched in October, because:

(a) I didn't trust Gono. He had already stolen our forex once, what would stop him from doing it again?

(b) The only legal forex in the country was emanating from friends and family living in the diaspora, who were sending money home each month for food and other living expenses.

(c) Our biggest customer base was the lower income groups, the majority of whom were civil servants, policemen, teachers and the military.

(d) Most importantly at US$20 000 per shop and with 196 shops, we would have had to find US$3.9 million just for the licence fee!!

There just wouldn't be enough money to sustain our business, buying stock, salaries and wages, rentals and other overheads.

I always believed that the day the state started paying civil servants in forex, that would be the day we would have a proper business again. Even Thembani jumped up from the front row and started giving everyone high fives. He too knew that such a development was the start of putting business back on track. Larry was tremendously excited. At last, after about five years, we could get back to what we did best: retail discounting.

In the meantime stories abounded about the struggles of the upper-end retailers. Even well-known pharmaceutical chains like Clicks or clothing stores like Express Mart now resembled basic food stores. Admittedly Clicks did have a few beer glasses and enamel pots for sale, but the shelves in the part of the shop that weren't blocked off, displayed Kellogg's rice crispies, peanut butter, salt, sugar and of course mealie meal.

Touring our shops in Bulawayo on Wednesday the 11th February 2009 was a real treat. All our members of staff were so excited. Prices had been painted on the windows a week before, one of the staff members was shouting out the bargains through a loudhailer and the music in the shop was blaring. After five years we were back in our element. The good Lord was smiling on us. The rains had been plentiful this season, optimism permeated everything.

By March 2009, four weeks into the new dispensation, reality was starting to dawn on everyone. Gone was the hype and excitement of this new beginning. Expectations had been created, both overtly by politicians, but also almost by default. After years of oppression, and now promises by the MDC of a wonderful free society, there was intense anticipation that, after the new government was sworn in, everything would be just perfect and life a bed of roses. But money did not pour into the country, potholes got bigger, power cuts occurred equally frequently. It became clear that the utopia everyone had been dreaming of remained just that

– a dream. Slowly people started coming to terms with the fact that it was going to be a long trek to recovery. We consoled ourselves that we could not sink any deeper, but how fast we rose out of the quagmire, would depend on ourselves.

I am not sure how many readers have had the privilege of living in a country where the economy is starting from scratch!

Where to begin? Like starting a new business, there has to be a business plan. The politicians drew up "STERP", the Short Term Economic Recovery Programme. Its details were never really spelt out to the public at large, but included, according to state newspapers, the freeing up of the media, the abolishment of oppressive laws and the encouragement of business through less stringent import controls.

Whilst these broad lofty ideals were great as a political tool, we in business were a little more stymied by practicalities! No one had any idea of the true value of the foreign currency in use! Local municipalities did not know how to charge for rates and services. Cellphone operators appeared to simply divide their total costs by the number of lines they had sold to arrive at their charges. They were ridiculously expensive at R4.20 or US$0.40 for a local SMS! Zesa's charges were just as outrageous. The Authority had not been sending out bills to households and businesses for 18 months. Quite understandable due to hyperinflation, but suddenly consumers received ridiculously high monthly electricity bills for thousands of Rands!

Obviously in the first three months of this fledging economy very few households or businesses paid these exorbitant fees. We opted to pay a portion to avoid disconnection or termination of the various services. So Jane would go to the post office and pay, for instance, R500 of R2 800 on our monthly phone bill. The company also paid phone bills proportionately. All attempts at finding a value level.

Eventually the new masters instructed all parastatals to bring their tariffs in line with regional players such as South Africa, Botswana, Zambia and Mozambique. In June all sorts of discounts were offered by service providers to encourage people to settle their bills. Free market forces were again determining the true economic value level of the charges levied by parastatals and service providers.

In the business, we were at a loss to know what our pricing structure should be. Unlike a new business starting out, we had huge overheads, which, after three months, we still could not quantify exactly. We realised it would take at least six months to a year to establish the correct level of company expenses.

What should our salary levels be? Minimum wage? Should we peg them to South African salaries and wages or to Zambian, which were much lower? But, service charges and rentals, which were initially also ridiculously high, were much higher than in South Africa or Zambia.

After spending a few days in Botswana and South Africa comparing prices and measuring these against local producer charges, we made a benchmark decision that initially we would pitch our selling price at between 10 and 30% higher than either Botswana or South Africa. This slightly higher pricing structure was largely due to transport costs from South Africa as well as to the duty structure for imports into Zimbabwe. However, if the company in South Africa was registered as part of the SADC, goods into Zimbabwe could be imported duty free.

We ran preliminary budgets with projected sales, cash flow forecasts and expenses as if we were starting a new business. After the first two months of trading, we had established a basis for making forward projections. We reverted to using 1999 figures as a performance target. Government's disastrous policies had effectively wiped out ten years of trading.

At this stage Elana and I recognised the important competitive strategy of "first mover advantage". We knew we would need to be first out of the starting blocks with the products we offered our customers. We realised that no longer would the customer simply buy whatever was in the shop. His dollar was not going to depreciate. Quality became of paramount importance. He could afford to exercise choice once more, something that the scarcity of product over the last few years had not allowed him to do.

As a starting point to determine remuneration, Government had decided to pay all civil servants a flat US$100 monthly allowance, since this was all it could afford. This figure became the basis for our minimum wages as well.

On the 12th of April, the new Minister of Finance, Tendai Biti, announced that, with immediate effect, the use of the Zimabwe dollar would be suspended for at least a year. Overnight, any money held in a bank, pension fund, medical aid society or any other financial institution, simply evaporated. From having a few quadrillion Zimbabwe dollars in the bank on the first day of April, companies and individuals woke up on the 13th of April with a zero bank balance. No individual or company was spared. This effectively forced everybody to start from scratch financially. Banks had no deposits, hence getting a loan was impossible. Thank goodness for our export earnings, which allowed our company some breathing space.

In July 2009 we decided to award a 50% increase to all staff across the board. This was based partly on the feedback received from staff on their living expenses, but more importantly on our three principles, on which we had fought many a wage battle in previous years and which had consistently worked for us, namely what the market was paying, what the company could afford and what the inflation rate dictated.

A visit to the doctor cost US$20. Medical aid societies had not yet started operating, and the only one that had, wanted members to wait six months before claiming, but was still insisting on members' subscriptions of US$40 per month. School fees ranged from US$5 to US$50 per month. Rent for a small room in the high density areas cost up to US$30 per month.

Our sales had also shown a monthly increase of about 20% since we re-opened our doors for trade in February.

Whilst it was true that everyone was far better off than in January, when monthly pay could only get you to work and buy one bag of sadza, expectations were high. We knew it wouldn't be long before we would have trouble on our hands if we did nothing.

Up until July we were still in a loss-making situation.

Fortunately for us, that same month Government decided to increase salaries for all civil servants by 40% to $140. This boosted our sales tremendously and allowed us to import duty-free product from South Africa, our closest southern neighbour. It was not easy, as all suppliers demanded cash up front before they would ship the goods. Our cash flow came under tremendous strain, but this expenditure was vital to secure first-mover advantage. We couldn't blame the suppliers for their circumspection. After all, historically, we certainly had not proved to be the most creditworthy country!

To our relief, after visits to their factories and various negotiations with the banks, quite a number of suppliers agreed to 60 and even 90-day payment terms. This allowed us to build up our stock levels and by the end of September 2009, they were back to where they were two years earlier in March 2007.

How the economy had been devastated in the last ten years becomes obvious when one compares 1999 versus 2009 customer figures. In July 1999 we served 458 000 customers in 170 shops. In July 2009 we only served 156 000 customers in 190 shops. A mere third of our customer base remained. We realised, as we obtained more information and statistics, that we were facing a long recovery period. Change was not just going to materialise overnight, but at least we were moving in the right direction.

Loss of Business Ethics

We had anticipated that we would need to do a lot of retraining once the situation normalised. What we had not been conscious of was the behavioural change that had taken place over the last five years and how we had reinforced these bad practices. The following case will illustrate what I mean.

During the really bad empty-shelf days in the shops, one day my management team and I arrived at one of our outlets in Bulawayo. Parked outside was our Area Manager's truck, loaded with bars of soap – *not* a product we sold. On questioning our employee, Larry was told quite unashamedly that he was helping out a friend to transport the soap to a rural area to sell. The friend was going to supply the fuel, so in theory there was no direct cost to the company. We simply turned a blind eye. The feeling at the time was, with the salaries we could afford to pay, with their money stuck in the bank, our staff, like everyone else was really battling to even feed themselves and their families, never mind buy any luxuries. If staff could make a few bucks on the side, and as long as it did not directly impact negatively on the business, we let it pass.

This was never a conscious management decision taken at a meeting, but an unwritten, undiscussed agreement between ourselves. We truly felt sorry for our battling staff, who, no matter what we did or paid, would still have to walk miles to work and struggle to find the absolute basics.

In another instance we called a shop manager in for a disciplinary hearing for stock loss, or shrinkage, which was higher at his shop than what the company allowed. Power cuts and staff absenteeism because of transport problems were quoted as reasons for the shrinkage. With the benefit of hindsight we now realise that in our sympathetic mode, we probably reinstated a lot of managers who were blatantly stealing from us!

A week earlier, we caught a staff member selling yellow dusters from his own stock in our shop. Yet another shop manager was reprimanded for being absent so often. Surprise, surprise, when we discovered that she had being running her own shop for the past three months, using our clothes' hangers and stationery! To correct these cavalier attitudes towards honesty would be a huge challenge.

We would have to carefully explain company policy to all staff members and enforce even the smallest of disciplines. The task ahead was massive.

As we traversed this once beautiful city of Bulawayo, we were struck by the abject filth and the deterioration of the roads. Garbage was strewn everywhere. Sanitary lanes between buildings were thigh high in refuse. Near the market, gutters were clogged with rotting vegetables, everywhere else old tattered plastic bags and household rubbish defaced open areas and streets. After the rainy season the smell of decay was pretty pungent. Up to about eight years ago Bulawayo had basked in the pride of being Zimbabwe's cleanest city.

The depressions, which with the last rainy season had become big, were now proper potholes, so that speeds in excess of 40 kilometres an hour were bound to buckle one or two rims. The section of road we had repaired two years ago was worse than before.

Some enterprising unemployed youths had taken it upon themselves to fix the potholes with clay and soil. The catch was, of course, that you had to stop in order to miss their buckets of sand and give them a chance to ask for a R5 fee for the work they were doing. They were pretty sharp, targeting intersections where motorists had to stop, because they realised that on the open road they were vulnerable to being knocked over by speeding cars and more likely to miss out on the bucks.

Obviously filling all the potholes swiftly would render them jobless and therefore penniless. Like good civil servants, therefore, they took their time. One or two really shallow potholes would be filled and a bucket of sand dumped next to the real big crater. As you stopped at the intersection, they would point to the fixed one and to the big pothole and then cup their hands expecting a few Rands. Forget about giving them Zimbabwe dollars! They would have buried you with the sand in the hole!

After watching them for two days at the same intersection, I managed to persuade them to fill the last big hole and move to the next intersection. In any case, I explained to them, rain had been forecast in two days time and their work would be undone in about a week. Then they could return! The more intersections they fixed and the more it rained, the more money they could make. Simple economics. It worked and they moved on after filling the biggest rim buster of them all!

In November 2008 we had placed an order for 190 000 metres of fabric from our Hong Kong suppliers. Because of the Chinese New Year, we knew the shipment would take longer than usual. We expected delivery on about 26 to 29 January 2009. Little did we know, when placing the order, that our friend Gono was going to dollarise in January – with immediate effect!

Our clearing agent advised us that the container with our fabric had arrived in Bulawayo on 10th February, but that unfortunately we were now required to pay the duty and VAT in foreign currency. Once again nobody at the RBZ had thought about the implications of this hare-brained decision on companies' forex cash flows.

Where were we going to find the cash? In the meantime, the transporter charged us a king's ransom for daily demurrage.

I decided to set up a meeting with our clearing agent and ZIMRA. One of our clearing agent's employees, Pienkie, was a former ZIMRA official who had terrorised us a few years back when she was on the other side of the fence.

Naturally Pienkie was now in our camp. We needed to ask ZIMRA to place an embargo on our shipment; we would offload it into our warehouse, section off an area containing the fabric, and apply at the same time for the area to be designated a bonded warehouse. ZIMRA could even keep the keys. In a bonded warehouse stock is kept under lock and key, and every time the user draws from it, he pays the proportionate duty and VAT, thus saving the company's cash flow. Without a registered bonded warehouse, ZIMRA would not allow this system to operate. Although we all reasoned that given ZIMRA's history of money grabbing and terror, waged over many years, we were wasting our time with our request – but we had no option but to try.

We met Pienkie at the Bulawayo Station Manager's office at Custom's House. Elana reminded me, as we walked into the lady's office, that we had sat in the same chairs three years earlier with our Tax Consultant, Fiona, trying to avoid going to jail for some petty trivialities ZIMRA had discovered during one of their surprise tax audits on the company. In those days we perceived ZIMRA to apply the law as they saw fit in order to intimidate and to extort as much money as possible. They backed down eventually, but we lived in fear as we knew they would want to get even.

This time you could have knocked me down with a feather. After exactly seven and a half minutes we walked out of the lady's office with broad smiles.

"Of course," she had said, "there are many customers like yourselves who have been caught unawares by this sudden turn of events. We must work together to rebuild our country, so we will agree to your request." Elana wanted to burst out laughing. How could this be happening? What a change! We walked out of ZIMRA's offices even more convinced that we were on the road to a bright future.

The following just serves to illustrate the tight control politicians had over the economy and every aspect of our lives. On the 18th July 2008 they introduced SI 103 dealing with Electricity Generators. For the last five years we had experienced power cuts of up to eight hours per day and they had been getting progressively longer. To circumvent the load shedding, we, like most other manufacturers, installed a 125kVa generator at our factory. It was a really big 12-cylinder truck-engine-sized generator. Many homes also had from 2 to 15kVa generators to make life more bearable.

On hearing about the SI we immediately took steps to comply, fearing another crackdown with the ensuing fines and court cases. Not surprisingly, the 14 days to comply with this SI were hugely inadequate. The government department concerned did not have the necessary application forms as somebody was still designing them, they could take up to three months to obtain and, to crown it all, no one knew what the licence fee should be. More ridiculous laws created more criminals and law breakers.

As with so many previous decrees, by February 2009, nine months later, no one was bothered or cared about the SI 103 and life continued as if the SI had never been issued.

On 17th November 2008, Professor Steve H. Hanke, of John Hopkins University, released a document estimating Zimbabwe's annual inflation at 89.7 sextillion percent or 65 to the power of 10. The monthly inflation he estimated at 79.6 billion percent as at 14th November 2008. Ironically, it was 11 years to the day since "Black Friday".

Multiple Currencies – Multiple Challenges

By the end of April 2009, just two months after the government allowed everyone to trade in US Dollars, South African Rands, Pounds and Botswana Pula, we took the decision to change all our prices from Rands to US dollars. The decision was prompted by the realisation that our daily takings throughout the country were mostly in US dollars. Rand deposits were down to 25% of all sales. In addition, the Rand was also strengthening against the US dollar, making our products more expensive in US-dollar terms. Shop staff also battled to convert the currencies when customers wanted to pay in US dollars while our stock was priced in Rand.

Of course the printing presses had stopped generating money on command, we were therefore relying on whatever money was floating around in the economy. This cash mostly originated from people in the diaspora, sending money back home through money-transfer agencies. Banks had limited cash, as everyone was simply withdrawing their full pay every month, but not depositing any.

The smallest denomination was the US$1 note, since no coins had found their way into the country's monetary system. As retailers we were forced to round our prices to the nearest 50 cents. Change, if needed, was in the form of loose sweets or lollipops!

A customer paying a lowly-priced item with a US$100 bill was the shop manager's biggest nightmare, especially in the early morning. He knew he would lose a sale because he didn't have any change to give the customer. It is impossible to estimate how many sales we lost as a result of this shortcoming. I thought it hugely ironic that we were crying for small change, when just six months previously we had been crying because the value of the notes was too small to draw all your money from the bank. How the wheel turns!

It would be a serious understatement to claim that the environment of trading in multi-currencies was challenging. One story – one of many – best illustrates this.

One day I received word that the Town Council had closed one of our shops for failing to pay the council rates. The company's finance department assured me all rates have been paid.

It turned out the council had supplied us with their Rand-account details, whilst we had correctly made a US dollar payment, as per their statement, into their account. The bank received the money and simply held onto it as it didn't have a US-dollar account number for the council. Eventually all was sorted out, but only after we had lost two days' sales in the shop.

Town councils were also battling to adjust to dealing with "real" money and more specifically "real" costs. Our council rates account from Victoria Falls, for instance, read as follows:

Assessment rates	US$145.00
Street light charge	US$ 40.00
Roads levy	US$ 15.00
Refuse removal	US$ 69.00
Education levy	US$ 20.00
Capital development	US$ 50.00
Environmental levy	US$ 30.00

Was there anything in Victoria Falls we weren't paying for?

Size Does Count

In March 2009, our shop managers inundated us with requests for men's trousers of a smaller size. One thing I have learned from all my years in the retail business, is never to take a salesman's word for what he needs in order to reach his sales target. It was critical to get proper information. Hence we sent out survey forms to all the shops, asking them to supply us with the sizes of men's trousers' stock left in the shops. We had the information of what sizes and quantities we had sent them, therefore it was easy enough to get the facts we needed to make an informed decision.

Traditionally we had purchased on a size curve for men's trousers from 28 to 40. This size curve followed a normal distribution or bell curve. An inflow of 4 500 pairs of trousers, which would be distributed across all our stores, was broken down into a so-called size curve – the smaller shops would receive one-size curve, while bigger shops would get more. One size-curve meant that the small shop would take delivery of a total of 15 units of men's trousers: one pair of sizes 28,

30 and 40; two of sizes 32 and 38; and four of sizes 34 and 36. A high-sales big shop would probably get four times this quantity. This size-curve had been in use for at least 12 years and is something that is not changed lightly, as it pretty much measures our customers' sizes through the sale of men's trousers.

The results that reached us, both from one of our store visits as well as from the information obtained from our store managers, was staggering. None of our stores had any trousers in size 28, 30 and 32, while they all had many of the big sizes left. We decided to input only size 28, 30 and 32 for the months of April through to August, or until we saw a change in buying behaviour. Our sales of men's trousers simply skyrocketed! We couldn't keep up with the demand in the smaller sizes.

After three months of trading, not supplying any trousers over size 34, we were still well stocked with size 36 and bigger. The population had got thinner since March 2008! This was clear from our own factory workers, who had been battling just to find mealie meal for months now. We realised that the effort of having to go across the border to purchase food as we had done in 2008, had not been in vain. We had statistical proof that the population of Zimbabwe had been starved to such an extent as to change the size curve on our men's trousers.

The good news is that since the multi-currency regime was introduced, shops have filled up and people have been eating properly. Thankfully, by our first order of men's trousers in September 2009, we were back to normal, with the shops requesting bigger trouser sizes, and our size curve back to where it was 18 months earlier. The nation had put on weight again!

SOAP And Pensions

Spare a thought for the pensioners during these times of change in the economy. Our pension fund, administered by a multinational, had obviously also been affected by the cessation of the use of the Zimbabwe dollar in February 2009. All of a sudden we woke up from having quadrillions of Zimbabwe dollars in our pension fund, to zero. Obviously the Zimbabwe dollars that the pension fund was holding for all our staff, and for thousands of fellow Zimbabweans, was worth nothing, and couldn't be exchanged for US dollars. This meant that all those years of contributions simply evaporated! We too had to start saving in a pension scheme from scratch. Someone who had worked for 30-odd years, was entitled to a payout of US$400. Their punishment, it seemed, for retiring in 2009. How do you tell loyal employees after 25 years of service that they don't have a pension?

The same scenario unfolded with medical aid funds. No claims could be paid out before six months of contributions had been received and then the maximum payout was three times the six months' contribution. We were inundated with medical loan applications, and as a result set up our own scheme to assist employees.

If survival was tough for people in employment, then the old-age pensioners were in dire straits. From 2001 pensioners saw their incomes slowly erode. By 2008 someone who had worked for a parastatal such as the railways and had retired after 40 years, received a monthly pension not enough to buy one loaf of bread! In early 2001 groups were set up to help the elderly. One such organisation had the acronym SOAP, which stood for Save Old Age Pensioners. Many of us made monthly contributions or bought toiletries on our shopping trips across the border.

Many people like Mags, her husband Rick, and Brett gave not only generously in financial terms but also of their time to keep the senior citizens in relative comfort. These and many others were and continue to be true angels of mercy to many old folk in Bulawayo. The number of heartbreaking stories would bring anyone with an ounce of human feeling to tears. The spirit of Ubuntu – caring for others – was not only alive during these dark days, but also put into practice by so many fellow Zimbabweans.

The Team and the Business Challenges

I really believe that the team we had was the root of our success, not withstanding everything the government and the business environment could throw at us.

Our organisational structure was very flat, consisting of only four levels. The operational level was made up of our team of five management members. Two Regional Managers and ten Area Managers each looked after approximately 20 shops, and our Shop Managers took care of 196 shops throughout Zimbabwe.

This allowed for quick decision-making, which was imperative in the prevailing environment. Formal meetings to discuss issues were rare. As a team we believe in sharing information, bouncing ideas off fellow team members and taking action. Centralised decision-making was critical, though going against the traditional management theories of empowering lower levels to make their own decisions. We adopted this style because the Reserve Bank Governor and his colleagues in government were making laws on a daily basis, which could have huge consequences for the survival of the business. The political climate was incredibly unstable, with fear and terrorisation pervading all aspects of life.

The absence of the rule of law was obvious and confusing. For instance, when a policeman entered a shop and demanded goods at half price, citing a speech made by a government minister, whom could the Shop Manager turn to? If he went to the police, he could be jailed on a trumped-up charge. Shop Managers and even Area Managers had been arrested and locked up during the famous price-cut blitz, hence they were loathe to question any person perceived to be in or associated with Government.

On a different occasion, ZANU-PF war veterans would enter a shop and insist on a donation from the Shop Manager for a planned political gathering in the town. These same war vets would demand posters advertising the meeting be prominently displayed in the shop windows.

We had sent out memos headed "To Whom It May Concern" spelling out our policy of being apolitical and instructing the Shop Manager to contact head office should any requests for contributions or participation in activities be demanded. This did not stop the lawlessness. I remember our shop staff in a rural town refusing to close the shop to attend a ZANU-PF rally scheduled for that afternoon. A group of war vets forced marched all the staff to a local school where the meeting took place. For failing to adhere to the instructions of the war vets they, together with others regarded as MDC supporters, were forced to sit through the meeting and they were held all night for a "pungwe".

They had to listen to and to repeat ZANU-PF slogans accompanied by the singing of and dancing to liberation songs. The government's version of *Strictly Come Dancing*, except that there were no winners, only beatings for those who didn't sing loudly or danced enthusiastically enough. This scenario played itself out in many rural towns in Zimbabwe.

Tragically neither the shop staff nor we had any recourse to the law. They were either part of it or were coerced into participating. The need for centralised decision-making in the company one could liken to a wartime scenario, where the commanding officer had to make all the decisions and determine how to react in the given situations.

Such tactics obviously put tremendous pressure on the five of us, as the calls from Area or Shop Managers came at any time – day or night. Motivation of all staff was therefore critical.

Business Challenges and Changes

The change to our business during the last five years, and especially since the price slash of 2007, was truly dramatic. With inflation at millions of percent per annum and our crucial weekly mark-ups, we had to take some hard decisions, which affected the nature and core of our business as a discount retailer.

Lay-bys were a sales scheme that, in normal circumstances, allowed a customer to pay a 10% deposit on goods, which were then held in-store and the customer had three months to pay off his debt. At first we reduced the repayment time to two months, then to one month, as inflation gained momentum. Ultimately, following the 2007-price slash, we had to suspend all lay-bys simply because price increases could not be passed on to the customer. The administrative aggravation and legal problems were nightmarish to say the least. Lay-bys were meant to help the lower end of the market from which we drew the customers who purchased our goods, making them feel good but knowing that they didn't have enough disposable income. This scheme formed 15% of our business. Stopping it therefore put a huge dent in our sales.

Money-back guarantee was part and parcel of our quality drive. Customers, who were not satisfied with their purchase, could return items to our stores and obtain their money back. One doesn't need to be a rocket scientist to see what would happen. A product bought for Z$100, today would cost Z$800 three weeks later. Of course the customer, who returns his Z$100 merchandise, would expect Z$800. Thanks to the vigilance of our store managers, who were being inundated with returned goods, this trend was discovered very early on. As the economy shrank and prices increased, it was a kind of saving scheme for some less-scrupulous customers! Wear the goods for a month and then replace them or get their money back a month later to buy food. For obvious reasons this scheme was terminated rather quickly.

Members of staff were allowed to purchase goods to the value of their monthly pay and deductions were made from their salary for three months until they had paid for the goods. In addition, a 20% discount was offered on these purchases. The scheme encouraged our staff to support our product and in so doing increase our sales and act as free advertising for our products. We had to suspend this scheme equally fast. Some unprincipled staff purchased at the 20% discount to the maximum limit allowed, then sold the goods in the townships at full price to customers who couldn't afford their bus fare to town anymore because taxi and bus fares were tracking the black-market fuel price.

To put hyperinflation in perspective, *one day's* sales in April 2008 equalled a *full month's* sales for February 2008. Advertising was curtailed. At first, we decided not to list prices in any adverts or brochures because the time between the selection of goods that should appear on our various leaflets and printed advertising media to the time of printing, could be as long as ten days by which time the price would have risen by over 200%. Obviously, after the government's 50%-off sale of 2007, we decided to stop all advertising. Moreover, customers had realised that it made more economic sense to buy goods as soon as they received their pay because after a few days the goods would be unaffordable.

Another challenge was the reprogramming of our cash registers. By early 2008, we had dropped the decimal point off our price, as our cash registers could only handle six digits including the point and one decimal. Reprogramming was a huge exercise as we were not on point of sale. No Area Managers were equipped with a reprogramming schedule, but somehow the decimal point had to be removed from our cash registers and hence they were tasked with the reprogramming. This exercise took over two months, with the result that by the time it was complete, our prices had risen to such an extent that three months later we had to do the exercise all over again, this time adding "Please add three zeros to the price shown" as a footnote to each cash register slip!

The shop staff would ring up the sale of goods selling for ZW$3 billion as ZW$3 million, with the customer aware of the system. Price cards in our stores now indicated prices as 10b or 2m indicating billions or millions. Customers quickly got used to this but for us, retail discounters, it was a big mind shift. Of course finding a 16-digit calculator was not easy and I am sure, as our prices moved to trillions (12 zeros) or quadrillions (15 zeros), many mistakes must have been made in all stores.

As a management team, we also had to write down the number of zeros to ensure we had not made a mistake when doing calculations of stock holding or sales figures. Disputes with banks over balances, because some clerk had left out a zero or two, became a common occurrence. Thank goodness, our kids had finished school, as the mind boggles at the amounts of tuck-shop money parents were giving their offspring! I can just imagine the situation. "Precious, here is 3 billion for tuck shop today. Don't forget to bring my change!" Teaching the 10-times table to schoolchildren must have been a real challenge when they were talking millions, billions and trillions.

In April 2008 Richard, our Buying Manager, decided to relocate his family to the UK. His British passport was his trump card. Our team was very sad but also understood that with three children at school, the financial challenge of maintaining any semblance of a decent lifestyle had become impossible. Therefore, he joined the estimated three million Zimbabweans, who became economic refugees in neighbouring countries, as well as in Australia, Canada or the UK.

Given the economic situation, we decided not to replace Richard but instead shift Fanuel from HR Manager to Buying Manager, while giving the HR responsibilities to his young second-in-command Mazwi. HR was a stand-alone function, which now would report to Elana, our Financial Director, adding more pressure to her function. In any case, finding a Buying Manager was a futile exercise: the brain drain had in fact made our decision relatively simple.

ZIMBABWE **WARM HEART** UGLY FACE

10

THE BULAWAYO GOLF CLUB AND OTHER STORIES

The secret to success is to learn to accept the impossible, to do without the indispensible, and to bear the intolerable.
NELSON MANDELA

Bulawayo Golf Club is the oldest in Zimbabwe, founded in 1895 by the early Rhodesian settlers. The oldest club in South Africa is The Royal Cape Golf Club in Cape Town, established only ten years earlier in 1885. The Club Champions Trophy in Bulawayo is the Rhodes Shield named after Cecil John Rhodes and was first presented in 1901, a few years before his death.

Being an avid golfer and having been brought up in a family where my mom and dad served on up to eight community committees at any one time, it was not long before I got involved in the Golf Club committee.

In 2000, the Bulawayo Golf Club had a membership of over 700 members. Sadly, by 2007, the number had dwindled to just 160. Over the years, especially since the farm invasions in 2001 and the subsequent free-fall of the economy, many members left for South Africa, Australia, New Zealand and other faraway countries. The pressure to keep the Club going was enormous, but there was a nucleus of members who were determined to see the history of the BGC preserved and the standards maintained.

In 2001, I was Captain and realised that we were not going to survive without outside help. My first fundraising competition was held at my old club in Somerset West. With the help of ex-Zimbabweans, we managed to raise R15 000. At the time, this was a huge amount of money and the gesture made me realise, that although they had left Zimbabwe, there were a lot of ex-Zimbabweans who wanted to help in our fight for survival.

Jane and I felt really blessed to have what we considered our two homes, one in Somerset West and one in Bulawayo. It was always great to get a week's break in the Cape. No power cuts, wonderful showers with high water pressure, dinners with ex-Zimbabwean friends like John and Marie. Of course, for me there was my old club, Somerset West Country Club, which I was privileged to captain in 1992/1993.

It was a great experience to have a game of golf at my old club, where childhood friends welcomed us every time we went down. Great mates, like Mike the lawyer, Patrick the mad Irish chemist, Dave, whose father had once been mayor of Bulawayo, Martin, Kriek, the Tonys and Kevin, were amongst the friends who made coming to Somerset West such a worthwhile and heartwarming break. We lived this double life, with good friends in Bulawayo and good friends in Somerset West.

Some memories of my time as Captain of the Somerset West Golf Club include the special AGM convened to get members' permission for juniors to play in a Saturday competition. The request came from parents of a special junior. Johan and June had wanted their 13-year-old son to get more competition experience. Permission was granted and had the desired effect: Trevor Immelman went on to win the prestigious US Masters golf tournament in 2008!

The distance from Bulawayo to Somerset West is over 2 000 kilometres. It was truly too far away to raise funds. In 2002 I decided to give Mike, the Captain of Polokwane – then Pietersburg – a call, to see if the Club would help us with fundraising. Mike was, and still is, one of the biggest chicken farmers in South Africa.

The following is an article about our struggles published in the *South African Golf Digest* and the *World Golf Magazine* in 2008.

"Imagine if the Committee at your golf club decided to change the payment of annual subs to payment on a three monthly basis. So in June 2007 you are sent an account for subs of R400 for July, August and September 2007, R900 for October, November and December 2007. But you also pay a top-up fee of R2 500 in November. For January, February and March 2008 the Committee decides to charge R9 000, come the middle of March you get a subs bill of R15 500 but this is only to cover April and May. During May you get a bill for June and July of R70 000. In all, you have paid R98 300 for a year's golf subs excluding green fees or caddy fees. Sounds incredible?! Well that's the reality at Bulawayo Golf Club in Zimbabwe. That's the reality of living with hyperinflation. Change the R400 to 4 million Zimbabwean Dollars and the R70 000 to 7 billion Zimbabwean Dollars and welcome to Bulawayo, Zimbabwe. How can a club survive in this environment?"

This is our story and epitomises the essence of the true golfing spirit of camaraderie.

Bulawayo Golf Club is the oldest golf club in Zimbabwe founded in 1895 (113 years old this year). The club champ has his name inscribed on the famous Rhodes Shield, donated by Cecil John Rhodes and first presented in 1901. Membership has dropped since 2001 (when the bottom dropped out of the economy) from over 700 to just above 200 of which 160 are full golf playing members. Foreign currency for spares, fertiliser, machinery, office equipment, etc. was and is still not available. So the famous Zimbabwean saying "We'll make a plan" came into operation.

In 2002, as Bulawayo Golf Club Captain, I called Mike Nunes, Captain of Polokwane, to ask if they would host a fundraising day for Bulawayo Golf Club to raise Rands for spares. Mike (of Mike's Chickens) agreed without hesitation and so started the relationship between Bulawayo Golf Club and Polokwane – home club of Retief Goosen, 2 x US Open Champion.

In August each year up to 30 Bulawayo Golf Club players travel down to Polokwane with indigenous prizes for the day (teak biltong cutters, leather products, etc.) and the Polokwane guys Mike Nunes and Ockie Jooste organise sponsorship for all the holes. An auction is also held to raise funds for Bulawayo. In November, Polokwane "manne" are hosted by Bulawayo Golf Club and bring with them the fantastic prizes (electric kettles, toasters, etc.), plus the much-appreciated funds raised.

Over the seven years, Polokwane has donated new green mowers, verticutters, score boards and a chlorinator, descaler, 5 000-litre water tank (from May 2007 until April 2008, the Club like most residents, received water once a week for eight hours) and all the piping, 7Kv diesel generator (power cuts in Bulawayo can last up to six hours per day, everyday) and much more. Financially the Bulawayo Golf Club should have closed its doors about five years ago. But thanks to a small group of die-hard golfers in Bulawayo and Polokwane, Bulawayo Golf Club is still a great tree-lined golf course.

Over the past seven years the Bulakwane Cup has brought together golfers, husbands and wives who would never have met. A camaraderie has developed between players who see each other once or twice a year when playing for the now infamous "Bulakwane" trophy, which Bulawayo Golf Club has only won twice in the seven years. Close friendships have formed which would not have otherwise happened. Of course many incidents have occurred over the seven years and are worth mentioning. Polokwane's Steve Rudd's run in with diabetes, sunstroke and alcohol. On the Sunday morning in his bed in Bulawayo, Doc Doolabh gives him a jab and implored him to drink as much fluid as possible on the way back to Polokwane. Steve's dry, slow reply, "But Doc I drank as much fluid as I could yesterday and look where I am now." Francois (brother of Retief Goosen) sms'd his brother in the UK (from the Bulawayo Golf Club bar) "At Bulawayo fundraiser, send donation." Reply – £500. Francois – "Not enough." Reply – OK £1 000. Francois – "Enough thanks." Then there was Ockie's car keys getting tossed into a croc-filled pond after a bet (retrieved next morning in the light of day).

In Bulawayo we are praying for our country to come right, and when it does (and we know it will), we hope to maintain the "Bulakwane Cup". To Mike Nunes and all the Polokwane guys, you have kept our golf alive and done more for golf in Bulawayo than you can ever imagine.

We salute and thank you!

I remember the phone call well. I could not hear a thing Mike was saying because of the noise. He told me he was in the middle of one of his chicken houses and asked me to phone him back. That one phone call in 2002 started a relationship, which exists to this day.

Once a year the Pietersburg guys (about 18 of them) would arrive on a Thursday morning after a nine-hour drive, including the notorious Beitbridge border post, and stay until Sunday. On Thursday they would arrive to play in our traditional Thursday Club competition, on Friday visit the Matopos, a fantastic rock-filled game reserve and site of Rhodes' grave. On Saturday they would compete against us for the Bulakwane – Bulawayo-Polokwane – Trophy. They would bring the prizes such as toasters, kettles or gas braais that at the time were very precious because they were no longer available in Zimbabwe.

All methods of fundraising took place. I clearly remember the incident described in the aforementioned article, where Francois squeezed Retief for his generous donation worth R16 000 at the prevailing exchange rate.

Like every club, Polokwane boasted some wonderfully colourful characters. Steve was one of those, with a slow, dry sense of humour. Steve was not an avid golfer, preferring to accompany the rest of the group up to Bulawayo just for the spirit. On one occasion, Steve had been walking round the golf course with his team-mates, cheering and encouraging them whilst sharing copious amounts of wisdom and beer with them.

It was October, commonly referred to as "suicide month" in Zimbabwe because of the high temperatures. After golf, everybody enjoyed the traditional braai and celebrations. Sunday morning we met the group at Banff Lodge where they were staying. According to our visitors, Steve was violently ill during the night and not well at all.

It took just one phone call and within ten minutes Doc Doolabh was at the hotel. He had witnessed the partying the previous night. Doc diagnosed severe sunburn, complicated by Steve's diabetes. A couple of injections started his recovery, and he was told by Doc to drink as much fluid as possible during the five-hour trip back to Polokwane.

Doc also castigated him for not taking in enough fluids the previous day, in the scorching heat. Steve's dry response was simply, "But Doc, I drank as much as I could yesterday and look what happened!" The generosity of people, who had no connection to Bulawayo, other than through golf, was truly overwhelming. Mike's personal commitment and generosity, as well as his remarkable fundraising efforts, deserves a special word of gratitude.

Polokwane trips started off small, with only eight golfers from Bulawayo, and took place on very few occasions. However, the number of jaunts became more frequent, when the need to obtain groceries was a good excuse for most golfers to convince their wives of the logic to combine shopping with golf. Eventually we boasted over 30 players. Some ex-Bulawayo golfers would even travel up from Johannesburg and from as far as Durban to take part in the fun reunions.

As you would expect, the liquor industries in both Bulawayo and Polokwane would show a growth in sales during these tournaments! Over the years, Polokwane supplied us with greens' mowers, spare parts, paint for the clubhouse and even a water system for the club. This consisted of a 5 000-litre water tank, pump, chlorinator and descaler, which finally enabled us to have the precious clear liquid in the club. This system had become a necessity because during 2006, 2007 and up to March 2008, the City Council rationed us to eight hours of water a week.

As soon as the borehole water was pumped through the toilets and showers, another problem presented itself. At 7:30 each morning, when the club opened, members and their families would arrive for their morning ablutions. At first we thought of banning anyone from using the showers, unless they had played a round of golf. Eventually, after much persuasion, the committee agreed that we were fulfilling a social responsibility by allowing all members who did not have water at home to use our facilities free of charge. No doubt there were many non-golfers in the queue, but all it cost us was the power – or diesel for the generator when there was no power – to pump the water from the borehole into the tank, and from the pressure tank into the clubhouse. All of this was only possible thanks to the Polokwane guys.

Many illustrious golfers have graced the BGC fairways in days gone by. Nick Price, Tony Johnston, John and Dale Hayes to name but a few. In fact John Hayes was the pro at Bulawayo and held the course record for some time. A record previously held by his own dad!

In 2008 Dale Hayes – in my eyes Mr. Golf in South Africa for his TV show and the promotion of golf in South Africa – held a "Save Bulawayo Golf Club" fundraising day at Zwartkops GC, his family's course in Johannesburg.

Famous Zimbabweans such as Peter Matkovich, the course designer, and Tony Johnston graced the occasion. All of us in Bulawayo were surprised beyond belief, when Dale e-mailed to tell us they had raised close to R30 000 for us! The goodwill and camaraderie that golf lovers experience, and which was shown to us over the years to save our historic club, was truly humbling.

One of the great traditions of BGC is "Thursday Club", a kind of club within a club, with the sole purpose to raise funds for machinery and equipment for the course. The captain of Thursday Club, who has no fixed tenure, has to my knowledge never been elected at a formal AGM but is simply nominated every year and voted in or out with a show of hands at a Thursday Club.

Great characters such as "Strongers" or Ian, a giant character in both girth and personality stands out in my mind and in my time. His booming voice and rugby ref's whistle, calling the prize-giving to order, were a tradition carried on by his successors. "Webby", or Craig, was his successor and was the exact opposite in size but not in mirth. Webby could have been a stand-up comedian in his previous life. He coined the saying, during our dark days of fear and intimidation in the country, "If you can't tell a good joke, you are allowed to start a rumour." Both were abundant at Thursday Club.

I remember one gathering when an upstanding member reported that one of our older golfers, who had been ill for a while, had sadly passed away. Without checking the facts, Webby duly held a minute silence, with all Thursday Clubbers standing, heads bowed. During the following week, to his great embarrassment, Webby discovered that the gentleman concerned had not passed away. Predictably, the "news bearer" and all those who had confirmed his story the previous week, received hefty fines, swelling the Club's coffers. Funds raised through such fines during Strongers' long tenure enabled us to build a concrete reservoir next to number six fairway, which we named "Strongers Pond".

A number of members were not only avid golfers, but also avid fisherman. Two such were Roger and Ron. Roger is an Ndebele and Ron is a white guy who fought on Ian Smith's side during the bush war in the 70s. Their talk on the golf course centred on the best fishing spots and whether fish were biting on slime, sadza or worms. Roger shares one story about the time he, Ron and two friends went fishing at a local dam.

Driving in the bakkie (pick-up truck) were Roger and his mate, while Ron, his friend, and all the fishing equipment were on the back. As Roger related he never realised how things had changed, when at every farm gate Ron would jump off the back to open the gate for Roger to drive through. In the old days, it was the white man driving and the black guy jumping off to open the gate. A product of South Africa's polarised society, even after the '94 elections and the emergence of the "rainbow nation", I acquired tremendous insight into how different races could become good friends, thanks to interactions at the Golf Club.

The Golf Club had many members who were wonderful characters and fantastic people. One of these was Sam. Sam was a Ndebele and General Manager of the National Railways of Zimbabwe. He lived with his family in the Railway House on 12th Avenue. "House" probably does not do justice to the property. It was a huge double-storey Victorian-style mansion with balconies all the way round, both downstairs and upstairs.

Sam, like so many of us, loved his golf and was an average 14 handicap. In early 2004 I got to know Sam and his wife very well when Jane and I travelled down to Nelspruit near the Kruger Park for the annual Nomad's golf nationals. Sam, his very good friend Mesheck, also a great Ndebele character, and their wives were billeted in the house right next door to Jane and me on a golf estate in Whiteriver. Everyday we travelled the 15 kilometres to and from Nelspruit to play in the tournament. The girls would go shopping or take part in the organised tours to game parks. Every evening we all had supper together.

In 2001 the country was in turmoil after the violent farm takeovers. The elections in 2002 were looming and the NRZ, like any other business in Zimbabwe, was suffering from a lack of forex to keep its train services running. Sam suffered from high blood pressure and was diabetic. He was under tremendous strain. To add to his woes the then Minister of Information, Jonathan Moyo, announced the launch of the "Freedom Trains" in his drive to win the election for his boss, Mr. Mugabe. Transport to and from work for most employees was arduous, to say the least. Fuel had become scarce with queues at garages stretching for kilometres. Obviously the cost of taxis had become astronomical, if you could find one at all. Some employees were walking up to 20 kilometres a day just to get to work.

Sam was ordered to run scheduled trains – two in the morning and two in the afternoon – to get people to and from work. The trains travelled from the high-density areas into town. There were designated stops where people had to be picked up and dropped off, but there were no stations in the middle of nowhere, forcing the waiting commuters to clamber aboard. Trying to collect fares was an impossibility.

When Sam tried to explain this to his bosses, he was ignored, I am told, and so the NRZ got deeper and deeper into trouble. Train breakdowns were not tolerated. Not surprisingly, this service proved very popular with the commuters and once started, put tremendous pressure on the rail staff and on Sam as General Manager.

I was in a management meeting one day, when I felt my phone buzzing in my pocket. I would normally just kill the call and phone back later. This time I looked who was calling and saw it was from Mesheck. I adjourned the meeting and called him back immediately. He told me the sad news that Sam had suffered convulsions the previous night and had passed away. I cannot help feeling that the myopic power addicts in Government contributed directly to Sam's untimely death.

I went to his house to see his wife and offer my condolences. On arrival the fires in the backyard were burning with huge cooking pots hanging over them. The kitchen was a hive of activity with ladies preparing food. As is custom, all the windows in the house were wide open. Mournful singing and wailing emanated from the lounge. I was ushered through. Lying under a blanket in the corner of the lounge was Sam's wife. I felt out of place and awkward. This was a new and strange experience for me, but also deeply touching. The sadness and grief permeated every corner. I quietly excused myself and left.

The cigars that my friend Sam had given me are still in my bar at home. Knowing I was a cigar smoker, he brought me some genuine Havanas from one of his business trips to Cuba.

In 2001, during the height of the farm invasions and the year of the formation of the opposition MDC, the City Council made some interesting discoveries on the 14th fairway at Bulawayo Golf Club.

Crossing the Golf Club fairways are underground sewerage pipes carrying raw effluent from Burnside, Bradfield and Suburbs to wherever sewage flows.

In 2001 the sewerage line running next to number 14 fairway was blocked once more, pouring raw sewage into the river running between 13 and 14 fairway and green. Our Club Manager Ken managed to get the Council to come and unblock the sewer. To their utter amazement, the blockage turned out to be body parts. They fished out feet with a shoe attached, a skull and some other bones.

The rumours abounded that MDC sympathisers had been killed and dumped by goodness knows who.

Unfortunately, with the deterioration of the infrastructure, we at Bulawayo Golf Club had a permanent stream of sewerage flowing alongside the fairway into the dam surrounding number three hole. After repeated attempts at clearing any blockage of roots from trees and other debris, the Council gave up 18 months ago. Not even the cholera epidemic in 2008 could motivate them to repair the line. We have got used to the smell and the surroundings, but they got progressively worse.

Hence, in June 2009, we decided to go across to Botswana and purchase 8mm high tensile steel sewer rods ourselves, for 2 400 Botswana Pula, tired of having to put up with the situation. The Council had informed us that they did not have enough rods to clear the blocked underground pipes, but at a meeting attended by Steve, our Club Captain, and myself, the Council agreed to use our rods and clear the blockage. Two Saturdays of overtime by Council workers and the blockage was cleared. I am sure that new pipes will have to be laid, when the money comes in.

Sadly this effort by us proved to be a temporary solution indeed, as after only three weeks sewage once again started flowing, now filling the dam on number three hole.

To prove what we had known for years already, on the 13th of August 2009 the headlines of the government-owned *The Chronicle* newspaper in Bulawayo reported that the Council had concluded the sewerage system in Bulawayo had collapsed and there were not enough funds to restore it. Therefore, we just have to get used to the smell and sights.

Despite this small inconvenience on one or two holes, the Golf Club still remains a fantastic tree-lined course, giving many hours of pleasure to us Bulawayo golfers.

The Frog in the Boiling Water

"If you put a frog in boiling water it will leap out as it hits the water, but if you put it in cold water and slowly heat the water until it boils, the frog will stay in the water and ultimately boil to death."

I use this story to illustrate how we Zimbabweans have adjusted to the slow deterioration of this beautiful country. Since 2000/2001 we have witnessed an ever-quickening pace of decline in service, infrastructure and business.

In theory Zimbabwe should be a net exporter of electricity similar to Mozambique, which exports electricity from its mighty Cabora Bassa hydroelectricity plant. Zimbabwe also has its Kariba hydroelectric plant with six huge turbines, sufficient to supply the whole country with power.

Unfortunately the steady deterioration, allowed to happen by really poor management, exacerbated by the lack of skills and finance to upgrade and maintain the operations, has left the Kariba hydroelectric plant able to deliver only a fraction of its potential power. Hwange power station, situated on arguably the largest coal deposits in Africa, if not in the world, has been hit by the same woes as Kariba.

Management at Hwange, like at most parastatals, is appointed by the ruling party. Ex-army generals and others of the same ilk have all had a chance at running the power utility.

A shortage of coal should be the last thing Hwange power station would suffer from. Well, in order to produce the coal, they need machinery and sophisticated equipment. Huge drag lines, which resemble front-end loaders of dinosaur proportions, scrape the earth for this "black gold". Hwange town used to be a bustling place, with all the major retailers represented in town, including our chain, boasting a beautifully manicured 18-hole golf course

We had three large shops in the city centre and in the outlying areas of Hwange.

As the foreign exchange dried up, mainly as a result of capital flight out of the country after the farm invasions and threatened nationalisation of businesses, Hwange mine, power station and town simply began to die.

Power cuts or "load-shedding" started as a minor irritation. ZESA, the Zimbabwe Electricity Supply Authority or as we now know it, an acronym for "Zimbabwe Electricity Sometimes Available", had sophisticated methods of load-shedding, which never really impacted too much on our lives.

Up until the serious load-shedding in 2002, ZESA could centrally disable household hot-water geysers, simply by sending a pulse down the electricity line to a device that had been fitted to the geyser specifically for that purpose. This enabled them to control the use of power in many households. Only very occasionally were we inconvenienced by a cold shower in the morning.

However, over the last three years, from 2006 to 2009, we have lived with up to eight hours a day (or night) of power cuts.

Give ZESA their due: they do try and stick to a sort of preset timetable that makes planning one's life a little easier. The 6am to 2pm power cuts are bearable, but the evening ones that can occur any time from 2 to 11 are definitely the worst.

Initially we tried a few board games or reading by candlelight, but eventually realised that, even if one went camping, it was limited to a few days. After three months we invested in a 5kVa diesel generator, which was enough to get our satellite TV (DSTV), kettle and all the home lights working.

We initially tried a small generator, but the frustration of its limited use e.g. switch off the TV to boil the kettle, switch off everything so Jane can blow-dry her hair, got the better of us and we went big.

Funny how one gets into a routine and we no longer swear, curse or regret our move to Zimbabwe. You walk outside and turn the key, changeover switch (from ZESA to generator), and you can carry on with life as normal. Like the frog in cold water, we have adjusted.

Of course during the serious diesel-shortage years it was more challenging than it is today with diesel more readily available. Jane gets a bit upset with the daytime power cuts because the borehole does not work and she cannot water her magnificent garden. When the power goes off it is fine. However, when it comes back on, there can be major problems.

You have to ensure that everything is switched off during the power cut, because when the power is restored, the supply could fluctuate between 110 volts to 320 volts as we discovered to our great cost. Three borehole pumps and motors, as well as our flat-screen TV have blown over the last few years.

Inverters do not work long-term either. An inverter is a 12-volt deep-cycle battery with a converter that turns the 12 volts into 220 volts enabling you to run a small TV or some house lights. The trick is that when the power comes on, the inverter battery is recharged automatically. But the charging time required is four times the length of time you have used the inverter i.e. the length of the power cut. An eight-hour power cut means we need to have at least 32 hours to fully recharge the inverter!

Unfortunately, after a maximum of 16 hours of power, you know you are going to have another cut, so the inverter battery slowly gives up the ghost. Like the frog in the cold water, the end is inevitable.

Water, Water Everywhere, and Nowhere

Bulawayo is the main city in Matabeleland and situated on the western side of Zimbabwe, sharing a border with Zambia (Victoria Falls) in the North and Botswana in the South West. Matabeleland is in a drought-prone area.

Good summer rains could average between 300 and 600mm or 12 and 24 inches over the six months of the rainy season. About 70 kilometres from Bulawayo runs the Nyamandhlovu aquifer – a huge underground water reservoir that the founding fathers of Bulawayo recognised as a potential source of drinking water for the city in the event of a drought.

Over the years, the 70-odd boreholes that were drilled have mostly ceased functioning due to lack of maintenance of pumping equipment. The same boring, but frustrating, scenario as at Kariba and Hwange power stations! In 2001 Bulawayo was struck by cyclone Eline, which besides causing havoc countrywide by washing away roads and bridges, ensured that our dams held enough water to supply the city with water for at least two years.

From 2001 to 2006, we had average to below-average rainfall. In the 2006/2007 season, rainfall was particularly low, and our dams fell to a dangerously low level. Drinking water from the taps at home in Bulawayo was accepted practice – up until December 2006. By that stage, the economy was in absolute free-fall.

In early 2007, the Bulawayo City Council was not only struggling to supply water to households, but they had also run out of the chemicals needed to take the mud sediment out of the drinking water.

As residents we suffered a double whammy. Water cuts could be anything from eight hours a week to only having water one day a week for eight hours, and when we did have some, it was muddy.

Where we live in Burnside, approximately one kilometre from the reservoir feeding the whole of town, the water could not be turned off as there was no valve between the reservoir and our property. We were one of about 15 households in Bulawayo that never experienced any water cuts at all! How lucky could we get! Power cuts paled in significance. You could live without power, but not without water.

This water shortage from 2007 until about March 2008 created a vast number of water technologists. At the Golf Club, braais or school rugby matches, everybody would compare their newly acquired water gadgets with those of others.

"We've just installed a new descaler that doesn't rely on power, but on rocks. The lime clings to the rocks and you only need to clean the rocks every six months. The great thing is we can use our borehole water now! Of course, only if we have power!"

"We went for the big blue filter, two of them in line with an activated carbon filter, which will take out any bacteria down to two microns. Coupled with this is the chlorinator with an electronic dispenser." Thus the conversations went, like proud parents comparing their children's academic achievements!

I learnt more about water purification, lime content or removal of lime from windows sprayed with borehole water, than I ever would have had if I had lived anywhere else.

Removing the mud from the municipal water was the greatest challenge and necessitated the most costly of filters. Who knows how much mud we Bulawayo residents have in our kidneys! Only time will tell.

The broken and leaking municipal pipes around Bulawayo are simply everywhere. The tragedy is not only that it is going to take years and a fortune to repair all these pipes, but that we will never know how many dogs and other animals will have drowned after falling into these sinkholes.

We take our hats off to the Council, who with their limited resources, always tried to bandage a leak if it was significant enough. The smaller leaks they just couldn't get round to fixing and would continue seeping water for years.

Potholes, Garbage and "Small Houses"

At first the potholes were not that bad and they were repaired on a regular basis. But from 2007 they have got bone-shattering, rim-bending worse. Each rainy season just sees them getting bigger and deeper.

Crushed red brick works best on those over 30 centimetres deep, while clay mixed with straw tends to work better on the shallower ones. The straw or dry grass seems to bind and hold the clay in the pothole. How much it will ultimately cost to resurface the roads in town one can only guess, but no doubt it will be affordable only a few years from now.

On 10th June 2009, Jane was ecstatic; one would swear she had won the lottery. For the first time in 16 months, our garbage had been collected outside our gate. According to the newspaper, we could now expect monthly bin collection on the 10th day of each month. Up to then we had been burning our own rubbish and what couldn't burn, we delivered to the municipal dump site at a cost of R230 or US$30 – payable at the gate! No reduction in rates, just like there was no reduction in water or electricity charges to make up for water or power cuts. Streets around the city and suburbs were littered with waste, dumped by residents too lazy, too poor or too hopeless to take it to the municipal dump.

I remember in 2004/2005 the Indians came to town. An Indian company had been contracted to lay cables for the introduction of a new digital telephone system. Indian labourers were in every street digging trenches, erecting poles and connecting our telephones. This hive of activity continued for almost nine months until we had our modern fixed-line digital telephone system, which I must add, works very well, especially for local calls. Sometimes late at night or over the weekend, calls will get through to a South African or UK landline number.

The land redistribution campaign in 2001 also had some strange twists. Burnside is regarded as an up-market low-density suburb in Bulawayo. In the middle of the suburb on the town's plans, an area of 25 acres has been designated for a primary and high school. Of course these plans were drawn up many years ago.

During 2002, about one year after the farm invasions had started, all the residents surrounding this 25-acre area received a notice stating that the area had been subdivided and five one-acre plots had been cut out along the one side.

At the meeting held at the government complex, the local Ministry of Lands informed the surrounding homeowners that it had been decided to re-zone these five acres to private land. Everybody was convinced the land was Council land and therefore had to go through a Bulawayo City Council re-zoning process. The simple response they gave was that all vacant land previously under the Council's control, was now declared state land.

Asked if the present surrounding homeowners could purchase the land to maintain it as a green belt or open space, the officials reiterated that it was now state land and would be allocated by the central ministry. In any case, so they said, we were homeowners already and owned one property, so why would we want another one?

The meeting was obviously a sham, called simply to simulate a measure of transparency. Nobody was surprised to learn that the recipients of the five plots were rumoured to be the head of CIO in Harare, plus Obert Mpofu, Minister of Trade – the 50%-off sale genius of 2007 – also the Bulawayo town planner and two other high-ranking chiefs. The price of the land– you guessed it – zero!

In African culture polygamy, i.e. having more than one wife, or in our Zimbabwe situation, having girlfriends while married, is broadly acceptable. The meeting place for the couples involved in what we would call extra-marital affairs, is normally a flat or house commonly referred to as a "small house". Today only two small cottages stand on two of the plots. Both are incomplete and have been under construction for the past five years, although one is occupied. Maybe unfinished "small houses"? The neighbours can only guess!

The frustration of not having any recourse to the law against these common autocratic decisions, only served to intensify the disgust toward the central government.

We, like the frog in the cold water, simply came to accept that all these devious practices were part of living in Zimbabwe. People get used to anything.

Don't Tell Tales

Doing business in Zimbabwe was not without its challenges due to cultural differences. As a white man used to a Eurocentric business culture, I realised there would be aspects that I would need to understand in order to be successful. Some concepts were definitely strange to me.

One Monday morning our HR Manager informed me that on the previous Friday our Loss Control Officer had been injured in a car accident on the way from Bulawayo to Victoria Falls. He had been on his way to investigate a break-in at one of our shops. Apparently he had swerved for a warthog and had left the road. The Loss Control Officer was fine, but the car was seriously damaged. In the same phone call, he also mentioned that one of our auditors was hospitalised with chest injuries after a soccer match on Saturday. On the same day, one of our female shop assistants in Bulawayo was also hospitalised, but with a broken arm.

Each incident sounded plausible in its own right. I had been a committed soccer player both in my youth and at university, so I did question Fanuel – he was still our HR Manager – how someone could sustain chest injuries playing soccer. He assured me this was the report the auditor had given to him.

It was only ten days later when he called and asked if he could have a private word with me. I wondered what it was about, afraid maybe that he too was contemplating leaving the country and join his father who lived in Botswana. He came into my office and closed the door. This had to be serious. After an uneasy silence and much humming and hawing, he blurted out his story. The Loss Control Officer, the auditor and the shop assistant, who was his girlfriend, were on the way to Victoria Falls for a naughty weekend with a bit of business thrown in, with the latter in the driving seat. They had been drinking and had left the road and crashed into a tree.

Why and how did this story only come out after ten days? Fanuel explained that he had been having sleepless nights since he had discovered the truth. He did not know how to break the news to me because it was culturally wrong of him to come and tell me. Eventually I might have found out, but he felt very uncomfortable. According to his culture he is allowed to discuss the issue with his colleagues but not with the chief boss, as he would be considered a snitch and would be frowned upon by his colleagues.

I explained to him that his role as HR Manager was in fact to keep me informed of what was happening in the organisation. It was a double whammy for him when we dismissed all three staff after disciplinary hearings. Not only had he broken a cultural code, but had also indirectly caused their dismissal, at least in the eyes of his colleagues. It took many hours of counselling before I could convince him that he had done the right thing.

Blessed – not his real name – was our Financial Manager reporting to the Financial Director, Elana. Although he was qualified, he was an SRB and not a "Salad Kid". SRB stands for "Strong Rural Background". This is a colloquial reference to someone who had spent his or her whole life in the rural areas, attended rural schools and as such had limited exposure to western manners and business values. A "Salad Kid" on the other hand, was someone brought up in the city and influenced by the ways of business and western culture through exposure to TV, magazines and various other means. The SRB, so the belief goes, exclusively ate sadza and relish, best described as boiled vegetables or meat eaten by hand with the sadza. The salad kid was used to hamburgers and city food, as well as to sadza and relish. When the salad kid was naughty, his parents would threaten to send him to his rural home by chicken bus (called this because of the type of baggage carried e.g. goats and chickens). These buses plied the city to the rural areas routes. Naturally, at his rural abode, he would have no TV, would have to walk barefoot in the veld, exposed to thorns and other vagaries of nature, much to the delight of his rural family who would no doubt regard him as a softie.

For a few weeks Elana had been discussing Blessed's performance, which had been deteriorating sharply. He was also late back from lunch, left early and was absent for long periods during the day ostensibly visiting banks to sort out problems. No amount of investigation and questioning of his colleagues cast any light on the reasons for this untoward behaviour,

One afternoon at 2.45, I happened to be driving through an obscure part of town when I spotted his car parked in a driveway. Knowing how Elana had been trying to solve the mystery, I decided to stop and see what he was doing. In his boot were four 20-litre plastic containers or drums of petrol ("chigubes"). I asked him what he was doing. He replied quite calmly that he was helping a friend with some fuel, but he would be on his way to the office without delay. Without further ado, "friends" started walking away, Blessed closed his boot and headed off to the office.

Elana and I decided to question him at once when I got back to the office. He stuck to his story. Next we inspected his car. The boot and backseat stank of petrol and were in a disgusting condition. We returned to the office and I decided to play the bad cop. I threatened him with dire consequences. If I reported him to the dreaded Task Force for unauthorised carrying of fuel in a company vehicle and for dealing in fuel, the immediate result would be a jail sentence. I reminded him of the government's threats against economic saboteurs, black marketeers and others considered to be a threat to the stability of the state!

Eventually he cracked. Every night after work, or slightly earlier as Elana had noticed, he would embark on the hour-long drive to Botswana. He would load up his car with 20-litre drums of fuel, return to Bulawayo and sell the fuel on the black market to desperate taxi drivers and other motorists, at up to ten times the price. The transactions took place in dark alleys and driveways, at all hours of the day and night. In the three months of this thriving trade, he had amassed enough cash to purchase a house for himself and his family.

He was fired after a lengthy disciplinary hearing on charges of moonlighting, which is against company policy, and misuse of company property. He did not understand what he had done wrong, the SRB background evident in the arguments he raised in his defence.

When we questioned his colleagues and co-workers, they all said they knew what he was doing, but had professed ignorance when we questioned them because it was culturally unacceptable to tell on others!

Forgive and Forget?

Another customary difference was what I call "forgive and forget", as opposed to our Eurocentric philosophy of "once bitten, twice shy".

Jonny was studying for his A-levels and was alone at home with Peggy and Rabson. Jane and I had gone to Durban for a week's break from the stress of Zimbabwe in 2004.

Jonny answered the gate bell to be told that a police officer and the next-door neighbour, a Nigerian, wanted to speak to Peggy. They asked him to take them to Peggy's quarters. Abandoning his usual caution, Jonny let them in, because it was a neighbour and a police officer. They went straight to Peggy's quarters and found a plastic bag with two pairs of shoes. They then marched her to the house, demanding to search the premises. There was an exchange of shouting, swearing and verbal abuse between the two visitors and Peggy, when suddenly the Nigerian slapped Peggy across the face. Jonny had been following this debacle, trying to find out what was going on. He was ignored. Peggy's slap in the face, however, was enough for Jonny to tackle him into the flower bed that lines the driveway. The previous year he had played lock for the Zimbabwe school's rugby team during the Craven week in Cape Town, and this made him pretty fearless. He then grabbed the Nigerian and told him in no uncertain terms that hitting a lady was unacceptable, or words to that effect. He then also decided to stamp his authority on the situation and told them that they were now trespassing, and unless they had a search warrant, they should leave.

Realising they had overstepped the mark they decided to leave. A tearful Peggy explained to Jonny that the Nigerian's maid had given her the two pairs of shoes to deliver to a friend of hers in the townships over the weekend. It turned out that the Nigerian was married to the daughter of the recently-appointed head of police in Matabeleland and they had been importing container loads of goods from Dubai, including shoes. They had discovered their maid had been stealing the newly-imported footwear.

Abusing Peggy's naïvety, the next-door neighbour's maid had used her as a courier of stolen goods. Later the same afternoon, the Nigerian returned with two other policemen, who promptly arrested Peggy for theft and carted her off to the Hillside police station, with Jonny in vigilant attendance. A prepared statement was already waiting for her, containing the admission that she had received stolen goods and which they forced her to sign with no chance to explain her side of the story. It was obvious the Nigerian was well connected and Peggy was locked up in the filthy holding cells. Jonny phoned us in Durban and assured us that he would take Peggy some blankets and food for as long as she was in custody.

We returned three days later and managed to secure Peggy's release on bail. Six months later Peggy had to appear in court. We engaged a local lawyer, who managed to convince the Public Prosecutor that Peggy's statement was coerced and not freely given. The case was postponed in order for the state to collect more evidence. I think the Nigerian had realised we were not going to be pushed around and had decided to back off.

Two years later we received a notice that Peggy was to appear at the Hillside police station because the Nigerian had reopened her case! Perplexed, I decided to phone his wife to find out what was going on. I was told her maid had been jailed for three years, but Peggy had not yet expressed any regret. I asked her if I could bring Peggy around to her house to apologise. She agreed. That afternoon we explained to Peggy what had happened and she accompanied Jane and I next door.

Mrs. Nigerian was dressed in her Sunday best, complete with headdress, sitting in the lounge. Jane and I were invited to take a seat, while Peggy sat on the floor in front of Mrs. Nigerian – a customary gesture of respect for somebody on a lower cultural level in African society. We accepted the tea the lady of the house offered. Small talk about the economy filled some awkward moments, whilst Mrs. Nigerian every now and then would berate Peggy for her misdemeanours. The whole situation was quite unreal. She lectured Peggy on how lucky she was to work for people who were doing so much for her, how fortunate she was to have a family. Peggy through all this held her head bowed, and the occasional agreement with a nod or a soft "Yes" were her only responses. This performance lasted for about an hour.

We then asked if we could leave. Mrs. Nigerian agreed and I decided to ask her what was now going to happen to Peggy's case. She informed us that Peggy had now apologised and was remorseful enough for the case to be withdrawn. I do not pretend to understand why Peggy, when innocent, had to ask for forgiveness, but I assumed it was because she had had the two pairs of shoes in her possession. She had been pardoned and the whole incident could now be forgotten!

Lovemore (not his real name) was an Area Manager in charge of 15 stores in the Lowveld area of Zimbabwe. He had been caught making inter-store transfers without the necessary paperwork ever reaching head office, and the stock never reaching the store to which he was supposed to send it. In common parlance, he was stealing. At the disciplinary hearing, he admitted his misdeeds, but pledged his undying love for the company he had served for over ten years. He apologised profusely and promised it would never happen again. The recommendation from the disciplinary committee was that he should be demoted, as he had shown remorse.

The final decision was passed on to me for approval. On going through his file, I had noted that he had numerous disciplinary cases against him and each time he had been given warnings.

To me it was clear-cut: he had stolen company property and should be dismissed.

For the next six months I received letters of appeal from him, requesting reinstatement since he had now learnt his lesson. Could I please forgive him? I ignored these pleas, until one day he phoned me, seeking clarification as to why I could not reinstate him because he had apologised for his wrongdoing.

I soon realised that whilst we in Eurocentric thinking based our decision on the adages "past behaviour predicts future behaviour" and "once bitten, twice shy", in African culture, if one apologised one should be forgiven because "everyone can make a mistake". This is fundamentally different from the way I tackle punishment for misdeeds.

It took a number of demotions for serious breach of policy and eventual dismissals for reoffending, before the HR staff accepted that "past behaviour does predict future behaviour".

This could possibly explain why in European politics a minister who committed an error of judgment would resign and disappear into the political wilderness. The same error of judgment in African politics would be forgiven, and the said minister would stay on in his post or, at the very worst, be redeployed to another government position. Examples of this thinking were plentiful, certainly in Zimbabwean politics, with the same ministers being recycled time and again in different ministries.

No more clearly was this principle of "forgive and forget" illustrated than by Gono himself. On 18th April 2009, Gono published a 20-page insert in *The Chronicle*, defending his quasi-fiscal activities over the past five years and the confiscation of our foreign currency without our permission (see appendix page 192).

He claimed all these actions were necessary because of the Western sanctions against the country. He listed all his good deeds, such as for whom he had bought vehicles, tractors, ploughs and other equipment!

He tried to justify why he took exporters FCA money and who got the cheap loans or BACOSSI forex money. In paragraph 1:58 he states: *"It was always a political problem and not an economic one that drove us into the difficulties this nation experienced and quasi-fiscal operations were a response to those political challenges, which have now been resolved through the inclusive government."*

1:61 continues, *"Our call is to let bygones be bygones and for everyone and every entity to start anew and open a new page."*

Unless one understands the African concept of "forgive and forget", one would, as I did, see this as not only an arrogant statement but also one totally devoid of any remorse. Gono negatively affected thousands of lives through his weak business policies and through his support of a dubious political agenda.

To simply call for bygones to be bygones, seemed to me to be very facile and naïve. The stress and anguish, fear and intimidation, which he caused our organisation and me, would need more than those trite statements to obtain absolution.

Renewed Hope [2009 – ...]

As I complete this story of our time in this wonderful country Zimbabwe, I reflect on the numerous times friends and family have over the years asked: "How long are you guys going to stay there?" or "Why are you still living in Zimbabwe, are you crazy?"

There is no trite answer. Maybe because of our personalities? My inflexible, never-say-die, love-a-challenge Sagittarius behaviour? Maybe Jane's heritage and her upbringing with a father, who loved the bush and was intimately involved in operation Noah, saving the animals threatened by the rising waters of lake Kariba in the early 1960s? Maybe it is the jovial warm-hearted local people whom we got to know. Never once did I see a local golfer beat the ground, swear profusely or throw a golf club in anger after hitting a really terrible shot. There would just be a laugh and a comment by someone like Evans or Smart "Aah, ah, ah, there is one in every village!" followed by more laughter.

The weather, with 364-and-a-half days of brilliant blue skies and warm sun definitely plays its part – at least it feels like 364 days, but apparently the bright sunshine warms us only about 354 days a year!

Going back to South Africa was definitely on our minds back in 2008, just after Jason died. I had this overwhelming need to protect my kids from any harm, and I thought, irrationally of course, that being closer to them would keep them safer. The impossibility, however, of a 50-something-year-old white male getting a job in South Africa with its fixation on affirmative action, ruled that out. Coupled with that was the fact Zimbabwe, in my opinion, was way ahead of South Africa with regard to race relations. In South Africa, you still have exclusive racially-segregated societies, like the Black Management Forum or the Black Lawyers Association, or the predominantly white union Solidarity. No such thing in Zimbabwe, except of course for the AAG – Affirmative Action Group – a not-so-structured group with unclear policies on reclaiming all they believe was stolen from them by the white man. Zimbabwe, in my opinion, has moved on. Of course societies of a segregated nature in South Africa, like the ones I mentioned, were justified and were not racist as they attempted to correct the wrongs of the past – or so those attempting to justify them would have us believe.

Owning our own beautiful home, waking to the cacophony of bird song and laughter every morning and throughout the day, also played a big part in keeping us in Bulawayo.

Yes, the politicians have over the past ten years destroyed a once thriving economy with their poor policies and poor ideological judgment, for their own reasons which to them and those who agree with them are justifiable. Just last week ZANU-PF ministers were acknowledging that the farm takeovers, or more euphemistically called "land distribution", had backfired.

What they could not do is break the spirits of those who sought freedom from oppression, fought for free speech and all those wonderful rights that people living in true democracies experience. They could not take away the weather, the beautiful sights and sounds which are unique to Zimbabwe. That's probably why we stayed, to be able to see the end of the horror movie that was Zimbabwe from 2000 to 2009.

Rebuilding Zimbabwe resembles a steep road ahead: it can only be travelled slowly and carefully. Infrastructure refurbishment will take years and millions of dollars. Banks have no money to lend as yet because no one can afford to save any part of their low salary and because nobody trusts banks anymore. This will change. Our business, which was decimated, has survived, and as I write in September 2009, the fragile Government of National Unity is holding. Our sales are growing day by day and as they grow, so does our optimism.

As the millions of skilled people come back home from far-flung lands, the country will be strengthened and continue to grow.

Once all the work has been done and the woman Zimbabwe has received her political and infrastructural face-lift, we will be able to say...

"Zimbabwe, warm heart, beautiful face."

Epilogue

The following events have occurred since completing the book:

- The Small House built across the road now has a wall around it and a family is living there, complete with satellite dish.
- The Reserve Bank of Zimbabwe has, according to newspaper articles, had five of its properties attached for failing to pay an import company US$2 million for tractors purchased for its farm mechanisation policy. Some companies have reportedly also instituted claims against the Central Bank for money taken from their foreign currency accounts for the same purpose, but without the companies' knowledge or approval. This was when Gideon Gono, who still is governor, was busy running the whole economy through quasi-fiscal loans, purchases and handouts.
- The Government of National Unity is still wobbling along, with serious disagreement between the parties over certain issues, which appear to the man in the street to be leading to its disbandment, with the accompanying fallout for the country.
- Ryk, Caren's husband, sadly passed away in October 2009 of pancreatic cancer.
- Farm takeovers continue unabated, despite the Government of National Unity. Some white farmers, who remained on their land, have 24 hours to leave their farms or face two years in jail, while youths camp on their farms, cut off water and power supplies, and beat up farm workers.
- Working Capital, in the form of loans from banks, is still very hard to come by. Short-term money is available, but at very high rates.
- Inflation, or rather deflation, for 2009 is reported to be -7%.
- Civil servants went on strike as salaries are still pegged at US$150 per month.
- Estimates put those employed in the formal sector, including civil servants, at 800 000 out of a population of around 12 million.
- Optimism in the economy is rising, as most products are available and production is slowly picking up.
- Tobacco deliveries in 2009 increased to 56.5 million kilograms up from 45 million in 2008.
- Cotton output declined to 210 000 tons in 2009, down from 241 700 tons in 2008.
- Sugar output declined by 4% from 298 000 tons in 2008 to 286 000 tons in 2009.
- Gold output increased from 3.07 tons in 2008 to 5 tons in 2009.
- Platinum output increased to 5.6 tons in 2009 up from 5.4 tons in 2008. [source: Monetary Policy Statement, 29 January 2010]

EPILOGUE

- The US dollar is now the currency of choice, with change being given in Rand, as these coins are readily available, but the smallest denomination of the American currency circulating in Zimbabwe is the US$1 banknote.
- Black or parallel market dealers from two years ago are back in business, swapping Rands for US dollars and vice versa on the street, albeit at lower profit margins than before.
- Power cuts have got worse as South Africa prepares to host the 2010 Soccer World cup and as a result is drawing power from its neighbours, limiting the export quantity Zimbabwe needs to import.
- On 30th January 2010, Worldspace, our satellite radio, ceased operations, apparently closing a number of offices worldwide. After ten years of keeping abreast of world happenings, while travelling and bringing great music to head office, we are back to listening to CDs.
- Road Toll checkpoints have been introduced throughout the country. Although very rudimentary, they have managed to collect much-needed US dollars from motorists.
- Bulawayo City Council has embarked on a large-scale pothole-fixing exercise, with money received from the tollroad project. This has been most welcome after the thousands of bent rims and damaged shock absorbers!
- On 1st March 2010 the indigenisation bill came into force. All business people in Zimbabwe, owning companies with assets exceeding US$500 000, had to complete forms on their business assets and how they planned to sell 51% to a black Zimbabwean within the next five years. They had 45 days to file the form with the Minister of Indigenisation. Confusion reigned as the Prime Minister said the law was null and void, and President Mugabe said, at his 86th birthday bash in Bulawayo, that it was as irreversible as the land issue.
- Zimbabwe still remains a cash society. The only other form of payment is a bank transfer, which requires forms to be completed in triplicate, for even the smallest payment. An administrative nightmare. No cheque payments yet, or credit cards.
- Gono is quoted in the *Zimbabwe Times* of 19th March 2010 as saying that there are "vulture-style" attempts to wrest stakes from foreign-owned banks. He says one cannot equate and apply the land-reform type of indigenisation with indigenisation of other sectors of the economy. As he did in 2007, he argues against disturbing foreign investors' confidence by Government spokespersons and media sending confusing signals.

Appendix

Gono's apology

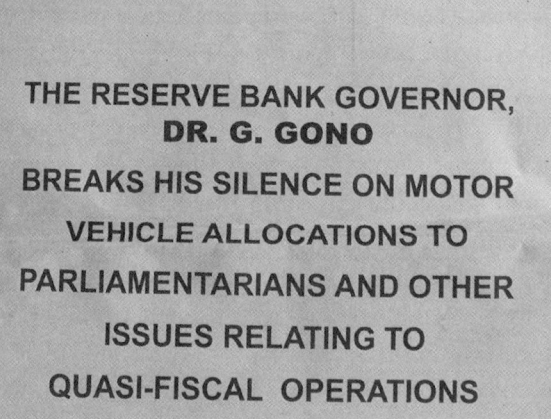

THE RESERVE BANK GOVERNOR, DR. G. GONO BREAKS HIS SILENCE ON MOTOR VEHICLE ALLOCATIONS TO PARLIAMENTARIANS AND OTHER ISSUES RELATING TO QUASI-FISCAL OPERATIONS

1.57 As often stated by the Governor, the Team at the Bank, which is full of energy, enthusiasm and cutting edge skills of all kinds, is proud to have stood by the country, feeding friends and foe alike, at the country's hour of greatest need in the face of maximum danger.

1.58 Also, as stated before, it was always a political problem and not an economic one that drove us into the difficulties this Nation experienced, and quasi-fiscal operations were a response to those political challenges which have now been resolved through the Inclusive Government.

1.59 For anyone to therefore continue focusing on these quasi-fiscal operations as the main cause of our economic difficulties and therefore demanding that the Governor should leave on that account, smacks of an attempt to believe that the ordinary Zimbabwean is not smart enough to know where the problem truly lies.

1.61 Our call is to let bygones be bygones and for everyone and every entity to start anew and open a new page, as repeatedly called for by the Principals to the Inclusive Agreement, namely His Excellency the President R. G. Mugabe, the Rt. Honourable Prime Minister Mr. M. R. Tsvangirai, Deputy Prime Minister Prof. A.G.O. Mutambara, the Vice Presidents and the Deputy Prime Minister Hon. T. Khupe.

APPENDIX

Mpofu's letters (i)

Handwritten note at top: Met @ 4pm 3rd/7 in my office

All correspondence should be addressed to
"THE SECRETARY"

Telephone: 730081/7; 791823/7; 702731
Facsimile: 704116/723765/729311
E-mail: minind02@samara.co.zw
Telegrams: "TRADEMIN", Harare
Private Bag 7708, Causeway, Zimbabwe

ZIMBABWE

Reference: ....

MINISTRY OF INDUSTRY
AND INTERNATIONAL TRADE
Mukwati Building
4th Street/Livingstone Avenue
Harare
Zimbabwe

29 June 2007

The President of Confederation of Zimbabwe Industries, Mr C. Jokonya

The President of the Zimbabwe National Chamber of Commerce,
Mrs Mara Hativagone

The Chairman of the Wholesalers and Retailers Association, Mr W. Zireva

Dear Sir/Madam

<u>CABINET TASK FORCE OF PRICE MONITORING AND STABILISATION</u>

As you are well aware, the above Task Force has been set up to deal with unjustified price hikes that have wreaked havoc on our economy.

The Task Force has put in place the attached measures to deal with the situation.

Your members are obliged to abide by the directives of the Cabinet Task Force on Price Monitoring and Stabilization and co-operate fully in the exercise to curb unjustified price increases.

Yours sincerely

C. M. Katsande
<u>SECRETARY FOR INDUSTRY AND INTERNATIONAL TRADE</u>

Mpofu's letters (ii-iii)

PRESS STATEMENT BY THE CHAIRMAN OF THE CABINET TASKFORCE ON PRICE MONITORING AND STABILIZATION HON O. M. MPOFU, MP

The Government has noted with great concern that manufacturers, wholesalers and retailers have unjustifiably increased their prices over the last few weeks. Prices have been hiked on a daily basis without proper justifications being given. This has been a cause for concern considering that business was part of the historic signing of the three protocols including the Incomes and Pricing Stabilisation Protocol, which formed the basis of a social contract.

Government is aware that these escalating price increases are a political ploy engineered by our detractors to effect regime change against the ruling party ZANU PF and its government following the failure of illegal economic sanctions. As a Government, we cannot stand idly by, while this situation continues. The Task Force on Price Monitoring and Stabilisation recently constituted by the Government is, therefore, with immediate effect, going to take appropriate action against unscrupulous and insensitive economic players.

APPENDIX

It is against this background that we direct all the players in the business sector to revert back to the prices as of Monday 18 June 2007, whilst their justifications for increases are being looked into by the National Incomes and Pricing Commission (NIPC). We would like to sensitise the public that the ruling and official prices are as listed in the table below:

PRODUCT	Prices as at 18-06-07 (Retail)	Unjustified Current Market Prices as at 24-06-07 (Retail)
Controlled		
Bread	$22,000.00	$45,000.00
Self Raising Flour 2kg	$66,000.00	$120,000.00
Refined Maize Meal 10kg	$85,000.00	$130,000.00
Roller Meal 10kg	$41,500.00	$41,500.00
Monitored		
Cooking Oil 2ltrs	$250,000.00	$420,000.00
Cooking Oil 750ml	$90,000.00	$240,000.00
Salt 2kg	$86,000.00	$180,000.00
White Sugar 2kg	$33,940.00	$70,000.00
Yeast 125g	$65,000.00	$115,000.00
Stock Feed Growers 5kg	$97,000.00	$200,000.00
Tyres 670-14 8PR	$1,134,993.00	$2,600,000.00
900-20 14PR	$3,472,781.00	$9,000,000.00
Maize Seed 10kg	$4,710.00	$97,000.00
Milk 500ml (fresh)	$27,180.00	$30,000.00
(steri)	$32,970.00	$45,000.00
Fertiliser 50kg "AN"	$500,000.00	$1,200,000
"D"	$450,000	$1,000,000
Cement 50kg (masonry)	$300,000	$800,000
Beef (1kg)	$120,000	$355,000
Packaging 10 kg pack	$12,000	$37,000
Other		
Bath Soap Geisha (250g)	$65,000	$190,000
Mazoe Orange Crush 2ltrs	$120,000	$600,000
Petrol (1 Litre)	$60,000	$180,000
Diesel (1 Litre)	$55,000	$170,000
Herald	$15,000	$25,000

2.

Mpofu's letters (iv-v)

Sunday Mail		$25,000		$35,000
Bus Fares 0-10km		$8,000		$30,000
10.1-20km		$10,000		$40,000
20.1-30km		$15,000		$80,000
Above 30km	$500/KM		$2000/KM	

This unruly behaviour is unacceptable and as such Government will mobilize all the powers vested in the State to protect consumers. The Government has set up a Crack Unit comprising all the security agencies who will work with the NIPC inspectorate to enforce the prices shown above and root out all forms of corruption and economic sabotage.

The Task Force is hereby calling upon all producers, manufacturers, wholesalers and retailers to desist from unjustified price increases and revert back to the indicated prices. Manufacturers of monitored or controlled commodities must follow the proper procedure in adjusting their prices.

PRESS RELEASE BY THE CHAIRMAN OF THE CABINET TASK FORCE ON PRICE MONITORING AND STABILIZATION HON O. M. MPOFU MP

As a follow up to the press statement of Monday 25 June 2007 by the Cabinet Task Force on Price Monitoring and Stabilization, the Task Force further directs the following:

1) That the correct prices for all controlled and monitored products shall be as approved by the Government.
2) That all other goods and services that were previously neither controlled nor monitored shall **with immediate effect** be monitored in terms of Statutory Instrument 125 of 2003
3) That prices of all goods and services should revert to those ruling on Monday 18 June 2007 whilst their justifications for increases are being looked into by the National Incomes and Pricing Commission (NIPC).
4) That all Small and Medium Enterprises (SMEs) and Vendors that connive with the large manufacturers, wholesalers and retailers will not be spared either by the Taskforce Crack Unit.

Mpofu's letters (vi-vii)

5) That all manufacturing and production value chains shall be fully monitored to ensure that no hoarding or removal of goods from shelves is effected. Any goods recovered from any act of hoarding shall be forfeited to the State.

6) That those who do not comply with all the above shall face the full wrath of the law.

7) All members of the public with information on issues involving price violations and hoarding should urgently report such information to the nearest police station.

Hon O. M. Mpofu, M.P
<u>MINISTER OF INDUSTRY AND INTERNATIONAL TRADE</u>

PRESS STATEMENT BY THE CHAIRMAN OF THE CABINET TASK FORCE ON PRICE MONITORING AND STABILIZATION, HON O. M. MPOFU, M.P

The Cabinet Task Force on Price Monitoring and Stabilization further reminds the public of the following:

1) That it is illegal for real estates management companies or individuals to either sell or rent out properties in foreign currency.

2) That an immediate moratorium is imposed on rent increases of both Commercial and Residential properties pending the finalization of appropriate regulating formulae by both the Commercial and Residential Rent Boards.

   It is an offence to evict a tenant without providing the stipulated three months notice.

3) No Tariff adjustments should be effected by public utilities forthwith without the approval of the Cabinet Task Force

4) In accordance with the First Schedule section 4(2) of the National Incomes and Pricing Commission Act, the Chairman of the Commission Mr David Govere has been relieved of his duties as Commissioner with immediate effect.

HON O. M. Mpofu, M.P
MINISTER OF INDUSTRY AND INTERNATIONAL TRADE

Taskforce (i-ii)

PRESS RELEASE

BY THE CHAIRMAN OF THE CABINET

TASKFORCE ON PRICE MONITORING

AND STABILIZATION,

HON. O. M. MPOFU

21 August 2007

APPENDIX

    iv)   Intra-city Passenger Service

    v)   Inter-city Passenger Service

    vi)   Telecommunication Tariffs

3. The benchmark for all other prices of commodities not covered by this Review is manufacture's/supplier's price as of 18 June 2007 until further notice. Implementation of the manufacturer's price of 18 June 2007 will guarantee uniformity and standardization going forward.

4. The Retailers are allowed to put a maximum mark up of 20% and charge Value Added Tax (VAT) of 15% on a commodity. As an example, a supplier charging a price of, say $100 000 will see the product sold by the retailer at a maximum price of $138 000.

5. In order to ensure consistency and uniformity, Price Inspectors and Monitors (Police Crack Teams and

Taskforce (v)

Research Teams) will use the manufacturer's price of 18 June 2007 as the benchmark, and **a mark up of 20% plus 15% VAT** as the price of basic goods and commodities in retail shops.

6. Furthermore, please note that when Price Inspectors and Monitors visit business premises to check on compliance to prices of 18 June 2007, they will be accompanied by uniformed Police Officers.

APPENDIX

Police case

TO : OPERATIONS MANAGER (MR L. MUKOMBWE)
FROM : BEATRICE SHOP MANAGER (MOSES JONGWE) 71
DATE : 20 AUGUST 2007

RE : **WITHDRAWAL OF THE CASE BY THE POLICE**

I just want to inform you that the police told me that, I am now free as from 15/08/07 refering to the case of being arrested by the price control team. The docket was closed the reason being that the Supa baths they had opened the docket for, were supposed to be going for $990 000-00 because we increased them from $599 000-00 to $990 000-00 on the 15/06/07. So we photocopied the memo N° B1085 for Supa baths as well as the PR N° 171438 and they attached them on the docket as proof of innocence. As for blankets they did not say anything since they had not opened a docket for them.

Thank you very much for your concern and support. Together we can left the red and yellow giant flag.
Thank you.

Letter to Katsande

3rd September 2007

The Secretary
International Trade
13th Floor, Mukwati Building
HARARE

Attention: C M Katsande

Dear Sir

We are a retail chain with 196 shops throughout Zimbabwe. All our goods are received from our suppliers into our distribution centre in Bulawayo. At our distribution centre the goods are checked for quality and quantity and are then priced according to SI 142 of 2007 (Control of Goods - Price Control Amendment Order 2007 (No. 11).

The goods are then dispatched already priced to our 196 shops country wide. All original invoices from suppliers are kept in Bulawayo at Head Office.

Operation price control officers are now visiting our shops (the latest being Banket on Saturday 1st September) and demanding all the invoices for the goods in the shop. On being told that all the invoices are held in Bulawayo the Shop Managers are being locked up overnight. (In Banket's case a woman) and charged with not producing invoices.

We would like to please appeal to your office to allow these price monitors to contact their counterparts in Bulawayo who can check on all the invoices which we hold and can then verify that we are within the law. These Bulawayo Officers can then report back to the enquiring officers wherever they may be in Zimbabwe.

To fax through all the invoices for any one of our shops from over 520 suppliers for all the products in the shop is not only practically impossible, but also a huge cost, both for ourselves and the office receiving the faxes.

I am sure these consequences of the price controls could not have been foreseen and as a result would humbly ask that you agree to our request in order to achieve what we all wish for, stability in our economy. This will also bring to an end the incarceration of innocent women and men who are honestly employed by our Company.

Thanking you in advance.

Yours sincerely

JEROME GARDNER
MANAGING DIRECTOR

Please could I request that you stamp this letter in recognition of receipt and request that it be faxed back to me on fax number:

Staff letters (i)

12 NOVEMBER 2008

To the M.D. MR Guardian

Dear Sir

I Alice Sithole, one of the committee members' appealing to you sir on behalf of the workers of ■■■■■ to help us with providing of Meilie-meal, Cooking oil and Soap. We are struggling to buy those commodities because of that $500 000 we are getting at the bank.
I believe once we get these staffs it will reduce the absentism of people at work. limitation of withdrawals at bank is causing starvations at homes
I know that you are trying you level best to do withdrawals on our behalve but we spend two to three days without getting the money, which will force us to go on our own. Never think that we are doing this deliberately but hungerness is forcing us. All of us likes our JOB AND OUR COMPANY. NOONE WANT TO LOOSE HIS OR HER JOB. I Put my trust in you that you will RESPOND TO US AS SOON AS POSSIBLE BEFORE OUR FAMILIES DIE OF HUNGER.
SIR HELP US WE ARE STARVING. ~~————————~~

YOUR FAITHFULL
ALICE SITHOLE (WORKERS COMMITTEE)

Staff letters (ii-iii)

Bulawayo.

11-11-08.

Dear (sir) Management,

We a have as requesting from people They are saying as management can you heep us to pay us with rand if we are going for shutdown. we are saying This issue in case of transport. If are coming back as you are seeing everything here in Zimbabwe They are using Rands. because if I have a rand I can fight hard to come back at work. because If you have a rand you can say my friend I have got a rand he can give you are raid Ok. to buy us some coupons sp. like 20 litres. I can give bus 10 litres of petrol or diesel If I come I can find some to give a 10 litres They I come back at work, The other can you please buy us some daily commodities like, c/oil, meat mealie and soap etc. and These Those Things like c/oil, mealie and soap it can reduce absentism of people at work because If a person have got These Things can come to work, and can work with his powers.

And I can sympatise you as our management to help us w. These things. I Kindly you can understand our request or problems, please help your workers.

APPENDIX

[Handwritten note: att Jerome / Copy of letter received from workers today. / Regards / R.]

The Management

20/01/09

Dear Sir,

We really do appreciate your efforts in trying to alleviate us from the economic hardships we face these days by awarding us our January salary early.

From the look of things, it seems these economic hardships we are experiencing are going to continue for some time. We really love our work but we feel that this work can no longer continue to sustain us anymore as long as we are paid in Zimbabwe dollars.

We are asking your good office to consider paying our salaries in <u>Rands</u> and give us loans in Rands too. The reason for this is because no shops or service providers will accept our Zim dollar anymore. In order to survive these days, one needs to be pay for the following basic commodities in Rands:

Rent	R250
Mealie meal	65
Cooking oil	35
Transport	10 (daily)
Soap	10

As at today, one needs about Z$50 trillion to buy only R100 on the street. We would really appreciate if you could bail us out from these hardships.

Yours faithfully,

<u>Committee</u>

Price mark ups (i-ii)

National Incomes and Pricing Commission
3rd Floor Runhare House
P.O. Box 8970
HARARE

26 October 2007

The Secretary
Ministry of Industry and International Trade
Col. C.M. Katsande

RE: MARK-UPS AND ALLOWANCES FOR OVERHEADS FOR THE RETAIL SECTOR

The NIPC has approved the following allowances for overheads for the retail sector. In addition the statutory retail mark-up of 20% will apply.

CATEGORY	ALLOWANCE FOR OVERHEADS
Food	5%
Butchery	20%
Takeaways and delicatessens	40%
Housewares/hardware/furniture/electricals	35%
Clothing	40%

These allowances for overheads will not apply to the 3 + 16 controlled and monitored products for which retail prices have already been approved.

E. NDLOVU
ACTING CHIEF EXECUTIVE OFFICER
NATIONAL INCOMES AND PRICING COMMISSION

c.c. Confederation of Zimbabwe Industries
c.c. Zimbabwe National Chambers of Commerce
c.c. Retailers Association of Zimbabwe
c.c. Police General Headquarters

VERY URGENT!

TO THE OPERATIONS MANAGER.
MR. L. MUKOMBWE.
FROM. R.D. MATASA (AREA 4)
DATE. 24/09/07.

RE: INVOICES FOR STOCKS

THE PRICE-CONTROL TEAM VISITED OUR JURU SHOP ON FRIDAY 21/09/07 IN THE AFTERNOON WHEN CHECKING OUR PRICES THEY SAID SOME OF OUR PRICES ARE HIGH. THEY WANT TO KNOW IF WE HAVE AN APROVAL FROM THE MINISTRY.

HERE WITH A LIST OF ITEMS

#	Item	Price	Codes	
1)	MENS T/S SELLING AT	1230 000 -	349450 1	BELMOR 20647
2)	M/SANDLES	472 000 -	270940 1	SPOONBILL 035
3)	M/T/S	2560 000 -	350830 1	MAT CLOTHING 584 27/MAI
4)	SUPER BATH	(1359 000) -	655220 1	CROWN 219778
5)	G/SKIRTS	789 000 -	762250 1	BELMOR 20545+
6)	G/SOX	184 500 -	765960 1	ZIMHOS RUSH 784
7)	BEER MUGS	183 000 -	27119 0 1	BENDEL DOUG 103946
8)	W/GLASS SETS	496 000 -	27117 0 1	BENDEL DOUG 0053
9)	GLASS PLATES	173 000 -	27118 0 1	BENDEL DOUG 103947

PLEASE SIR THEY ARE COMING TO THE SHOP TO SEE THE RECEIPTS TOMORROW 25/09/07. IF YOU CAN SEND THEM BY OVER-NIGHT TODAY TO HRE OFFICE SO THAT I CAN PICK THEM AND GO WITH THEM TO JURU ON MY WAY TO MUREWA ON MY TRIP.

Thank you SIR.